Economic Analysis of Music Copyright

Ivan L. Pitt

Economic Analysis of Music Copyright

Income, Media and Performances

 Springer

Ivan L. Pitt Ph.D.
American Society of Composers, Authors and Publishers
ASCAP Building
One Lincoln Plaza
New York, NY 10023
USA
ipitt@ascap.com

Important Disclaimer

Before we begin our analysis, we offer a disclaimer to the reader of this monograph. It is virtually impossible to write about performing rights societies in the United States without illustrating some aspect of U.S. copyright laws. This monograph is written by an economist, not an attorney, intended for limited economic analysis purposes only and should not be used as a substitute for legal advice.

The information, data and tables presented here do not contain or convey legal advice, and should not be used or relied on with regard to any particular facts, circumstances or situations. Laws can change over time and some of the material discussed here can be out of date by the time the monograph is published. Given this time lag, the reader is advised to consult with legal counsel for expert advice and interpretation of U.S. copyright laws or any subject matter presented here. Furthermore, the opinions expressed here are solely those of the author and should not be construed to represent any particular organization or person.

ISBN 978-1-4899-8623-8   ISBN 978-1-4419-6318-5 (eBook)
DOI 10.1007/978-1-4419-6318-5
Springer New York Dordrecht Heidelberg London

Springer is part of Springer Science+Business Media (www.springer.com)

Preface

Introduction

This book began an initial study of the skewness in royalty income data after I joined ASCAP as their Senior Economist for Licensing Distribution and Member Services Analysis. We were trying to determine if Chris Anderson's *Long Tail* actually applied to the income distribution of members in a Performing Rights Organization. Many economists in arts administration were intrigued by Anderson's theory on niche markets which at the time appeared to turn on its head, the conventional wisdom that the vast majority of royalty income is earned by a few songwriters, the so-called 'superstar effect.' The first question that came to mind what not so much the niche markets, given the many radio formats, but how to measure the skewness in the apparent data. This monograph handles the measurement of skewness and heavy tails in income data in the performing rights music industry.

In addition to recorded music revenue—with declining CD sales and digital media that failed to meet income and future cash flow expectations—music publishing has other more diverse revenue sources such as royalty payments from performance licensing and publishing. Performance royalties are a steady income stream that could be collected from a wide variety of established music users such as radio and broadcast stations through ASCAP, BMI, and SESAC and are not subject to the problems associated with mechanical royalties such as declining CD sales and online piracy.

Anderson began his 'Long Tail' analysis in an article that first appeared in *Wired* magazine in October 2004. His book on the same topic was released in 2008. Anderson's work came out just as the wave of mergers and acquisitions in music publishing and radio were sweeping the industry; the number of radio formats and genres increased dramatically while the number of publishers and radio station owners was consolidated under a growing mountain of debt that would soon have other economic implications; and many potential investors were interested in maximizing the 'economic value' of the copyright assets in music publishing catalogs.

In Anderson's theory, hidden gems, long forgotten and dormant musical works in publishers' catalogs that were not part of their 'Top 25' best-known hits would soon invigorate the music industry struggling with falling retail sales and shrinking advertising budgets, as digital technology expanded the way in which consumers bought and listened to music. Music industry executives began looking for Anderson's 'Long Tail' effect and with it the implied redistribution of income, and the ability of music publishers to maximize the value of their copyright assets (lyrics and melody) in their existing music catalogs. The competition for music publishing catalogs by investors, the exploitation of the copyright in musical compositions and the income they generate from radio, television, Internet, advertising, and movies made existing music catalogs of old hits more valuable as the demand for digital music in the Internet age increased dramatically.

Many older recording artists made 'comebacks' as their previous works were met with some renewed commercial success when used by new recording artists in what *Billboard* magazine called a 'multi-formant cross-generational' appeal. Hip and Hop and Rap artists were credited with refocusing attention on older hits and songwriters by use of the popular music composition technique called 'sampling' in which recognizable snippets of older songs were used in current recordings. With renewed interest in some older hits, performing artists soon began touring and giving live performances again.

ASCAP, BMI, and SESAC are the major performing rights organizations (PROs), sometimes called performing rights societies, which control the non-exclusive licensing rights to millions of musical compositions, the lyrics, melody and musical notation, in the United States. These organizations grant a blanket or per-program license to music users for the public performance use of copyrighted music in their catalogs. As it stands today, recording artists (as distinct from the songwriter/composer) are paid performance royalties through SoundExchange, another PRO, for their digital sound recording use on a limited basis on the Internet, satellite, digital cable, and other subscription services. Recording artists (vocalists and background musicians) are paid only for the audio transmission of the sound recording, including voice, sound, and audio effects, and not the underlying music copyright in the music composition, the melody and lyrics, which would still be handled by ASCAP, BMI, or SESAC.

This important distinction between the performance licensing of music compositions—the melody and lyrics—by ASCAP, BMI, and SESAC, and the licensing of– the audio sound recording– by SoundExchange should be kept in mind by the reader for many reasons, including the fact that a single song title may have more than one copyright attached to it, and there is important pending legislation such as *The Performance Rights Act* that will have an impact on audio performance rights for terrestrial broadcasters and others. Both types of licenses by these agencies could be required now or in the future depending on whether the musical works are used on terrestrial or on digital and satellite broadcasts.

PROs then track musical performances or airplay use on television, radio, the Internet, live venues, and other media, determine which music has been performed, and pay the appropriate copyright holders a royalty income when their musical compositions, called performances, are performed in those licensed media. There are different types of performances such as features, themes, jingles, background/foreground music, and promos that are weighted differently and each earn different royalty amounts. This performance royalty is distinct, and it is collected and paid out separately from other types of income agreements such as mechanical royalties as spelled out in recording contracts.

Songwriters, composers, and publishers, the copyright holders of the musical compositions, may have other sources of royalty income (both domestic and international) such as from mechanical and synchronization sources, and we do not model the returns from those incomes sources. Songwriters and composers, unlike other salaried workers who are engaged in making a tangible product or providing a business service and may receive a regular paycheck each week, are producers of what is known as *intellectual property*. There are several types of intellectual property such as a copyright, a trademark, or a patent. For example, the music copyright in terms of intellectual property is the protection from infringement given to original musical compositions or songs. A trademark protection is granted for a name or symbol used to identify products and services. Patent protection is given to new inventions and designs.

This book continues the study of art and culture from a royalty income perspective, an area in royalty income analysis that has received very little academic attention for various reasons. The main reason is that most of the data on royalty income at the individual member or affiliate level is proprietary and generally not made available for analysis by the various performing rights agencies or the industry group, CISAC. The focus of this book is limited to the economic analysis of domestic members—songwriters and composers (as distinct from the recording artist), the publishers—and the income they earn from performance copyrights from one of those societies, ASCAP.

This study is based on limited ASCAP internal and licensed external proprietary data, we do not identify any of the individual members, radio station owners, nor do we analyze individual royalty statements from an accounting perspective. Individual songwriters, publishers, and radio station owners are only mentioned if there is publicly available information in popular magazines and newspapers such as *Billboard, Playback*, and the *Wall Street Journal* to further illustrate a complex topic that otherwise would be confusing to the reader. The reader should keep in mind that there are considerable differences in the way PROs handle members, affiliation, survey data collection, royalty payment methods, procedures, and policies. These are factors that should be considered if any comparisons are made to other PROs. Some performing rights organizations are more transparent than others and periodically report some of their financial and membership data, while others do not follow this practice.

It would impossible to conduct a study of popular culture without relying on popular music magazines since few academic studies have been conducted on songwriters and composers in a PRO and those magazines contain a slew of rich data that could augment other studies. In the review sections on songwriters, composers, publishers, media, and skew theory of the monograph, each chapter in itself could easily fill an entire volume.

The aim of this monograph is to cover the basic essentials of skew theory and music copyright from a performance right perspective in a brief and constructive fashion. In the interest of brevity every topic could not be covered, and I am sure that some topics that others would find important may have been omitted. I am entirely responsible for that omission and I apologize in advance. A reference section at the end of each chapter provides a list for further reading for anyone who wants to learn more.

Intended Audience

The scope of this monograph has been designed to meet the needs of three groups of readers. For general readers and professionals in the music publishing industry, this monograph provides a general introduction into the economics of music copyright from the perspective of performing rights organizations. For undergraduate students in media and cultural economics, the monograph can serve as a principal undergraduate text on the economics of the arts and culture or on arts administration with a focus on music copyright in performance rights organizations or as a supplementary text on a broader economic survey of the musical arts. Statisticians, graduate students, and academics interested in statistical theory and data modeling applied to music copyright would benefit from this study because it bridges the empirical gap between the theoretical and practical analysis of songwriters and music copyright.

Chapters Organization

This book is divided into two parts. The first part is a general introduction to the many supply and demand economic factors that are related to music performance royalty payments. The second part is an applied econometrics section that provides modeling and in-depth analysis of songwriter, publishers, and blanket licensing income data using utilizing skew theory.

Part I: Economics of Music Copyright (Chapters 1 through 4)

In Chapter 1, we introduce the reader to the factors that would motivate one to undertake an in-depth economic analysis of non-dramatic performance copyright in the performing arts from the perspectives of performing rights organizations. From the perspectives of performing rights organizations such as ASCAP, BMI, and SESAC, we provide a basic economic model of supply and demand to illustrate the dynamic economic interplay of music creators—the copyright holders such as composers, authors, songwriters, and publishers— who create and supply the music, and music users— the media companies in television, the Internet, and other venues— who use copyrighted music in a variety of performance (airplay) types such as features, jingles, promos, or background music.

Chapter 2 explores the media segments such as radio, cable, television, and the Internet in the US music industry from a revenue perspective as one source of licensing fees and royalty income for songwriters, composers, authors, and publishers from music performances.

Chapter 3 is devoted to the economics of music copyright such as performance rights licensing from the perspective of music publishers, one of the suppliers of copyrighted music.

In Chapter 4, the songwriter/composer/lyricist, as distinct from the recording artist or vocalist, is analyzed from a creative perspective.

Part II: Econometric Analysis (Chapters 5 through 9)

Chapter 5 reviews the skew-Normal and skew-t statistical distribution theory and presents a model that can be used to estimate regression models when the distribution is highly skewed and asymmetrical.

In Chapter 6, the first of three econometric case studies is presented. The effects of member type (writer or publisher), license type (blanket or per-program), type of medium (broadcast TV, local TV, radio, etc.), performance type (features, themes, etc.), tenure (length of membership in years), and tail segment variables on performance royalty income are estimated using the skew-Normal and skew-t distributions in a parametric approach.

The second of the three econometric case studies is presented in Chapter 7. This chapter looks at the dynamics of 'superstar' effects of age, length in membership in a PRO, and the number of song titles registered on songwriter's income when publishers are excluded.

Chapter 8 is the third case study, an econometric model has been developed that looks at the licensing fee structure involved in the radio blanket license, and explains the variation of the blanket fees in terms of radio format, station owners, region, market size, and recorded plays.

Chapter 9 concludes our study and suggests a few areas for research.

Acknowledgment

An initial survey of the economics of art and culture revealed that there was a gap in the literature that focused on economics of music copyright, particularly as it related to songwriters, composers, and authors of musical compositions. This monograph bridges that gap with a focus on performance rights.

This monograph would not have been possible without the constructive criticism of colleagues both within and outside of ASCAP. The manuscript was greatly improved by their many suggestions. I would like to acknowledge Peter Boyle, the Chief Economist at ASCAP for his insights of an earlier draft. Professor John R. Norsworthy (retired) of Rensselaer Polytechnic Institute, Troy, New York, is also graciously acknowledged for his generous contributions in improving the manuscript. I must also thank Jonathan Berger, Tom Hauner, Mike Riley, and Pavlos Mourdoukoutas for their generous assistance in reading parts of the manuscript or providing graphical assistance. I also owe a special thanks to Clint Cummings of TSP International for his technical assistance. I also owe a debt of gratitude to Jon Gurstelle, the U.S. Economics Editor at Springer for shepherding the manuscript through the various channels at Springer and getting its approval for publication. I am also pleased to thank Felix Portnoy and Gillian Greenough at Springer for preparing the final version of the manuscript. Finally, I would like to thank, you, the reader, for making the choice of reading or buying the monograph.

Contents

List of Figures

List of Tables

xx

List of Tables

Part I
Economics of Music Copyright

Chapter 1
Economics of Music Copyright: Income, Media, and Performances

Abstract In this volume, we begin our economic analysis of the non-dramatic *performance* copyright in the performing arts from the perspectives of performing rights organizations (PROs) such as ASCAP, BMI, and SESAC. We continue with the further expansion of the discipline of cultural economics. A basic economic model of supply and demand is used to illustrate the dynamic economic interplay of the music creators who supply the music and the demand by music users who market culture in various media industries and other venues. A general overview of the economics of music production is discussed. We end the chapter with a brief overview of performing rights organizations and music licensing.

1.1 Introduction

There is a huge demand for the use of music catalogs by many music users in the terrestrial and satellite radio, local, cable and satellite broadcast television, Internet, and cell phone industries. Other music users include bars, restaurants, hotels, retail shops, colleges, and universities. There is also a demand for music on music channels on an airplane, music at a convention, or music on hold on a telephone.

All of these music users have arranged for blanket licenses with performing rights organizations (PROs) to use their music catalogs in a variety of music *performance types* such as a song or musical composition performed live or recorded, theme music used in the beginning and ending of programs, jingles used in advertising, underscores, ring tones, or promotional announcements. The purchaser of the blanket license is allowed the non-exclusive and unlimited use of the PROs library of songs, once the fee for its use has been negotiated and the license had been granted.

The PROs would then make performance royalty payments (less administration fees) to the copyright owners registered on record. These royalty payments become one source of income for the songwriters, composers, and music publishers. Popular music, when conveyed through tone, tempo, harmonization, melody, and lyrics, are thought to reflect the popular culture, nature, and values in a society.

Millions of song titles created by hundreds of thousands of songwriters and composers who belong to performing rights organizations and decades of royalty payments and income to songwriters, composers, and publishers have resulted in

I.L. Pitt, *Economic Analysis of Music Copyright*,
DOI 10.1007/978-1-4419-6318-5_1, © Springer Science+Business Media, LLC 2010

a vast collection of proprietary data compiled by performing rights organizations, sometimes referred to performing rights societies. The licensing fees (less administration costs) collected by these PROs become the royalty payments or income made to copyright holders, the songwriters, composers, and publishers whose musical compositions are licensed by the PROs.

We will be using the terms song, title, or work interchangeably to refer to a musical composition. Similarly, when we speak of a songwriter, he or she may be a performing or a non-performing songwriter, and it is to be assumed that the composer, lyricist, and author of a musical composition is also included in the term songwriter. Some PROs refer to the copyright holders as members or affiliates depending on the organization structure and we will refer to the terms interchangeably as well.

The proprietary data in this study include the fees collected by a single PRO from licensing the various music users in media industries such as television, radio, cable, and the Internet, and others such as bars, restaurants, theme parks, colleges, and universities. In addition, the proprietary data used in this study is from a single PRO, and is limited to a small sample meant to illustrate skew analysis. Furthermore, this analysis may not be applicable to other performing rights organization or other situations. Licensing procedures, survey processes, and administration may vary across different PROs. This study also includes external licensed data or copyrighted material from Mediaguide, comScore, *Billboard* magazine, Magna, and other sources who granted us copyright permission to reprint, publish, and modify their data. Some of the data used here were obtained from website links and these links may or may not be available for future use.

This study is different from other studies that focused on the performing arts from a theater, opera, dance, and luxury art works using census, survey, or organizational design data. With this limitation in mind our focus will be on the publishers, songwriters, and composers with regard to income earned from the performance copyright of music as laid out in the copyright laws of the United States.

Songwriters, composers, authors, and publishers can have other sources of income that would be beyond the scope of our analysis in Part II of the monograph. We will also examine the various factors affecting the licensing fees by radio broadcasters. In our analysis, demand for a songwriter's song is determined by many factors including the various new and existing genres of music on radio, television, and the Internet.

1.2 Motivation for the Study

The compact disk (CD) has now become both a blessing and a curse in the music industry. Perhaps, the biggest economic and technological change affecting sales and profitability has been the consumer's preference for music in a digital format instead of the physical format of a CD, which earlier replaced vinyl records and cassettes. In the late 1980s and early 1990s, CDs fueled the boom in the sale of digital recordings as consumers replaced their older music with the better sound quality and portability of CDs.

But as the Internet and its technological changes became apparent with the introduction of the digital music file formats such as MP3s and CD burners, digital music became a threat to the long-established business model in the music industry. Traditionally, consumers purchased their music at specialty stores like Tower Records, but with the entry of big-box retailers like Wal-Mart and other discount retailers, these music specialty retailers were driven out of business.

The music industry is now an industry in transition with new business models emerging everyday on the many ways to profitably exploit digital technology. The hope had been that digital sales would offset the decline in sales of the CD format. But this has not happened for many reasons, which we analyze and discuss below. The compact disc used to be one of the main products in the music industry that accounted for most of its sales. Initially, revenue increased as music fans replaced their older album collections with new CDs. But as the Internet gained widespread use with the ability to transfer and share music files, CD sales began to plummet.

Physical album sales have been falling dramatically since 2005 as music sales have evolved from CD album purchases in brick and mortar retail music stores, many of which are now closing, to purchases of digital songs from online retailers such as Apple's iTunes store. Table 1.1 from the Recording Industry Association of America (RIAA) illustrates what has happened over time to the sale of music in various physical formats. Physical formats of recorded music such as CDs, cassette tapes, and vinyl records once dominated and represented 91 percent of shipments as late as 2005, but by 2008 the physical format had shrunk to 68 percent.

In addition, as the 2009 recession worsened, advertising spending, a key source of performance, mechanical, and synchronization royalty income, also declined. Tables 1.2 and 1.3 summarize the recent data published in *Billboard* magazine and

Table 1.1 Percent Physical and Digital Shipments, 2005–2008

Format	2005	2006	2007	2008
Physical	91	84	77	68
Digital	9	16	23	32

Source: http://www.riaa.com/keystatistics.php.

Table 1.2 May 2009 Y-T-D Overall Unit Sales and Shares

Unit Sales* (000)	2008	2009	Year/year change	Year/year % change
Albums	164,579	142,998	−21,581	−13.11%
Albums % Share	27.18%	22.07%	−0.051	−18.82%
Digital Tracks	440,280	504,379	64,099	14.56%
Digital Tracks % Share	72.71%	77.83%	0.051	7.04%
Store Singles	651	662	11	1.69%
Store Singles % Share	0.11%	0.10%	−0.0001	−0.0498
Total Overall Units Sales	605,510	648,039	42,529	7.02%

*As of May 24, 2009.
Source: Based on data from *Billboard* magazine, June 6, 2009, p. 57. Used with permission of e5 Global Media.

Table 1.3 May 2009 Y-T-D Album Format Sales and Shares

Album format* (000)	2008	2009	Year/year change	Year/year % change
CD	138,723	111,577	−27,146	−19.57%
CD % Share	84.29%	78.03%	−0.063	−7.43%
Digital	25,151	30,404	5,253	20.89%
Digital % Share	15.28%	21.26%	0.060	39.13%
Cassette	43	18	−25	−58.14%
Cassette % Share	0.026%	0.013%	0.000	−51.82%
Other	662	999	337	50.91%
Other % Share	0.40%	0.70%	0.003	73.68%
Total	164,579	142,998	−21,581	−13.11%

*As of May 24, 2009.
Source: Based on data from *Billboard* magazine, June 6, 2009, p. 57. Used with permission of e5 Global Media.

provide a snapshot of the accelerating slide in CD sales that has occurred in the music industry over many years.

The year 2009 is showing the same trends as in past years in term of royalty income from *mechanical* sales. May 24, 2009 year-to-date sales data show that album sales dropped by 13.11 percent in 2009 when compared to the same period a year ago. Albums slumped to a mere 27.18 percent of unit sales in 2009. Paid digital tracks saw an increase of 64,099,000 units in 2009 over 2008, or a 14.56 percent. Although there is a large demand for digital songs and consumers continue to purchase large amounts of digital music, most are buying one or two individual tracks rather than the higher-margin albums. Today, an 'album' has taken on a new meaning and can simply be just a 'play list' of digital songs compiled from many Internet sites by consumers based on their listening habits, tastes, and preferences.

When overall album sales are broken out by CD, digital, cassette, and other formats and shown in Table 1.3, CD sales declined by 27,146,000 units and sales plunged by nearly 20 percent in May of 2009 when compared to the same period in May of 2008. Digital tracks saw an increase of 5,253,000 units or an increase of 20.89 percent, but may not have been enough to offset the decline in CD sales and revenue.

Today's music consumer may not be willing to pay for an entire higher priced CD when they are merely interested in only one or two 'hit' songs to complete their library. Furthermore, the sale of higher priced CD albums are being replaced by selected single song downloads that may cost as little as 99 cents.

1.3 Economic Model of Performance Rights and Copyright Holders

The traditional arts industry include many categories such as literary works; musical works; dramatic works; pantomimes and choreographic works; pictorial, graphic, and sculptural works; motion pictures and other audiovisual works; sound recordings and architectural works. These categories make up what is sometimes referred to as the *cultural industry*. When the 'original works of authorship' within these categories are fixed in a tangible form of expression such as books, poems, articles, songs including lyrics, musical notation and sound recording, operas, choreography, paintings, drawings, designs, sculptures, photographs, videos and motion pictures, including screenplays or other forms, these works are protected under US copyright laws from infringement.

US copyright laws grant the owners of such copyrighted works the exclusive and legal right to or authorize others to do the following:[1]

1. To reproduce the work in copies or phonorecords;
2. To prepare derivative works based upon the work;
3. To distribute copies or phonorecords of the work to the public by sale or other transfer of ownership, or by rental, lease, or lending;
4. To perform the work publicly, in the case of literary, musical, dramatic and choreographic works, pantomimes, motion pictures, and other audiovisual works;
5. To display the work publicly, in the case of literary, musical, dramatic, and choreographic works, pantomimes, and pictorial, graphic, or sculptural works, including the individual images of a motion picture or other audiovisual work; and
6. In the case of sound recordings, to perform the work publicly by means of a digital audio transmission.

A songwriter, composer, or performer can earn significant amounts of income from the performance, mechanical, synchronization, and digital recording rights to their music. Many media companies (music users) in radio, broadcast television, cable, satellite, the Internet, and others are granted the right to use these copyrighted works once a compulsory license has been obtained, royalty fees have been paid, and without the need to contact each individual copyright holder for permission to use their works.

Agencies such as ASCAP, BMI, and SESAC handle some of the performance rights licensing of musical compositions, while SoundExchange handles the rights for audio-sound recordings on behalf of the copyright holders. The Harry Fox Agency (HFA) handles the rights for mechanical distribution of a song. A single song can have multiple copyrights attached to it. For example, a song to be broadcast on radio can have both a *performance right* for the underlying musical composition—the musical notation, melody, and lyrics—and the *sound recording rights*—the audio, voice and sound effects attached to the song—depending on whether the medium used to broadcast the song is considered terrestrial or digital.

The copyright holders in the case of performance rights would include the publishers, songwriters, and composers (music creators) who are paid royalty income when their copyrights works are broadcast on radio, television, the Internet or cell phones, or used in retail outlets. For sound recording rights, the copyright holders would include the vocalists and the background musicians when their musical works are played on certain digital radio, cable, and satellite television transmissions.

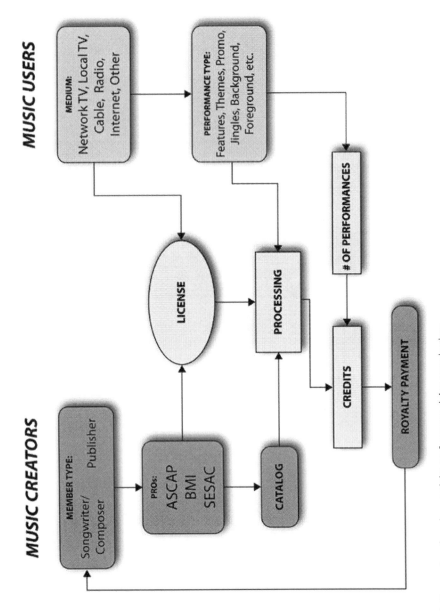

Fig. 1.1 Economics of music copyright: performance rights organizations

In order to receive an income stream from their copyrighted songs, songwriters, composers, and music publishers rely on performing rights organizations such as ASCAP, BMI, and SESAC to license and track the many non-dramatic recorded uses of their song titles on radio, television, the Internet, and elsewhere. These recorded uses are sometimes called performances or airplay. The copyright holders are then paid based on factors that include the number of performances. The need to efficiently compensate songwriters, composers, authors, and publishers, the copyright holders of musical compositions, in the form of performance royalty payments has evolved into a model of supply and demand as shown in Fig. 1.1.

The focus of this study is mainly on performance royalty income for musical compositions, the lyrics, melody, and musical notation, not the sound and audio recording. As such you will notice that SoundExchange is not included in Fig. 1.1 as a PRO. Figure 1.1 illustrates the dynamic economic interplay of the music creators who supply the music, and the demand by music users for copyrighted music compositions in various media industries and other venues. Figure 1.1 is adapted from the performance and credit-based royalty payment philosophy currently in place at ASCAP. The methods used by BMI and SESAC for translating non-dramatic musical performances into royalty payments may be slightly different and may not be entirely depicted in the figure.

The end result for all PROs, nonetheless, is the same in making sure that the copyright holders, the songwriters, composers, authors, and publishers, are paid in a timely and efficient manner when their licensed copyrighted musical compositions are used on television, radio, the Internet, and other venues.[2]

1.4 Economic Characteristics of Music Production

The demand for access to a PRO's catalog of licensed songs is determined by music users in many media industries such as television, radio, cable, the Internet, and other venues such as bars, restaurants, theme parks, and colleges and universities. Unlike other entertainment industries, the music publishing business is said to follow the same business cycle fluctuations in consumer spending (which in turn is driven by personal income) like many other firms.

During the boom phase of the economic cycle record, sales increase as disposable income increases and record companies are flush with profits. During downturns and recessions, the sale of music declines as consumers cut spending, shift to other forms of entertainment, and company profits decline. In terms of the demand and supply of labor in music, record labels and music publishers must constantly develop, sign, and promote new performing and non-performing songwriters with the potential of selling millions of records, while generating revenue from the existing recordings in their catalogs.

Large record labels (that are sometimes owned and housed under the same roof a major music publisher) have several advantages over smaller independent labels in terms of being able to offer large upfront advance payments (as an offset to future royalty income to artists) to recording artists, marketing, and distribution in both domestic and international markets. Independent or smaller record labels lacking the ability to offer large advances focus on a few music genres, perhaps in a local marketing area.

There is said to be an oversupply of both artists and songs because many recording artists may be involved only on a part-time basis, may have other interests or jobs, and some recording artists are popular enough that works are constantly in demand. The difference between a full-time recording artist and a part-time artist may be determined by whether he or she has a recording contract, a key barrier to entry in the music recording industry that is now being reshaped by the Internet.

Throsby (2006, p. 9) describes the three features of artistic labor that combine to set artists apart from other workers:

1. Financial rewards to professional artistic practice are generally lower than in other occupations with other similar characteristics (education and training requires, etc.); thus artists' labor markets profiles typically exhibit multiple job holding.
2. The level of variability of artistic earnings is generally higher than in comparable occupations, making an individual artist's attitudes to risk an important determinant of his or her labor market participation.
3. Non-pecuniary motives are important in the allocation of an artist's time between alternative labor markets, i.e. the 'inner drive' to create art may dominate financial incentives or at least mediate their influence.

Grant and Wood (2004) describe the many non-labor related economic attributes that characterizes cultural products, and we have selected some of these attributes as they relate to the music industry to discuss below.[3] According to Grant and Wood, music, like books and movies, when compared to other physical commodities such as cars, is considered a *cultural good* with several unique economic attributes. Music is designed to communicate ideas, entertain consumers, enhance other social activities that do not require total concentration, and affects the audio and visual senses more directly that some other products. Music is said to be an *experience good* in that listeners must first 'consume' the good before deciding whether to purchase it or not. Consumption of music is said to be *non-rivalous* in that one's person consumption of a song does not reduce its availability to millions of other consumers in the future.[4]

Competition among the record companies is in quantities rather than prices, with consumers being charged similar prices for practically all records released. As profit margins are significantly higher on albums than on singles, success is usually judged in terms of albums sold.[5] From a product perspective, there is a vast collection of recorded music in the catalogs of music publishers where each song is said to be a unique creation. The nature of the production process in popular music is that of high risk, high fixed capital costs, upfront artistic labor costs, and low marginal cost of production.[6]

The risk level involved in each investment in each new artist or even existing successful artists is highly speculative and significant because the level of expected future sales cannot be determined even using past success as a guide. The pressure is always on music publishers to produce 'hit albums,' and for existing artists to meet or exceed previous record sales goals in an industry with constant changing consumer tastes in music and genres. Music success is often measured using Billboard Album Charts, based on album sales from Nielsen SoundScan, and Billboard's Singles Charts, based on airplay data from Nielsen Broadcast Data Systems (BDS).[7] Table 1.4 indicates that cash flow in the music industry is seasonal and a large percent (30 percent or more) of physical music sales such as CDs occur during the Christmas selling season each year, even though since 2006 that share has been steadily declining year over year.

Table 1.4 Seasonal Cash Flow Trends In Music Sales

Year	Q4 sales	Year-end sales	Q4/year-end (%)
2004	218	681	32.01
2005	204	619	32.96
2006	195	588	33.16
2007	163	501	32.53
2008	131	428	30.61

Source: *Billboard* magazine, July 18, 2009, pp. 10–11. Used with permission of e5 Global Media.

Most of the fixed capital cost, including the advance paid to recording artists, upfront marketing and promotion costs, is sunk upfront in producing the first physical copy where also the intellectual property and copyright ownership are first created. It may take years before the capital costs can be recovered from CD sales, digital downloads, and other copyright exploitation.

'Any or all of the copyright owner's exclusive rights may be transferred, but to be valid, the transfer of exclusive rights must be in writing and signed by the owner of the rights.'[8] The need to transfer a copyright can occur as the result of legal proceedings in the case of a divorce or bankruptcy. The copyright can also be transferred to the estate or heirs in a will or, however, a writer's property is disposed of by various state laws upon the copywriter owner's death.

The publishers pay nothing for being assigned their share of the copyright, except for an upfront payment or 'advance' to some recording artists to cover living expenses which must be recouped from the songwriter's share of future royalty income. In some cases, the advance paid can be substantial if the recording artist has a previous history of recording success. Advance payments can have a direct impact on the earnings of songwriters depending on record sales and airplay.

The ability to offer advance cash payments to sign a recording artist is a key distinguishing between the major record and the independent labels. In addition with all the mergers and acquisitions, music publishers are now large conglomerates with a wide international footprint that may outweigh some of the benefits of signing with a small independent label.

Thall (2006) illustrates the many advantages and disadvantages of the advance payment system. His analysis explains why some artists may earn very little in mechanical royalty income from the exploitation of their copyrighted material. With the advance, the record label in some cases may be taking a gamble with some unknown artists in which they hope to recoup the advance from future royalty payments earned by the artists. On the other hand some artists, without another source of income, rely on the advance payments to enable them to write and perform their music. The advance payments made to artists are more like a loan with all the implications of repayment that come from a loan. For many recording artists living expenses, attorney fees, income taxes, recording, marketing, and other costs can often magnify the burden of repaying the advance. In some cases it make years before an advance can be repaid, particularly if the artists do not have a large backlog of music. Yet, even if the advances are recouped, the publisher or record company will end up owning the writer's or artist's valuable copyright assets in both musical compositions and recordings assets in perpetuity. In addition, growing segments of the music industry's lawyers and accountants are no longer inclined to encourage artists to accept substantial advances given the potential risks versus income. For example, some writers can choose to pay for their own demos, or hire their own promotion teams, rather than have the music publisher handle it.[9]

Keep in mind that songwriters, composers, authors, and publishers are paid *separately and directly* by ASCAP, BMI, and SESAC for the performance rights to a song that would have nothing to do with retail album sales. This means that ASCAP, BMI, and SESAC disburse the songwriters' share of performance royalty check directly into hands of the songwriters/composers, and the publishers' share directly into the hands of publisher and there is no co-mingling of income.

From a technological change and productivity perspective, the costs of producing and distributing digital music are far lower today than the comparative costs of earlier physical products such as the CD. The marginal cost of producing an additional unit of a song or album is insignificant once the master copy has been created. In the case of digital recordings, the marginal cost of producing another unit may simply be just the cost of the physical compact disk itself, if it is distributed in that physical form.[10]

The intellectual property —usually the lyrics and melody— can then be stored, duplicated, and delivered by several transmission modes, including the cell phone or iPod. Music publishers will attempt to recoup their investment over time after the initial investment of creating each new song title. Unlike other products in which capital can be substituted for other key inputs, music is said to be of limited substitutability because the copyright laws protect the monopoly on each unique title. The copyright laws protect the uniqueness of each song title by prohibiting the unauthorized distribution or sale of copies. The monopoly quality of each composer or songwriter and their unique works may be thought of as the so-called 'no substitutes' rule.[11]

Initially, the major music publishers and record labels, with a well-known stable of artists and hit songs and control over the means of production and distribution channels built up over many decades, would have been a barrier to entry for independent distributors or labels who wanted to become alternative suppliers of music.

The overhead costs such as advertising, retailing, and cross promotions alone would have made it difficult for independent labels to enter the market for music distribution. But the Internet, computers, CD burners, camcorders, iPods, and large-box retailers have dramatically changed the economics of music distribution and made it easier for independent artists and labels to reach thousands of listeners.

In terms of the physical demand for music, it is difficult to predict which individual song or album might sell in the millions or which new artist might rise to the top of the charts in *Billboard* magazine. Several factors affect the demand for music as we shall see later when we discuss the various music users, such as radio stations, with so many segments and sub-segments that cater to the many diverse listeners and tastes in local communities.

Grant and Wood suggest that the risk factor in launching new works of popular culture is impossible to overestimate because the vast majority of cultural products do not succeed and some music publishers may fail to recoup their investment in the creation of the intellectual property. This might help to explain the so-called '80-20' split in the music business in which 20 percent of artists may earn the lion's share of performance royalty payments, creating a skewed distribution of earnings. The demand for 'superstars' and their music is heavily influenced by the taste of the listening audience and consumer spending.

Another factor that affects the demand for music is that the demand for each new title may be independent of the demand for other titles, given the fickle nature of music listeners, particularly young listeners whose taste and buying habits can change overnight. Consumers in certain age brackets may only be interested in a particular genre and may limit their purchases of other music genres. With music downloads (both free and paid), file-swapping, the CD burner, and various other music choices such as HD and Internet radio, it is the consumer who is the ultimate decision maker in the demand for music.

The time line of demand for music is such that demand falls off sharply after the first introduction of a song. The rapid decay, using the terminology of Grant and Wood, of a song title on Billboard's charts can be measured in weeks, if not months, judging from the number of charts chronicled by *Billboard* magazine each week. For example, as reported in *Billboard* magazine, Nielsen Soundscan counts albums as current only if sales occur within the first 18 months of an album's release (12 months for classical and jazz albums). Titles that stay in the top half of the Billboard 200 however remain as current. Titles older than 18 months are considered 'catalog.' 'Deep catalog' is a subset of catalog for titles out more than 36 months and still in physical CD production.[12] Pricing of cultural goods is said to be discriminatory between markets, particularly when a film is involved and distributed in different geographical regions and countries.

The selected attributes described above when taken together demonstrate what Grant and Wood call the 'curious economics' of the business of popular culture. They cite three observations about cultural products: Most cultural products are risky investments that fail to achieve commercial success and it is virtually impossible to predict ahead of time which products those will be. Once the sunk costs of producing a cultural good has been recovered, the marginal cost of producing the next unit is tiny.

Cultural products marketed to consumers in large geographical areas have a lower risk because there are more consumers in which to amortize the fixed costs associated with the making of the master copy. Grant and Wood help to explain why record companies might only be interested in signing new acts that have already established a fan base on the Internet. Record producers would rather focus resources on a few diminishing top selling artists whose catalog of previous songs can be exploited as 'best of' type compilations and folios. Royalty income is, therefore, skewed toward artists with recording contracts and previous recording success, making it difficult for some independent artists to break through.

1.5 Brief Overview of Performing Rights Organizations

The American Society of Composers, Authors and Publishers (ASCAP), Broadcast Music, Inc. (BMI), and SESAC are the major performing rights organizations, sometimes called performing rights societies, that control the non-exclusive licensing rights to millions of copyrighted musical compositions that include the lyrics, melody, and musical notation. These organizations represent the vast majority of copyright holders—songwriters (composers and lyricists) and music publishers in the US and some foreign affiliates. These organizations grant a blanket or per-program license to music users for use of the music in their catalogs.

SoundExchange is responsible for collecting royalties on behalf of the recording labels and performing artists for the digital sound recordings on digital radio and satellite cable.[13] PROs then track music use on television, radio, the Internet, live venues, and other media, determine which music has been performed, and pay the appropriate copyright holders a royalty income when their musical compositions—called performances—are performed in those licensed media. This performance royalty is distinct, and it is collected and paid out separately from other income agreements as spelled out in recording contracts.

There are some differences among the various PROs in the US in terms of organizational structure, music performance weighting schemes, survey sampling, and payment methods. ASCAP is the oldest and largest performing rights *society* in the United States since its founding in 1914, and is a membership association of 350,000 US composers, songwriters, lyricists, and publishers of every kind of music. BMI is a corporation, organized in 1939 by members of the radio broadcasting industry, with which writers and publishers affiliate. BMI's ownership now also includes television as well as radio stations. The eligibility requirements for both ASCAP and BMI are practically the same for songwriters, composer, and publishers. Privately held SESAC was formed in 1930 and is much smaller than both ASCAP and BMI in terms of members. These PROs, through agreements with affiliated international societies, represent hundreds of thousands of music creators around the world.

1.6 Music Licensing

ASCAP, BMI, and SESAC bundle together the creative output of songwriters, composers and publishers in a collective license in what is known as a *blanket license* and licenses the use to music users for use on radio, television, cable television, Internet websites, and in concert halls and retail establishments.

The purchaser of the blanket license is allowed the non-exclusive and unlimited use of the PROs library or repertory of songs, once the fee for its use has been negotiated, for *non-dramatic public performances*. In addition to a blanket license, ASCAP also offers the *per-program* license in which the variable fee is based on programs containing ASCAP music not otherwise licensed.

Liebowitz and Margolis (2009) suggest that 'the blanket license has economic attributes that are superior to á -la-cart pricing. Because a musical composition is an information good—a *non-rivalrous* good with zero marginal reproduction costs—there are no social benefits to excluding users from using particular songs or having them economize on the use of already created music. This means that the blanket license induces the efficient use of music for all consumers who take the license.'

ASCAP, BMI, and SESAC collect licensing fees on behalf of the copyright holders, the publishers, composers, and songwriters, and not the recording artist. SoundExchange collects royalty payments for certain digital performances for the recording artist, other background musicians and the record labels, which may be a subsidiary of a large publisher. This distinction is important to keep in mind in this section. The issue of performing artists (as distinct from the songwriters/composers who already receive performance royalty payments) from terrestrial radio and TV stations is now a major legislative battle that involves creating a new and separate category for performance royalties.

The Harry Fox Agency handles the royalty payments for some mechanical rights for physical products such as CDs, DVDs, and tapes. Many major publishers also handle their own mechanical licensing, rather than using Harry Fox. Mechanical royalty payments for independent songwriters not affiliated with a major publisher and who own the exclusive rights to their songs are handled by the American Mechanical Rights Agency (AMRA) and the Songwriters Guild of America (SGA).

With the widespread use of the Internet, individual songwriters can register their own song titles with a PRO online without the need of a publisher. However, there is still the need to register the song formally with the US Copyright Office to prevent other infringement issues. Table 1.5 describes the many types of licenses that may be required to use a single song, and the various agencies involved in licensing the copyrights and the owners of the copyrights. With a 'compulsory' license as defined in the Copyright Act as long as the royalty fee is paid, the license granted by the PRO and the terms and conditions of the license are met, the music user is free to use the music without having to worry about being sued for infringement or having to contact each individual copyright holder. However, ASCAP, BMI, and SESAC

Table 1.5 Music Royalty Multiple Licensing and Collection Agencies

License	Music use	Agency	Copyright owners[1]
Public Performances (Non-Dramatic)	Live or recorded music used on TV cable, radio, Internet, cell phone, in bars, restaurants, retail outlets, hotels, colleges, gyms, theme parks, etc.	ASCAP BMI & SESAC	Publishers Songwriters
Mechanical	Physical products (CDs, cassettes, etc.) or permanent digital downloads, interactive streaming and ring tones	Harry Fox	Publishers
Mechanical		AMRA & SGA	Independent Songwriters
Digital Audio/ Sound Recording Performances	Sound recordings performed on digital cable, satellite TV the Internet & satellite radio	SoundExchange	Record Labels Performers
Lyrics Reprint Worship Services[2]	Lyrics reproduced in Church bulletins & overhead projectors to aid singing	CCLI	Publishers Songwriters
Synchronization[3]	Music used with moving images in theatrical and TV movies, commercials and DVDs	Negotiated	Songwriters Publishers Producers
Live Dramatic Performances[3]	Music for the stage that includes scenery, props, costumes and reserved seating	Negotiated	Publishers Songwriters Producers

[1] Songwriters include composers and authors.

[2] Royalty fee for reproducing lyrics not for performing the works.

[3] Negotiated separately between the producers and copyright owners.

have a 'non-exclusive right' to the copyrights of their members or affiliates because composers and publishers do retain the right to license their songs directly should they choose to do so.[14]

Music publishers can be affiliated with all of the performing rights societies at the same time because they often represent individual songwriters who are registered with the various organizations. In this case only a partial catalog may be registered with each of the PROs. A songwriter, on the other hand, can only be actively registered or affiliated with one performing rights licensing organization at a time in the United States. Writer members would have to resign from one society to join another within the United States. Writers, however, are permitted to have dual affiliations with foreign societies outside of the United States and still maintain membership in the United States.

There are some cases where a songwriter may have resigned from one PRO but because a co-writer or co-publisher of the same song elects to remain with the PRO, the song remains with the original PRO. The resigned member may continue to receive distributions for the song provided that the song is not licensed by any other PRO in the United States.

The PROs will then monitor the airwaves, public retail establishments, bars, clubs, restaurants, and other places for music performances based on their individual catalogs of registered song titles, and when necessary file infringement lawsuits on behalf of publishers and songwriters for the use of copyrighted music without a license.[15]

The standard method for determining the fee for a blanket license issued by ASCAP, BMI, or SESAC is usually based on a percent of the music users' revenue with annual minimum fees built into the licensing agreement. There may be other ways of assessing fees in the cases of new business start-ups who may not be generating revenue, but whose input expenses include the cost of using copyrighted music. For example, some industries have the option of negotiating an industry-wide association multiple-year licensing agreement with the PROs that is then allocated to individual members using a complex formula based on ratings, market size, and other factors. These fees are then adjusted by music-use factors depending on the amount of music used or deductions are made for advertising agency commissions and other items not directly related to music.

From the royalty fees collected (less administration costs) publishers and writers are paid separately and directly in the case of ASCAP, BMI SESAC, and CCLI. SoundExchange will collect royalty payments for certain digital audio performances on behalf of records labels and recording artists. Table 1.6 shows the substantial amounts collected by the two largest PROs in the US in 2008 for distribution.[16] Privately held SESAC does not make their financial data public unlike ASCAP and BMI. It is clear, however, that performance rights licensing fees collected now run in the billions of dollars each year.

Table 1.6 Royalty Receipts by PRO, 2008

Agency	Affiliates/ Members	Receipts ($ mil.)	Distribution ($ mil.)	Distribution (%)
ASCAP	350, 000	933	817	87.57
BMI[1]	375, 000	901	786	87.24
SoundExchange[2]	34, 600	148	100	67.57
Harry Fox[3]	37, 000	307	283	92.25
SESAC[4]	NA	NA	NA	NA

[1] BMI's fiscal year ends in June.
[2] Statutory Royalties only. Members include 3,600 recording copyright holders and 31,000 featured artists. Note that SoundExchange's distribution ratio is smaller than that of the other agencies for the 2008 reporting period. The data on SoundExchange's royalty is taken from pp. 5–6 of the *SoundExchange Draft Annual Report For 2008.*
[3] Harry Fox admin. fee is 7.75% or $24 million.
[4] SESAC is privately held and does not provide financial information.

BMI reported that they generated $905 million in licensing fee revenue in its fiscal year that ended June 30, 2009. That amount represented an 0.44 percent increase over $901 million collected during the same period in the prior fiscal year, despite one of the most difficult economic environments in the company's history.[17]

Although we focused on performing rights agencies in the United States, many do have reciprocal agreements with foreign affiliates in other countries. These foreign performing rights societies will collect royalty payments for the use of American music abroad. Similarly, American performing rights organizations will collect and transmit royalty payments for foreign music used in the United States and its territories. For example, in Britain the *MCPS-PRS Alliance Limited* agency handles both mechanical and performance rights for musicians there, these functions are handled separately in the United States as shown in Table 1.5.

1.6.1 Performance Rights Licensing

The distinction between a non-dramatic and dramatic public performance is very important, and the subject of many court challenges. A dramatic performance could be a Broadway show or opera in a theater with scenery, elaborate costumes, and reserved seating. In general, the show producers and the artists (or their representatives) negotiate their own royalty payments, artistic control, and so on in individual transactions.[18] In contrast to a dramatic performance in a theater, non-dramatic public performances occur everywhere in thousands of commercial establishments every day. *Performance rights* income is income derived from licensed copyrighted musical compositions, the melody, and lyrics, when performed in public whether it is live or recorded.

There is no charge or fee to perform hymns or songs of a religious nature in a worship service. But when lyrics are reproduced and printed in the church service bulletin or used in an overhead projection to aid the congregation in singing, the copyrights owners of such works must be compensated for the use of those lyrics through Federal copyright laws. The Christian Copyright Licensing Incorporated (CCLI) is the agency that handles the licensing and the distribution royalty payments for Christian publishers and songwriters.[19]

1.6.2 Mechanical Rights Licensing

The Harry Fox Agency handles the mechanical licensing for a variety of physical formats, including lyrics, tablature, and more; collections; and distribution of royalty payments for US music publishers. Mechanical royalties are based on Federal copyright laws designed to compensate songwriters and publishers for the use of their creative output such as songs. Mechanical revenues, based on the volume of CDs or albums produced, and digital downloads are two of revenue segments for the music publisher.

Songs on a CD are typically licensed to a record label by the copywriter holders. The record label will then sell the CD to retailers or digital downloads for Internet use. The record label then pays *mechanical* royalties to the publisher based on *sales volume*. The publisher then shares these receipts with the songwriter. The mechanical royalty is totally different from the recording artist royalty that is paid from retail sales price of an album.

The Mechanical Statutory Rate is derived from the rates set by the Copyright Board under the US Copyright Code in October 2008 and shown in Table 1.7. Songwriters and music publishers are paid a mechanical royalty rate of 9.1¢ per unit for both physical products and digital downloads, while a rate of 24¢ is applied to each ring tone.[20]

Table 1.7 Statutory Mechanical Royalty Rates for Songwriters and Music Publishers

Type	Rate per song (5 min or less)	Per minute (Over 5 min)
Physical Records	9.1¢	1.75¢
Permanent Digital Downloads	9.1¢	1.75¢
Masterone Ringtunes	24¢	–
Limited Downloads	Varies	Varies
Interactive Streaming	Varies	Varies

Source: www.harryfox.com/docs/HFARoyaltyRatePR10-2-08.pdf.

The market for ring tones declined in the 2007 and 2008 year over period as shown in Table 1.8. Two reasons are cited in explaining the decline of ring tones. First, ring tones may not be as popular as in previous years among young users because of the proliferation of other mobile music options such as ring back tones. Second, the price differential between higher-margin ring tones—which typically retail for $1.99 for a snippet of a song—and 0.99¢ full-track downloads of the same song is another factor.[21] In most publishing deals, the publisher is traditionally paid 50 percent of royalty income from *mechanical* licensing such as the physical reproduction of CDs, tapes, vinyl, and digital downloads, and the other half going to songwriter.

Table 1.8 US Ring Tone Sales 2007–2008 by Volume (in million)

	2007	2008	Change	% Change
Masterphone	201.2	159.6	42.6	21.2
Polyphonic	14.6	6.4	8.2	56.2
Voicetone	4.2	2.3	1.9	45.2
Total	220.0	167.3	52.7	24.0

Source: Based on *Billboard* magazine, January 17, 2009, pp. 22–24. Used with permission of e5 Global Media.

Physical albums— such as CDs, cassettes, and LPs that once made up 91 percent of the record industry main product lines— dwindled to a mere 26.54 percent of album sales at year-end 2008, but accounted for 77.88 percent of retail sales in dollar value. Digital tracks which are now replacing physical formats accounted for close to 73.46 percent unit sales, while contributing 22.12 percent in dollar value as shown in Table 1.9. This might explain why a band such as Radiohead would choose to give away their digital downloads for free in certain cases in the hopes that fans purchase CDs, lyrics, and other bonus material at their website.

Table 1.9 Year-End 2008 Retail Physical Units and Dollar Value (by Format)

Format	2008 Units (mil.)	2008 % Share	2008 ($ mil.)	2008 % Share
Physical	401.8	26.54	5,758.5	77.88
Digital	1,112.3	73.46	1,635.4	22.12
Total Units	1,514.1		7,393.9	

Source: Based on data from www.riaa.com, 2008 Year-End Shipment Statistics.

It might also explain why there is some difficulty in 'monetizing' digital sales. Music fans can simply download their favorite music for free from websites, use a CD burner to burn tracks of their favorite music from their friends, or pirate the music from websites. It is not uncommon to hear music industry insiders speak of the so-called *80-20 split* in which 20 percent of the artists are generating 80 percent of the revenue. At the rate, CD sales are declining, the *80-20 split* might also be applicable to the digital tracks vs. CD/album unit sales judging by Table 1.9, but the revenue split would be different.

The *80-20 split* has become the subject of a heated debate in the music industry, and in academic circles since Anderson (2008). Anderson published his *Long Tail* analysis in which he described a scenario in which 'niche' artists were presumably changing this dynamic based on sales at an online retailer. However, Christman (2009) reports that music publishing executives are lamenting that 'they don't believe the celebrated "long tail" effect is playing out in the market for digital downloads, adding however that it is hard to predict when an obscure song will suddenly find itself in the spotlight. Cheery Lane Music publishing CEO Peter Primont noted that the Harry Belafonte song *Day-O* enjoyed a revival thanks to the 1988 movie *Bettlejuce*, while [Sony/ATV Chairman/CEO Martin] Bandier pointed out that the 2000 movie *O Brother, Where Art Thou?* gave new life to songs that had been virtually dormant for 60 years.' We will much more to say on the 'long tail' controversy when we examine the distribution of royalty payments in Chapter 6.

When physical unit sales are broken down by album format, shown in Table 1.10, CDs album sales represented the largest category of 511.1 million units sold in 2008, and had plunged by 27.73 percent or 126.4 million units from the year 2007. In terms of revenue for the CD albums, revenue declined by $1,981 billion or 26.58 percent. Overall physical units declined by -141.9 units or -26.11 percent and revenue by $2,227.3 or 27.89 percent in the year over year RIAA data. Table 1.11 shows the sales volume and revenue from digital music that have offset the decline in C.D. sales. For example, digital revenue climbed to approximately $1.022 billion for year-end 2008. The sale of previously released albums also showed a decline in 2008 as shown in Table 1.12. In terms of market share by the major music publishers, Universal Music was the market leader in terms of digital music sales in May 2009, followed by Sony with 25 percent, and Warner Music at 21 percent as shown in Table 1.13.[22]

It is not just the music publishers who have been affected by the slide in recorded music sales, but the Harry Fox Agency as well. In a March 24, 2009 press release

Table 1.10 Physical Unit Sales and Dollar Value, 2007–2008 (by Format)

Physical units (mil.)	2007	2008	Change	% Change
CD	511.1	384.7	−126.4	−24.73
CD Single	2.6	0.7	−1.9	−73.08
Cassette	0.4	0.1	−0.3	−75.00
LP/EP	1.3	2.9	1.6	123.08
Vinyl Single	0.6	0.4	−0.2	−33.33
Music/DVD Video	27.5	12.8	−14.7	−53.45
Total Units	543.5	401.6	−141.9	−26.11
Dollar value ($ mil.)	2007	2008	Change	% Change
CD	$7,452.3	$5,471.3	−$1,981	−26.58
CD Single	12.2	3.5	−8.7	−71.31
Cassette	3	0.9	−2.1	−70.00
LP/EP	22.9	56.7	33.8	147.60
Vinyl Single	4	2.9	−1.1	−27.50
Music/DVD Video	484.9	218.9	−266	−54.86
Total Value	$7,985.80	$5,758.50	$−2,227.3	−27.89

Source: Based on data from www.riaa.com, 2008 Year-End Shipment Statistics.

Table 1.11 Digital Unit Sales and Dollar Value, 2007–2008 (by Format)

Digital units (mil.)	2007	2008	Change	% Change
Download Single	809.9	1,033.0	223.10	27.55
Download Album	42.5	56.9	14.40	33.88
Kiosk	1.8	1.6	−0.20	−11.11
Music Video	14.2	20.8	6.60	46.48
Total	868.4	1,112.3	243.90	28.09
Digital dollar value ($ mil.)	2007	2008	Change	% Change
Download Single	$801.6	$1,022.7	$221.10	27.58
Download Album	424.9	568.9	144.00	33.89
Kiosk	2.6	2.6	0.00	0.00
Music Video	28.2	41.3	13.10	46.45
Total	$1,257.3	$1,635.5	$378.20	30.08

Source: Based on data from www.riaa.com, 2008 Year-End Shipment Statistics.

Table 1.12 Sales by Album Category (as of 12/07/08)

Category (000)	2007	2008	Change	% Change
Current[1]	270,467	221,213	−49,254	−18.21
Catalog[2]	172,009	160,073	−11,936	−6.94
Deep Catalog[3]	122,546	115,347	−7,199	−5.87

[1] Sales with 18 months of album release
[2] Titles in top half of the Billboard 200
[3] Titles out more than 36 Months
Source: Based on data from *Billboard* magazine, Special Double Issue, December 20, 2008, p. 159. Used with permission of e5 Global Media.

Table 1.13 Market Share of Digital Music Sales (Y-T-D May 15, 2009)

Publisher	Market Share (%)
Universal Music	31
Sony Music	25
Warner Music	21
EMI Group	9
Others	14

Source: Based on Smith (2009), *Wall Street Journal.*

Harry Fox announced that its total 2008 royalty collection from all sources totaled $307.1 million, a 22 percent decline from the year 2007. Of the 2.44 million mechanical licenses issued in 2008, 84 percent was for digital formats, which included permanent digital downloads (Table 1.14). HFA's President, Gary Churgin, attributed the slide in record sales to the closing of retail stores and the reduction in floor space dedicated to music sales. He also suggested that the growth of digital sales, while still robust at the time, was slowing and he did not expect digital to offset the losses of CD sales any time soon.[23]

Table 1.14 Harry Fox Agency 2007–2008 Fees (Year over Year Change)

	Y/Y Change	Y/Y % Change
License Collections All Sources	$307.1 m	−22
Number of Licenses*	2.44 m	62

* 84% of 2.44m are for digital formats, including permanent digital downloads.

Source: http://www.harryfox.com/docs/2008HFARecapPR.pdf.

1.6.3 Synchronization Licensing

Music used in a movie televised on broadcast or cable television would require a synchronization license to reproduce the song in synchronization with a visual moving image, a 'Master Use' fee, and a public performance license when the movie is broadcast to the general public. The 'Master Use' fee for use of the sound recording master copy may be lumped in with the synchronization license, if the Master and copyright owners are the same entity.

Synchronization royalty income is generated when music is used with audio-visual moving images in movies, DVDs, and in broadcast and cable television shows and commercials. The publisher will split the royalty fee 50-50 or at some pro-rata share with the credited writer or writers. As shown in Table 1.15 income generated from synchronization can be substantial, particularly if used in movies and commercials.

Unlike the mechanical license, there is no fixed or statutory rate for a synchronization license or specific collection agency involved. Synchronization licenses are negotiated between the copyright owners (publisher and songwriter) and the production company of the film, the television show, or the commercial based on some mutually agreed on economic value.

Table 1.15 Selected Synchronization Income (Songwriters and Music Publishers)

Media	Income ($, per year)	License Type
Television	1,750–3,500	Worldwide 5-year free television
Motion Pictures	15,000–60,000	Depends on film budget music use & distribution
Commercials	75,000–1,000,000	Depends on use on radio or TV, local or national spots

Source: Brabec and Brabec (2008, pp. 34–46).

Notes

1. See *Copyright Law of the United States and Related Laws* contained in Title 17 of the US Code available at http://www.copyright.gov/title17/circ92.pdf.
2. See Brabec and Brabec (2008, pp. 283–328) for an analysis of the payment philosophy at ASCAP, BMI, and SESAC, or the individual websites of these PROs.
3. See Grant and Wood (2004, pp. 44–60) and Strobl and Tucker (2000) for a full comparison of the features we discuss here.
4. Grant and Wood (2004, pp. 44–60).
5. See Strobl and Tucker (2000).
6. Grant and Wood (2004, pp. 44–60).
7. See the Charts Legend at the back of a current issue or online at http://www.billboard.biz. SoundScan uses point of sales data from retailers to compute its measures.
8. Walker (2008, p. 160).
9. Thall (2006, pp. 17–21)
10. Grant and Wood (2004, pp. 44–60).
11. Grant and Wood (2004, pp. 44–60).
12. See the weekly charts and national music sales report data at the back of any issue or online.
13. See www.ascap.com, www.bmi.com, www.sesac.org, Walker (2008), Krasilovsky and Shemel (2007), and Brabec and Brabec (2008) for detailed information on these organizations.
14. ASCAP uses the term 'member' to describe their songwriters, composers, and publishers while BMI and SESAC may use other designations such as affiliate. We will use member or affiliate interchangeably.
15. ASCAP does not survey public retail establishments, bars, clubs, and restaurants.
16. Data obtained from the following websites:

1. http://www.ascap.com/press/2009/0309_financials.aspx;
2. http://www.bmi.com/news/entry/537154;
3. http://www.harryfox.com/docs/2008HFARecapPR.pdf and
4. http://www.soundexchange.com/assets/download_forms/2008/Annual/Report/PDF/203-23-09_PRE-AUDIT.pdf

Note that the SoundExchange distribution ratio is smaller than that of the other agencies for the 2008 reporting period. The data on SoundExchange's royalty distribution and royalties collected are taken from pp. 5–6 of the SoundExchange Draft Annual Report for 2008.
17. See BMI's August 25, 2009 press release, 'BMI Tops Previous Year in Revenues with $905 Million in FY 2009' at http://www.bmi.com/news/entry/539505.
18. Koenigsberg (2002).
19. See Keen (2007).
20. See http://www.loc.gov/crb/proceedings/2006-3/dpra-public-final-rate-terms.pdf and www.harryfox.com/docs/HFARoyaltyRatePR10-2-08.pdf.
21. *Billboard* magazine, January 17, 2009, pp. 22–24.

22. See Smith (2009).
23. See their March 24, 2009 press release, *HFA Collects almost $307.1 Million in Royalties for its over 37,000 Affiliated Publishing Clients in 2008* at http://www.harryfox.com/docs/2008HFARecapPR.pdf.

References

Anderson, C. (2008). *The Long Tail*. Hyperion, New York, NY.

Brabec, J. and Brabec, T. (2008). *Music Money and Success: The Insiders Guide to Making Money in the Music Industry*. Schirmer Trade Books-Music Sales, New York, NY, 6th edition.

Christman, E. (2009). 'Stormy Weather'. *Billboard* magazine. March 21, p. 16.

Grant, P. and Wood, C. (2004). *Blockbusters and Trade Wars: Popular Culture in a Globalized World*. Douglas and McIntyre, Vancouver, BC.

Keen, D. (2007). 'How Are Royalties Created?'. http://www.ascap.com/musicbiz/christian_music_faq.

Koenigsberg, I. (2002). *Performing Rights in Music and Performing Rights Organizations, Revisited*. White and Case, LLP, New York, NY.

Krasilovsky, W. and Shemel, S. (2007). *This Business of Music: The Definitive Guide to the Music Industry*. Billboard Books, 10th edition.

Liebowitz, S. and Margolis, S. (2009). Bundles of joy: The ubiquity and efficiency of bundles in new technology markets. *Journal of Competition Law and Economics*, 5(1):1–47.

Smith, E. (2009). Universal music takes another stab online. *Wall Street Journal*. May 15, p. B8.

Strobl, E. and Tucker, C. (2000). The dynamics of chart success in the UK pre-recorded popular music industry. *Journal of Cultural Economics*, 24:113–134.

Thall, P. (2006). *What They Will Never Tell You About the Music Business: The Myths, the Secrets, and the Lies (& a Few Truths)*. Billboard Books.

Throsby, D. (2006). Introduction and Overview. In Ginsburg, A. and Throsby, D., editors, *Handbook of the Economics of Art and Culture*, volume 1, pp. 4–21. North Holland.

Walker, J. (2008). *This Business of Urban Music: A Practical Guide to Achieving Success in the Industry, From Gospel to Funk to R&B to Hip-Hop*. Billboard Books.

Chapter 2
Economic Analysis of Music Copyright: Music Users

Abstract The US media industry includes many segments not just radio, cable, television and Internet, but newspapers and films as well. The industry as a whole is reliant on the growth in advertising revenue to sustain profitability. This chapter explores the many music users and how their revenue becomes the source of licensing fees collected by PROs to compensate the copyright holders in the form of performance royalty payments for the use of their music. We will also examine the various types of music performances, their methods of collection, and the way in which royalty payments are computed.

2.1 Introduction

In many cases, the fee for a blanket license from ASCAP, BMI, or SESAC is determined by a percent of advertising or subscription revenue from various music users or media firms with adjustments made for music use and other factors. Media firms are in turn funded by advertisers with a need to make consumers aware of their products and services. Media firms play a dual role in which they must first attract advertisers by their content, and then the content must attract consumers (viewers, eyeballs, web surfers, etc.). Close attention is paid to the economic trends that will affect the demand and supply of advertising from an input cost and output perspective.

2.2 Media Industry Advertising Revenue

Advertising expenditures (or amount spent) and revenue (or amount earned) are both useful measures depending on their strategic importance in marketing. Advertising as a percent of gross domestic product (GDP) is one measure that has been used as a leading indicator of the health of advertising demand.[1] However, personal consumption and industrial production are also now being used by some in the advertising industry as macro-economic drivers to model the demand for advertising. The basic formula for calculating GDP is as follows:

I.L. Pitt, *Economic Analysis of Music Copyright*,
DOI 10.1007/978-1-4419-6318-5_2, © Springer Science+Business Media, LLC 2010

$$GDP = C + I + G + X,$$
where C = Consumption spending; I = Investment spending;
G = Government spending; X = Net of exports over imports.

In July of 2009, Magna, a corporate unit of Interpublic, changed its media forecast from an advertising expenditures–based model to an advertising revenue–based model. Magna's new model appears to be using disaggregated GDP as some of the key inputs. Table 2.1 gives a selected view of some of the changes in the advertising media model produced by Magna.[2] Magna's new advertising media forecast now focuses on advertising revenue with personal consumption and industrial production as primary drivers in the broader macro economy.

Whether the key driver of advertising expenditures is GDP or the key drivers personal consumption and industrial production correlated with advertising revenue, the story has been the same in terms of the direction of these variables. Table 2.2 indicates that beginning in 2006, some of the key drivers correlated with advertising revenue that are used in the Magna's January 2010 forecast show a downward trend.

Mass media advertising revenue, broken down by direct, national, and local categories, is shown in Table 2.3, and is expected to decline to $161.18 billion in 2009.

Table 2.4 shows the percent share of direct, national, and local media advertising revenue over time, direct media revenue has been increasing over time. For example, direct media advertising revenue grew from 20.74 percent in 2005 to an expected 28.19 percent in 2010. Overall, local media advertising has seen a larger share of advertising spending, but that has been declining over time. Local media made up

Table 2.1 Changes in Magna's Old and New Advertising Media Forecasts

	Old Media Forecast	New Media Forecast July 2009
Data Change	Advertising Expenditures	Advertising Revenue
Media	Categorized as National and Local	Categorized as Direct, National Mass or Local Mass
Selected Key Macroeconomic Drivers	Gross Domestic Product	Personal Consumption and Industrial Production

Source: Based on data from B. Wieser, Magna, July 2009.

Table 2.2 Key Drivers Correlated with Advertising Revenue Used in Magna's January 2010 Forecast

Year	Personal Consumption*(%)	Industrial Production(%)
2004	6.16	2.49
2005	6.44	3.32
2006	5.71	2.30
2007	5.40	1.50
2008	3.09	-2.25

*Nominal
Source: Based on data from B. Wieser, www.magnaglobal.com.

Table 2.3 US Mass Media Advertising Revenue ($mil.), January 2010 Forecast

	2005	2006	2007	2008	2009E	2010E
Direct Media	$40,567	$44,400	$47,649	$47,322	$43,617	$45,407
National Mass Media Ex-Olympics	60,746	63,482	64,643	62,276	56,229	57,316
Local Mass Media Ex-Political	94,258	93,469	91,680	79,070	61,333	58,369
Total Media Advertising Ex-Political & Olympics	$195,571	$201,352	$203,972	$188,668	$161,179	$161,092

E = Estimated

Source: Based on data from B. Wieser, www.magnaglobal.com.

Table 2.4 US Mass Media Advertising Revenue (% Share), January 2010 Forecast

	2005	2006	2007	2008	2009E	2010E
Direct Media	20.74	22.05	23.36	25.08	27.06	28.19
National Media Ex-Olympics	31.06	31.53	31.69	33.01	34.89	35.58
Local Media Ex-Political	48.20	46.42	44.95	41.91	38.05	36.23

E = Estimated

Source: Based on data from B. Wieser, www.magnaglobal.com.

48.20 percent of advertising revenue in 2005, but is expected to decline to 36.23 percent in 2010, almost even with expected national advertising revenue of 35.58 percent in 2010.

Tables 2.5 and 2.6 show the year-over-year change in dollar amounts and the corresponding year-over-year change in percentage terms of advertising revenue by media categories. As the US economy worsened, the biggest decline in 2008 over 2007 occurred in local mass media which saw a decline of $12.61 billion or 13.75 percent, while national media adverting declined by $2.38 billion or 3.66 percent. Direct media has the smallest decline of $327 million or 0.69 percent.

Table 2.7 provides a granular look at actual and estimated advertising revenue broken down by the components of direct, national, and local advertising revenue for the years 2008, 2009, and 2010. An inspection of Table 2.7 shows a few of

Table 2.5 US Mass Media Advertising Revenue (Y/Y Change), January 2010 Forecast ($mil.)

	2005	2006	2007	2008	2009E	2010E
Direct Media	3,104	3,833	3,249	−327	−3,705	1,790
National Mass Media Ex-Olympics	2,995	2,736	1,160	−2,367	−6,047	1,087
Local Mass Media Ex-Political	3,405	−789	−1,789	−12,610	−17,737	−2,964
Total Media Ex-Political and Olympics	9,505	5,780	2,620	−15,304	−27,489	−87

E = Estimated

Source: Based on data from B. Wieser, www.magnaglobal.com.

Table 2.6 US Mass Media Advertising Revenue (Y/Y % Change), January 2010 Forecast

	2005	2006	2007	2008	2009E	2010E
Direct Media	8.29	9.45	7.32	−0.69	−7.83	4.10
National Media Ex-Olympics	5.19	4.50	1.83	−3.66	−9.71	1.93
Local Mass Media Advertising Ex-Political	3.75	−0.84	−1.91	−13.75	−22.43	−4.83
Total Media Ex-Political & Olympics	5.11	2.96	1.30	−7.50	−14.57	−0.05

E = Estimated
Source: Based on data from B. Wieser, www.magnaglobal.com.

the bright spots in the Magna forecast. Direct online media is expected to show an increase in advertising revenue of $386.60 million or 2.86 percent over 2009 when the final numbers are tablulated. Overall, the advertising picture for 2010 is expected to improve for direct and national advertising revenue, while a continued decline is forecast for local advertising revenue.

2.3 Music Users: Radio, Broadcast, Cable Television, and Internet

2.3.1 Radio

The radio broadcasting industry consists of two groups of stations, commercial and non-commercial stations. These 'terrestrial' commercial and non-commercial radio stations may also retransmit their programming over the Internet. It has long been the case that commercial stations are paid by advertisers and corporate sponsors to deliver a listening audience defined by certain content and demographic profiles. Non-commercial stations, 'educational' or 'public' stations, earn revenue from government subsidies, subscriptions, or contributions through membership drives, or in the case of colleges and universities from student activity fees collected by the institutions that they represent.

In light of the recent year-over-year decline in radio advertising revenue as shown in Table 2.7, the *Wall Street Journal* reported that for-profit radio stations with financial problems were considering asking their listeners for donations through paid membership drives and other fund raising to partially offset the decline in advertising revenue.[3] Asking the listening public for donations during 'pledge week' has long been the practice of public stations. Not to be out-done, the same article reports that National Public Radio stations are now recruiting ad-sales professionals to drum up corporate sponsorships. The distinction between a non-commercial station and a for-profit station is increasingly becoming blurred in this environment, leading to some confusion among listeners.

The radio programming format, genre, or audience segmentation refer to the type of content that radio stations broadcasts over the air or on the Internet to its many

Table 2.7 Change in US Advertising Revenue, 2008–2009, January 2010 Forecast (in $mil.)

Media	2008	2009E	Change	% Change	2010E
Direct					
Lead Generation	$1,690.00	$1,546.30	−$143.70	−8.50%	$1,618.40
Internet Yellow Pages	1,336.70	1,444.40	107.70	8.06	1,621.70
Paid Search	10,500.00	10,922.60	422.60	4.02	12,377.10
Direct Online Media	13,526.70	13,913.30	386.60	2.86	15,617.20
Directories[a]	12,182.20	10,601.10	−1,581.10	−12.98	9,906.80
Direct Mail	21,613.50	19,102.60	−2,510.90	−11.62	19,883.40
Total Direct Media	$47,322.40	$43,617.00	−$3,705.40	−7.83%	$45,407.40
National					
National Newspapers[a]	1,180.30	873.90	−306.40	−25.96	775.70
Network and Satellite Radio	1,219.90	1,097.90	−122.00	−10.00	1,119.50
National Digital/Online Media[c]	6,186.40	5,551.70	−634.70	−10.26	5,772.50
Magazines[a]	19,191.80	15,437.70	−3,754.10	−19.56	14,311.50
Network Broadcast TV - English[a,b]	13,614.20	12,816.40	−797.80	−5.86	13,249.10
Network Broadcast TV - Spanish	1,062.80	1,035.10	−27.70	−2.61	1,118.60
National Syndication	1,934.80	1,816.60	−118.20	−6.11	1,774.50
National Cable TV[a]	17,885.70	17,599.80	−285.90	−1.60	19,194.70
Total National Media	$62,275.90	$56,229.10	−$6,046.80	−9.71%	$57,316.10
Local					
Local Digital/Online Media[c]	3,829.00	3,367.10	−461.90	−12.06	3,493.00
Outdoor	6,991.40	5,953.60	−1,037.80	−14.84	5,954.70
Local Radio - National	2,929.00	2,349.40	−579.60	−19.79	2,319.30

Table 2.7 (continued)

Media	2008	2009E	Change	% Change	2010E
Local Radio - Local[a]	13, 607.00	10, 736.60	−2, 870.40	−21.10	10, 439.00
Local Cable TV[d]	3, 337.10	2, 810.40	−526.70	−15.78	2, 861.50
Local Broadcast TV[a,d]	14, 817.10	11, 673.90	−3, 143.20	−21.21	11, 482.90
Local Newspaper - National[a]	4, 815.70	3, 554.60	−1, 261.10	−26.19	3, 221.20
Newspaper Classifieds	9, 975.00	6, 110.50	−3, 864.50	−38.74	4, 904.60
Local Newspaper - Retail[a]	18, 768.60	14, 777.00	−3, 991.60	−21.27	13, 692.50
Total Local Advertising	$79, 069.90	$61, 333.10	−$17, 736.80	−22.43%	$58, 368.70
Total National & Local	$141, 345.70	$117, 562.20	$ − 23, 783.50	−16.83%	$115, 684.80
Total Advertising Excl.-Political & Olympics	$188, 668.20	$161, 179.20	−$27, 489.00	−14.57%	$161, 092.30
Total Media Advertising	$191, 653.50	$162, 019.70	−$29, 633.80	−15.46%	$164, 322.90

E=Estimated

[a] Excludes online advertising revenues.

[b] Excludes incremental Olympic advertising revenues.

[c] Includes Banner/Display, Sponsorship, Slotting, Mobile and Other Revenues prior to 2000), Excludes Paid Search and Lead Generation.

[d] Excludes local political advertising revenues.

Source: Based on data from B. Wieser, www.magnaglobal.com.

listeners. It is quite common for some stations to broadcast multiple genres such as part talk, part sports, or part music on a fixed schedule that might vary by time of the day or day of the week. Table 2.8 describes the dramatic increase in the number of radio formats or radio audience segments that were introduced over many years, and their evolution into many radio niches and sub-niches that define radio segmentation. This is only a partial list and many other sub-divided formats are not listed as they are far fewer in number.

Table 2.8 Total US Radio Stations by Format (Commercial and Non-commercial March 2009)

Format	Comm.	Non-Comm.	Total	% Total	Cum. %
News/Talk	1, 382	686	2, 068	13.88	13.88
Country	2, 005	15	2, 020	13.56	27.44
Religion (Teaching, Variety)	300	1, 083	1, 383	9.29	36.73
Spanish	785	137	922	6.19	42.92
Contemporary Christian	137	762	899	6.04	48.96
Oldies	683	33	716	4.81	53.77
Variety	41	647	688	4.62	58.39
Adult Contemporary	623	14	637	4.28	62.67
Sports	624	0	624	4.19	66.86
Classic Hits	578	10	588	3.95	70.81
Top 40	471	33	504	3.38	74.19
Classic Rock	477	8	485	3.26	77.45
Hot AC	402	12	414	2.78	80.23
Alternative Rock	109	260	369	2.48	82.71
Adult Standards	340	18	358	2.40	85.11
Rock	301	11	312	2.09	87.20
Southern Gospel	211	90	301	2.02	89.22
Black Gospel	240	21	261	1.75	90.97
Soft Adult Contemporary	210	1	211	1.42	92.39
Classical	23	155	178	1.20	93.59
Modern Rock	118	53	171	1.15	94.74
Urban AC	163	4	167	1.12	95.86
R&B	131	26	157	1.05	96.91
Ethnic	115	17	132	0.89	97.80
Jazz	45	83	128	0.86	98.66
Pre-Teen	53	0	53	0.36	99.02
R&B Adult/Oldies	38	4	42	0.28	99.30
Gospel	26	9	35	0.23	99.53
Easy Listening	16	9	25	0.17	99.70
Modern AC	20	1	21	0.14	99.84
Rhythmic AC	18	0	18	0.12	99.96
Format Not Available	7	0	7	0.05	100.00
Total Operating Stations	10, 692	4, 202	14, 894	100%	
Stations off the air	197	59	256		
Construction Permits	345	977	1, 322		
Total Stations and CPs	11, 234	5, 238	16, 472		

Comm. = Commercial, Non-Comm. = Non-Commercial and Cum. = Cumulative
Source: Based on data from http://ftp.media.radcity.net/ZMST/insideradio/Mar2009TOTAL Formats.html,
The Radio Book 2008–2009 Edition, © 2009.

For example, 'rock music' has been sub-divided into 'classic rock,' 'modern rock,' 'alternative rock', and many other categories such as 'hard rock Christian-themed,' 'soft rock,' and 'light rock.' Jazz has been sub-divided into 'traditional,' 'smooth jazz,' or 'new age.' Christian music has many sub-niches such as 'Black Gospel' with an emphasis on music heard in predominantly Black churches. 'Contemporary Christian' music can be rock-driven or the type of Gospel music heard in evangelical southern states. Music intended for Spanish-speaking listeners can be broken down into 'Tejano,' 'regional Mexican,' and 'Spanish adult contemporary.'

Other stations focus their musical content based on nostalgia and musical time-periods such as 'hits' from the 1960s, 1970s, 1980s, and 1990s, or offer a 'mix' of these time periods in a 'Top 40' context. Many of the radio formats are designed to reach a specifically defined segment or niche of the listening population based on such demographic criteria as age, ethnicity, religion, sports, political viewpoints, and hobbies. Stations owners hope that with so many formats and sub-segments targeting men, women, the young and the old, and with the right blend of music, information and entertainment programming (that is both meaningful and relevant to their segments), their intended listeners tunes in and keep listening.

One interesting observation from a music royalty and demographic perspective shown in Table 2.8 is the popularity of the interactive and low music use news/talk radio format where on-air hosts comment on the latest issues affecting listeners and then take their telephone calls. News/talk, country and religious radio formats cumulatively account for 36.73 percent of all radio stations even when all types of gospel and contemporary Christian formats are excluded. Country radio format (most are in rural areas) dominates all other formats in the United States, while the news/talk (mostly in urban areas) format follows country.

Over the course of many decades FM radio developed a larger listening audience than the AM format, in part due to better sound quality. As the popularity of music on FM gained momentum, music on AM radio waned. AM radio stations then began offering more news and talk content to attract and keep their listening audience. In New York, largest radio media market, you will find more AM radio stations (28) than FM stations (22).

The passage of the Telecommunications Act of 1996 had a dramatic effect on radio stations as radio station ownership rules were relaxed, and several companies acquired a large number of radio stations. The most significant change that occurred was that the FCC relaxed its radio duopoly ownership rules and regulations. A duopoly is defined as owning two AM and/or two FM radio stations, up to four in total, in the same media market.

Tables 2.9 and 2.10 show the revised rules on radio and television cross-ownership in which a single party could now own or control both an AM and an FM duopoly in individual markets. While no nationwide limits on the number of stations AM or FM radio that a single entity could own were put in place, there was a set limit on local radio ownership and local radio and television cross-ownership. For example a single radio entity can own up to five radio stations in a market, but no more than three stations can be on the same AM or FM service, and the market must have fewer than 14 radio stations. No single entity can own, operate, or control

Table 2.9 Local Radio Ownership Limits

Single entity ownership	Restrictions (AM or FM)	Market size
Up to 5 Stations	Not more than 3 stations	Fewer than 14 radio stations
Up to 6 Stations	Not more than 4 stations	15–29 radio stations
Up to 7 Stations	Not more than 4 stations	30–44 radio stations
Up to 8 Stations	Not more than 5 stations	45 or more radio stations

Source: GAO (2007), Report-GAO-08-330R.

Table 2.10 Radio and Television Stations Cross-Ownership Limits

Television stations	Radio stations	Market restrictions
1	1	Regardless of Independently Owned Media Voices
1	7	At least 20 Independent Owned Media Voice Post Merger
Up to 2	Up to 6	If Permitted Under LTMO & LRMO Caps
Up to 2	Up to 4	At least 10 Independent Owned Media Voice Post Merger

Source: GAO (2007), Report-GAO-08-330R.

more than 50 percent of the stations in a market. Limited local media ownership reflected the FCC concerns on the needs of local residents for such coverage of local news, political campaigns, and public affairs that nationwide media owners might not otherwise provide.

In addition, media companies may have cross-ownership of both radio and television stations in the same market with Local Radio Multiple Ownership (LRMO) and Local Television Multiple Ownership (LTMO) caps and other restrictions.[4]

While the Telecom Act of 1996 addressed the issue of terrestrial radio ownership, the act did not adequately address the issues of the soon to emerge new technologies such as the Internet, HD, and satellite radio broadcasts. By 2008, the radio industry consolidation, which had begun following the 1996 Telecommunications Act, had mostly been completed. This changed the industry makeup considerably, aided in part by advertisers.

The top 10 radio station owners in terms of 2008 estimated revenue and station ownership now included Clear Channel Communications Inc. with $2.92 billion in revenue and 845 stations; CBS Radio with $1.59 billion in revenue and 130 stations; Citadel Communications with $720 million and 205 stations; and Cumulus Media with $520 million and 305 stations as shown in Table 2.11. In aggregate, the Top 10 radio station owners in term of revenue generated an estimated $7.82 billion in revenue in 2008. Table 2.12 shows that selected segments such as satellite and local radio in the radio industry are expected to see double digit declines in advertising revenue in 2009.[5]

While the number of station-owners was becoming concentrated, the number of radio formats targeting specific local community segments expanded rapidly. This sort of radio station differentiation created a huge opportunity for advertisers to connect with their targeted audience in special local marketing niches. Radio station owner concentration shown in Table 2.13 reveal that the Top 10 radio station

Table 2.11 Top 10 Radio Owners 2008 Estimated Revenue and Stations

Owner	2008 Revenue ($b)	% Share	Stations	% Share
Clear Channel	2.92	37.34	845	45.48
CBS Radio	1.59	20.33	130	7.00
Citadel	0.72	9.21	205	11.03
Cumulus	0.52	6.65	305	16.42
Entercom	0.47	6.01	112	6.03
Cox Radio	0.45	5.75	85	4.57
Univision	0.41	5.24	72	3.88
Radio One	0.27	3.45	52	2.80
Bonneville	0.25	3.2	28	1.56
Emmis	0.22	2.81	23	1.24
Total Top 10	7.82		1, 858	

Source: Based on revenue data from *Wall Street Journal*, 12/21/2009, p. B3.
Station owner data based on licensed data from www.bia.com.

Table 2.12 Selected Radio Advertising Revenue, 2008–2009, January 2010 Forecast ($mil.)

Media	2008	2009E	Change	% Change	2010E
Network & Satellite Radio	1, 219.90	1, 097.90	−122.00	−10.00	1, 119.50
Local Radio - National[a]	2, 929.00	2, 349.40	−579.60	−19.79	2, 319.30
Local Radio - Local[a]	13, 607.00	10, 736.60	−2, 870.40	−21.10	10, 439.00

E = Estimated
[a] Excludes online advertising revenues.
Source: Based on data from B. Wieser, www.magnaglobal.com.

owners in terms of stations owned controlled 57.56 percent (or 2,003 stations) of the Top 50 commercial radio stations. Radio concentration came with a steep rise in company debt that would later leave many station owners unable to service their debt payments as advertising revenue declined due in part to the on-going economic downturn, increased competition from Internet broadcasting, and shifts in consumer habits for pre-recorded music using devices such as iPods and commercial-free satellite radio broadcasts.

The viability of Clear Channel to remain as a going-concern during the recession of 2009 was raised in several media reports and summarized in Table 2.14. Clear Channel's nationalized ad sales model is being questioned since it contrasts sharply with the localized segmentation model that radio specializes in. 'Clear Channel not only became the nation's largest radio station owner, but also the biggest leveraged buyout ever in the media business after it was taken private by Thomas H. Lee Partners and Bain Capital. The company has $16 billion of bank debt and another $6 billion of junior debt'.

'In the first quarter of 2009, Clear Channel's revenue plummeted by 23 percent and its cash flow declined by 47 percent, making it harder to meet the payments on the billions in debt accumulated in the process of buying out its public investors. Furthermore in April of 2009, the company laid off 590 employees after cutting 1,850 employees in January, for an overall staff reduction of 12 percent since the acquisition.'[6] However, by December of 2009, it was Citadel Broadcasting

Table 2.13 Top 50 Station Owners Ranked by Stations

Rank	Station owner	No. of stations	% Stations	Cum. %
1	Clear Channel Communications Inc	845	24.28	24.28
2	Cumulus Broadcasting Inc	305	8.76	33.05
3	Citadel Communications	205	5.89	38.94
4	CBS Radio	130	3.74	42.67
5	Entercom	112	3.22	45.89
6	Salem Communications Corporation	93	2.67	48.56
7	Saga Communications Inc	91	2.61	51.18
8	Cox Radio Inc	85	2.44	53.62
9	Univision	72	2.07	55.69
10	Cherry Creek Radio LLC	65	1.87	57.56
11	Regent Communications Inc	62	1.78	59.34
12	Gap Broadcasting LLC	58	1.67	61.01
13	GAP Broadcasting II LLC	54	1.55	62.56
14	Three Eagles Communications Incorporated	54	1.55	64.11
15	Radio One Inc	52	1.49	65.60
16	Bicoastal Media LLC	49	1.41	67.01
17	Entravision Communications Corp	47	1.35	68.36
18	ABC/Disney	46	1.32	69.68
19	NRG Media LLC	45	1.29	70.98
20	Nassau Broadcasting I LLC (New Members)	44	1.26	72.24
21	Beasley Broadcast Group	43	1.24	73.48
22	Midwest Communications Incorporated	43	1.24	74.71
23	Mapleton Communications LLC	41	1.18	75.89
24	MultiCultural Radio Broadcasting Inc	41	1.18	77.07
25	Max Media LLC	39	1.12	78.19
26	Aloha Station Trust LLC	37	1.06	79.25
27	NextMedia Group Inc, Debtor in Possession	36	1.03	80.29
28	Armada Media Corporation	35	1.01	81.29
29	Cumulus Media Partners LLC	34	0.98	82.27
30	MCC Radio LLC	34	0.98	83.25
31	Withers Broadcasting Co	34	0.98	84.22
32	Journal Broadcast Group Inc	33	0.95	85.17
33	Pamal Broadcasting Ltd	33	0.95	86.12
34	Qantum Communications Corp	33	0.95	87.07
35	Triad Broadcasting Company	33	0.95	88.02
36	Double O Radio LLC	32	0.92	88.94
37	Forever Broadcasting Incorporated	32	0.92	89.86
38	New Northwest Broadcasters, LLC	31	0.89	90.75
39	Backyard Broadcasting	29	0.83	91.58
40	Bustos Media Enterprises LLC	29	0.83	92.41
41	Flinn Broadcasting Corporation	29	0.83	93.25
42	Bonneville International Corp	28	0.80	94.05
43	Frontier Radio Management Inc	28	0.80	94.86
44	Cochise Broadcasting LLC	27	0.78	95.63
45	First Media	27	0.78	96.41
46	Lotus Communications Corp	27	0.78	97.18
47	Birach Broadcasting Corporation	25	0.72	97.90
48	Renda Broadcasting Corporation	25	0.72	98.62
49	Citadel/ABC	24	0.69	99.31
50	GoodRadio.TV, LLC	24	0.69	100.00
	Total Top 50 Station Owners Only	3, 480		

Source: Based on licensed data from www.bia.com, January 2010.

Table 2.14 Clear Channel Cash Flow Crisis, April 2009

Purchase Price	$18b plus	
	$5b in Outstanding Debt	July 2008
Debt	$16b (Bank) plus	
	$6b (Junior)	April 2009
Annual Interest Payments	$1.3b	April 2009
Revenue (Decline)	$1.2b (−23%)	1Q 2009
Layoffs (Overall Reduction)	2,440 (−12%)	January & April 2009
Cash on Hand	$1.4b	April 2009
Company Worth	$6.3-$12b	April 2009

Source: Based on Fabrikant (2009), www.nytimes.com, $b=Billion.

Corporation that had filed for bankruptcy protection with listed assets of about $1.4 billion and more than $2.4 billion in debt.[7]

Arbitron Inc. and The Nielsen Company are two of the businesses that measure network and local-market radio and television audiences across the United States, among other things. The Nielsen Company uses a designated marketing area (DMA) to rank television households into 210 markets, while Arbitron uses a similar ranking system broken down in finer detail by age and city groupings in 302 radio markets. There is considerable overlap between the two company media market rankings. Some media outlet's residents may be able to receive television and radio signals located in adjacent markets. All of the rankings are based on projections using US census data last collected in the year 2000.

The number of media outlets and station owners generally increase with the size of the market. For example, markets with large populations have more television, radio stations, and newspapers than less populated markets.[8] According to the radio rankings by population displayed in Table 2.15, the three largest media markets are New York with an audience size of 15.35 million people, aged 12 years and older, Los Angeles follows next with an audience size of 10.90 million, and the Chicago area audience is 7.78 million. From a cumulative share perspective, the largest three media outlets have a combined share of 15.75 percent of the US total audience for radio and television content. The Top 25 large media markets contain close to 50 percent of the radio and television audience. The next 100 medium media markets account for about 35.73 percent of the radio audience and the last remaining 177 small media market total 15.13 percent. All 302 radio media markets reach an estimated 216.07 million viewers or listeners.

2.3.2 Internet Radio

One of the most important technological changes in broadcasting has been the switch from analog to digital transmission of both radio and television signals. With the widespread introduction of web technology and high-speed Internet access, a new medium—Internet radio—emerged that lowered barriers to entry, made radio

Table 2.15 2008 Radio Rankings by Population Size

Market Name	Metro 12+ Pop.	Market size	Region	% Share	% Cum.
New York, NY	15, 345, 000	Large	NE	7.10	7.10
Los Angeles, CA	10, 902, 400	Large	WE	5.05	12.15
Chicago, IL	7, 784, 400	Large	MW	3.60	15.75
San Francisco, CA	5, 969, 400	Large	WE	2.76	18.51
Dallas-Ft. Worth, TX	4, 973, 000	Large	MW	2.30	20.82
Houston-Galveston, TX	4, 639, 000	Large	MW	2.15	22.96
Philadelphia, PA	4, 350, 000	Large	NE	2.01	24.98
Atlanta, GA	4, 267, 500	Large	SO	1.98	26.95
Washington, DC	4, 210, 000	Large	SO	1.95	28.90
Boston, MA	3, 874, 600	Large	NE	1.79	30.69
Detroit, MI	3, 866, 500	Large	MW	1.79	32.48
Miami-Ft. Lauderdale-Hollywood, FL	3, 538, 400	Large	SO	1.64	34.12
Puerto Rico	3, 328, 500	Large	SO	1.54	35.66
Seattle-Tacoma, WA	3, 328, 100	Large	WE	1.54	37.20
Phoenix, AZ	3, 173, 200	Large	WE	1.47	38.67
Minneapolis-St. Paul, MN	2, 683, 000	Large	MW	1.24	39.91
San Diego, CA	2, 515, 100	Large	WE	1.16	41.07
Nassau-Suffolk (Long Island), NY	2, 359, 300	Large	NE	1.09	42.17
Tampa-St. Petersburg-Clearwater, FL	2, 350, 000	Large	SO	1.09	43.25
St. Louis, MO	2, 308, 400	Large	MW	1.07	44.32
Baltimore, MD	2, 255, 100	Large	SO	1.04	45.37
Denver-Boulder, CO	2, 244, 300	Large	WE	1.04	46.40
Portland, OR	2, 049, 600	Large	WE	0.95	47.35
Pittsburgh, PA	1, 986, 600	Large	NE	0.92	48.27
Charlotte-Gastonia-Rock Hill, NC-SC	1, 886, 100	Large	SO	0.87	49.15
Top 25 Total	106, 187, 500	Large		49.15	49.15
Top 25 Average	4, 247, 500	Large			
Next 100 Markets Total	77, 191, 148	Medium		35.73	84.87
Next 100 Markets Average	771, 911	Medium			
Next 177 Markets Total	32, 687, 600	Small		15.13	100.00
Next 177 Markets Average	184, 676	Small			
All 302 Markets Total	216, 066, 248				

Source: Based on licensed data from www.bia.com.

listening interactive, eliminated coverage restrictions found with AM/FM stations, lowered overhead broadcast costs, and created unlimited space for radio content.

The options for mass communications and information technology grew rapidly so that anyone with a computer and broadband connection could now access thousands of radio stations' content such as music, sports, entertainment, and news via the Internet. Internet radio appeals to many displaced listeners who are away from their hometowns because of work, school, or other factors, and who listen to keep

Table 2.16 Selected Total Radio Online Revenue by Year, January 2010 Forecast ($mil.)

Revenue	2004	2005	2006	2007	2008	2009E	2010E
Radio Online	$76	$157	$237	$332	$380	$341	$355
Total Radio Incl. Online	$20,183	$20,336	$20,447	$20,034	$18,135	$14,525	$14,233
Share	0.38%	0.77%	1.16%	1.65%	2.09%	2.35%	2.49%

Source: Based on data from B. Wieser, www.magnaglobal.com.

up with news and current events in their home media markets. Table 2.16 provides a breakdown of the share online radio compared to total radio.

MagnaGlobal.com's January 2010 forecast estimates that online radio revenue was expected to surpass $341 million in 2009. In terms of revenue share, online radio is expected to account for 2.35 percent of total radio revenue by 2009.

2.3.3 HD Radio

Today, more and more traditional (terrestrial) radio stations are not just broadcasting their signals over the Internet, but in many areas, there are also digital HD (high definition) radio signals providing multi-casting programming. The website http://www.ibiquity.com describes HD radio as having the ability to broadcast multiple CD quality audio programs over a single FM frequency whether the listener is at home, at work, or in the car. HD radio offers on-screen programming choices that can include text information such as song titles, artists' names, weather, and traffic alerts broadcast directly to the HD receiver's display screen. In terms of multi-casting, HD radio stations can offer one channel of news and another channel of music; two different music formats or different music formats in different languages.[9]

In examining the largest radio media market—the metropolitan New York City area—in Tables 2.17 and 2.18, we can get a feel for the direction of this format in both commercial and non-commercial stations. New York is ranked number one in terms of radio listeners (and television viewers) with a total of 67 commercial and 29 non-commercial radio stations in the area.

In April of 2009, of the 67 commercial radio stations in the New York market, 28 or (41.79 percent) are AM stations, 22 (32.84 percent) are FM stations, 13 (19.40 percent) are HD/F2 stations, and the remaining 4 (5.97 percent) are HD/F3 stations. F2 and F3 are definitions assigned by Arbitron to refer to HD radio stations that offer two or three additional channels above and beyond their analog and main digital channels. The data also reveal that HD radio has just over 25.37 percent of the stations in the market. For station owners such as CBS, Clear Channel, Emmis, and Citadel, HD radio now accounts for 50 percent of their stations in the New York Market. Similarly, non-commercial radio stations in the New York market, WNYC Radio, Fordham University, Newark Public Radio, and Seton Hall University, account for five stations utilizing the HD/F2 or the HD/F3 radio format.

Table 2.17 NY Market Commercial Radio Stations by Service

Owner	AM	FM	HD/F2	HD/F3	Terr. Radio	HD Radio	Grand Total	HD % Share
CBS Radio	3	3	3	3	6	6	12	50.00
Clear Channel	0	5	5	0	5	5	10	50.00
Emmis	0	3	3	0	3	3	6	50.00
MultiCultural	5	0	0	0	5	0	5	–
Citadel/ABC	1	1	1	1	2	2	4	50.00
Cumulus	2	2	0	0	4	0	4	–
Pamal	1	2	0	0	3	0	3	–
Univision	1	1	1	0	2	1	3	33.33
ABC/Disney	2	0	0	0	2	0	2	–
Hudson West.	1	1	0	0	2	0	2	–
Inner City Bcstg.	1	1	0	0	2	0	2	–
Salem	2	0	0	0	2	0	2	–
Spanish Bcstg.	0	2	0	0	2	0	2	–
Access.1	1	0	0	0	1	0	1	–
Alexander Bcstg.	1	0	0	0	1	0	1	–
Blackstrap Bcstg.	1	0	0	0	1	0	1	–
Bloomberg	1	0	0	0	1	0	1	–
Buckley Bcstg.	1	0	0	0	1	0	1	–
Forsythe Bcstg.	1	0	0	0	1	0	1	–
Mariana Bcstg.	1	0	0	0	1	0	1	–
New York Times Co.	0	1	0	0	1	0	1	–
Polnet Comm.	1	0	0	0	1	0	1	–
Universal Bcstg.	1	0	0	0	1	0	1	–
Total	28	22	13	4	50	17	67	
Share (%)	41.79	32.84	19.40	5.97	74.63	25.37		

Terr. = Terrestrial

Source: Based on licensed data from www.bia.com, April 2009.

2.3.4 Satellite Radio

One of the limitations of most AM and FM radio is that those stations' signals covered only a limited geographical area. This limitation resulted in the thousands of individual stations first described in Table 2.8. XM Satellite Radio Holdings was founded in 1992 and was granted a satellite radio license in the US in 1997 by the FCC. XM was the first company to launch nationwide radio satellite service based on a revenue subscription model with commercial-free music.

In November 2001, satellite radio was operated on a subscription basis and was launched with scores of programming choices for listeners who just wanted an alternative to traditional radio, while driving. This was followed by a new competitor Sirius Satellite Radio Inc. in 2002. While satellite radio offers commercial free service in most cases and digital CD quality on a nationwide basis to listeners, the service sometimes suffers from the same 'dead zone' problems—long associated with TV satellite dishes and wireless phones—such as severe weather conditions, tunnels, skyscrapers, and other blockages that can momentarily block the satellite signal.

Table 2.18 NY Market Non-Commercial Radio Stations by Service

Owner	AM	FM	HD/F2	HD/F3	Terr. Radio	HD Radio	Grand Total	HD % Share
WNYC Radio	1	1	1	1	2	2	4	50
Fordham Univ.	0	1	1	0	1	1	2	50
Newark Public Radio	0	1	1	0	1	1	2	50
Radio Vision	2	0	0	0	2	0	2	–
Seton Hall Univ.	0	1	1	0	1	1	2	50
Auricle Comm.	0	1	0	0	1	0	1	–
City College of NY	0	1	0	0	1	0	1	–
College of Staten Is.	0	1	0	0	1	0	1	–
Columbia Univ.	0	1	0	0	1	0	1	–
Fairleigh Dickinson	0	1	0	0	1	0	1	–
Family Stations Inc	0	1	0	0	1	0	1	–
Hudson Valley Comm.	0	1	0	0	1	0	1	–
Kingsborough C.C.	0	1	0	0	1	0	1	–
Montclair State Univ.	0	1	0	0	1	0	1	–
NYC Board of Ed.	0	1	0	0	1	0	1	–
New York Univ.	0	1	0	0	1	0	1	–
Nyack College	0	1	0	0	1	0	1	–
Pacifica Foundation	0	1	0	0	1	0	1	–
Ramapo College	0	1	0	0	1	0	1	–
Union Free School Dist.	0	1	0	0	1	0	1	–
Westchester Community	0	1	0	0	1	0	1	–
William Patterson College	0	1	0	0	1	0	1	–
Total	3	21	4	1	24	5	29	
Share (%)	10.34	72.41	13.79	3.45	82.76	17.24		

Source: Based on licensed data from www.bia.com, April 2009.

The consolidation wave that swept through the terrestrial radio industry soon made its way to the radio satellite industry. By 2007 Sirius decided to acquire its rival XM Satellite Radio in a $13 billion merger, creating a monopoly in that industry segment. On July 28, 2008, the US Department of Justice approved the merger with many conditions and restrictions, despite the opposition by many industry critics. The companies were successful in convincing the Justice Department that the combined companies were not competitors because of incompatible proprietary equipment that prevented customers from accessing each other's signal. Furthermore, the companies viewed iPods, Internet radio, and the HD radio segments as their competitors. In Table 2.19, a quick look at selected quarterly performance metrics of the merged companies, now called Sirius XM, indicate that there was a 3.61 percent decline in subscribers acquired at the retail channel, while overall subscribers increased to over 19 million or a 9.54 percent. Similarly total revenue increased by $378 million in 2008.

Sirius XM satellite radios are primarily distributed through automakers or original equipment manufacturers (OEMs) as factory or dealer-installed equipment in vehicles. Therefore, Sirius XM radio relies heavily on the sales volume of new automobiles for its subscriber growth. However, dead zone problems may be the

Table 2.19 Selected Sirius XM Annual Performance, 2007–2008

Subscribers	2007 (000)	2008 (000)	Change	% Change
Retail	9, 239	8, 905	(334)	−3.61
OEM	8, 033	9, 996	1,963	24.43
Rental	77	103	26	34.16
Total Subscribers	17, 349	19, 004	1,655	9.54
Total Revenue	$2, 059 (mil.)	$2, 437 (mil.)	$378	18.37%

Source: Sirius XM 2008 Annual Report.

least worries in this industry as the recession in 2009 takes its toll on lowered new car sales, diminished consumer spending, an advertising revenue pullback by major advertisers, and the widespread use of alternative mobile listening devices such as iPods.

2.3.5 Radio Royalty Payments Controversy

With all of the terrestrial radio consolidation, the emergence of new digital segments such as Internet, HD and satellite radio, computers, and portable listening devices such as iPods and ring-back tones on cell phones, it soon became apparent that were as an explosion in the massive use of digital music. Naturally, in the new digital era, two important concerns were raised. The first concern focused on the right of *recording* artists to be compensated for the use of their creative works, and share in the revenues the new digital formats were generating. The second concern among recording artists, composers, music publishers, record labels, and others was the impact of digital music on (declining) sales of copyrighted works through CDs and other pre-recorded formats.

The radio industry controversy would soon center on the traditional way under current US copyright law, in which non-dramatic performance and publishing royalties were collected and remitted to the songwriters, composers or lyricists and publishers of a song, but not to the featured recording artist (vocalists or background musicians) for audio portion of the sound recording. 'Because ASCAP, BMI and SESAC pay the songwriter, composer and publisher directly and separately for radio, television and other types of performance of songs and scores, the writer (unless a co-publishing or participation agreement has been signed) will not share in the royalties received by the publisher.'[10]

This is an important point in the performance royalty controversy and turf battle: The distinction between the recording artist (singer/vocalist) and the composer or publisher of the song. When a performing rights agency collects licensing fees on behalf of its members (songwriters, composers, and publishers) from radio stations for the use of music from its catalog, the royalty payments are made to the assigned songwriter (or multiple songwriters) *and* the music publisher(s) of the song. Moreover, ASCAP, BMI, and SESAC are collecting licensing fees for the musical composition, the lyrics, and melody, and not for the sound recording. The recording artist would *only* receive performance royalty payments if he or she is also credited as a performing songwriter, composer, publisher or through SoundExchange for certain digital *audio* performances.

With the advent of the Internet and music composition software, it is becoming increasingly common today for the songwriter/composer to also be the recording artist and a self-publisher for fairly well-established artists. In general, the copyright owner and the music user seeking the use of copyrighted works would voluntarily negotiate the royalty rates.

In the case of ASCAP (songwriters, composers and publishers), there is a 'rate-court' process under the AFJ2 (2001) in which the parties unable to reach an agreement can petition the court to establish royalty rates. Congress in other cases (recording artists, record labels for example) has appointed the Librarian of Congress, through the Copyright Royalty Board (CRB), to settle royalty disputes among parties.

The US Congress passed two important pieces of legislation that affected sound recordings: The Digital Performance in Sound Recordings Act (DPSR) of 1995 and Digital Millennium Copyright Act (DMCA) in October 1998 in order to protect copyright owners from copyright infringement in the digital age. The DMCA established the copyright law for certain digital transmissions and required performance royalties to be paid for emerging radio segments on satellite radio and Internet radio broadcasts.

Copyright owners and music users such as webcasters had two choices: they could either negotiate a royalty rate for a blanket license among themselves or adopt the rates for the digital distribution of music set by the Copyright Arbitration Royalty Panel (CARP) created by the Copyright Board. The legislation granted a 'statutory license' (license provided by copyright law as opposed to one granted by the copyright owner) to webcasters giving them the automatic right to use digitally transmitted sound recordings in exchange for the payment of royalties to copyright owners.[11]

In 2002, the royalty rates recommended by CARP were rejected by the Librarian of Congress. 'The Librarian then attempted to set rates that would prove controversial to both copyright owners and to small webcasters. Copyright owners believed the new rates were too low, while small webcasters believed the rates were still too high, and small webcasters sought legislative relief to lower rates further.'[12] Congress then enacted the Small Webcaster Settlement Act of 2002 which allowed small webcasters and copyright owners to enter into an agreement that provides for the payment of royalties based on a percentage of revenues, expenses, both revenue and expenses, or a minimum fee (whichever was greater) for time periods, the historical period, which began on October 28, 1998, and then ended on December 31, 2002, and 2003–2004 as shown in Table 2.20.[13]

SoundExchange, a part of the RIAA until 2003, was one of the beneficiaries of the Small Webcaster Settlement Act of 2002 and was permitted to enter into agreements on behalf of all copyright owners (mostly record labels) and performers such as vocalists and background musicians. SoundExchange is an independent, nonprofit performance rights organization that represents over 3,500 record

Table 2.20 Summary Royalty Rates for Small Webcasters, 1998–2004 Based on Gross Revenue

Time period	Gross revenue rate	Expense rate	Minimum annual fee
10/28/98–12/31/98	8% of Revenue	5%	$500
01/01/99–12/31/02	8% of Revenue	5%	$2,000
01/01/03–12/31/04	10% of first $250,000 and		$2,000 for rev. less than $50,000
	12%in excess of $250,000	7%	in prior year or current license period
			$5,000 for rev. greater than $50,000
			in prior year or current license period

Source: GAO (2004), Report-GAO-04-700.

labels and over 31,000 featured artists and whose members include both signed and unsigned recording artists; small, medium, and large independent record companies; and major label groups and artist-owned labels. The record labels and artists are paid *digital* performance royalties when their sound recordings are performed on digital cable and satellite television music, Internet, and satellite radio (such as XM and Sirius). In contrast to performance rights organizations such as ASCAP, BMI, and SESAC (whose copyright holders are songwriters, composers, and publishers), SoundExchange distributes 50 percent of the royalties (minus operating costs) they collect to the copyright owner/record label, 45 percent to the featured recording artist, and 5 percent to a fund for non-featured vocalists and musicians.[14]

Legal disputes emerged among the copyright owners and webcasters as to how performance royalties and music-use factors should be assessed for blanket licenses in that industry. The Small Webcaster Settlement Act of 2002 failed in its intended purpose of improving the system of royalty payments and the resolution of disputes. The legal disputes stemmed from a complicated mix of contracts and lawsuits that focused on the economic arrangements that webcasters had with:[15]

1. Third party vendors (such as bandwidth providers, ad agencies, content providers, parent companies, and other suppliers) that were not included in revenue or expenses calculations;
2. Size of webcasters (small business, large business, or 'aggregator');
3. Medium (simulcast terrestrial radio vs. Internet only);
4. Business models (free vs. subscription or sponsorships);
5. Music use factor (amount of music used by visitors to a website); and
6. Fee calculations (gross revenue, advertising revenue per song) among radio stations, PROs, record labels, songwriters, and musicians.

Smaller independent Internet-only stations at the time felt they might not be able to afford the proposed rates given their smaller share of listening audience, the listener log documentation required to track users and the lack of revenue, unlike larger players like AOL and Yahoo with established customer bases. Even the larger players balked at paying performance licensing fees for user-generated music and video content uploaded to Internet sites and made available to the general public by relying on the 'safe harbor' clause under copyright law. At the request of copyright owners, these companies promised to remove copyrighted material that infringed on the rights of the copyright owners, a costly, ineffective, and inefficient endeavor. The legal wranglings just angered and confused consumers who were not interested in the arcane topic of intellectual property rights, and just wanted to listen to their favorite music online.

The conventional thought, among webcasters and other users of sound recordings, was that recording artists receive promotional benefits such as free publicity, name recognition and a boost in record sales, concert tickets and merchandise from traditional radio airplay offsetting the need for further performance royalty payments for vocalists and background musicians, while stations owners benefited from listeners and advertising dollars. Dertouzos (2008) examined the symbiotic relationship between radio airplay of music and sales of albums and digital tracks from 2004 to 2006 in the 99 largest DMAs. He found that a significant portion at a minimum of 14 percent and as high as 23 percent of music industry sales can be attributed to radio airplay. Furthermore, the incremental sales revenue or promotional sales benefit ranged from $1.5 to $2.4 billion annually, excluding concert ticket, merchandising, and licensing revenue.[16]

Since music is considered a *cultural good*, it is a product that is *experienced* (or an 'experienced good') rather than one that is conventionally consumed or employed for some subsidiary purpose (such as a hand tool or appliance).[17] This suggests that the individual audience member must first listen to a piece of music before deciding whether to purchase it. The Internet simplified the purchasing of music, in which the user after hearing a song at a website can now click, purchase and download the song to an iPod in a matter of minutes. The listening and purchasing habits of consumers on the Internet raised an important question as to whether higher royalty rates or a new performance fee (to offset declining CD sales) may result in some online radio stations going out of business may be doing more harm than good in the recording industry.

Dertouzos (2008) suggests that 'as the record industry advocates for direct payment from radio stations to music labels and arts through a new performance fee, it should be noted that disturbing the current symbiotic relationship that is found to exist between radio and the record industry could actually harm, not help, all parties. If a new performance fee were enacted, stations could reduce the amount of music airplay, change formats, or even cease to operate resulting in the loss of much of this promotional benefit.'

In March of 2007, the CRB set the new webcasting per play/per listener royalty rates for the years 2006–2010, retroactive to the year 2006 and with no increases for 5 years. The rates are displayed in Table 2.21 for webcasters operating non-

Table 2.21 CRB Webcasting Royalty Rates (Commercial Non-interactive Stations)

Year	2006	2007	2008	2009	2010
Rate	$0.0008	$.0011	$.0014	$.0018	$.0019

interactive radio stations. For non-commercial stations an annual fee of $500 per channel or station, up to a total of 159,140 aggregate tuning hours or (one listener listening per hour) per month was set by the panel. After 159,140 ATH are maximized, the per-play/per listener rate for commercial webcasters would be applicable.[18]

Finally, the CRB announced the royalty rates for the mechanical and digital reproduction of music in October 2008. Details of that agreement between National Music Publishers Association (NMPA), the Nashville Songwriters Association International (NSAI), the Songwriters Guild of America (SGA), Recording Industry Association of America (RIAA), the Digital Media Association (DIMA) and other interested parties are discussed here.[19]

The CRB set the mechanical royalty rates for physical records such as CDs, and digital downloads in October 2008 as shown in Table 2.22. Songwriters, composers, and music publishers will be paid a rate of 9.1 cents for digital downloads, while the mechanical rate for physical products such as CDs remained at 9.1 cents. In July of 2009, groups representing artists, recording labels, and SoundExchange negotiated and reached an agreement under the Webcaster Settlement Act of 2009, which gave SoundExchange the authority to negotiate alternative rates and terms to those set by the CRB in 2007 for sound recordings on the Internet. Commercial webcasters have the option of 'opting in' to this agreement or using the existing CRB-set rates.

Table 2.23 shows the three rate classes that were established for music websites streaming music over the Internet for the period 2006–2015, with retroactive rates and late fees going back to 2006. The three rate classes are as follows: Large commercial webcasters (earning more than $1.25 million in annual revenues), small commercial webcasters (defined as those earning $1.25 million or less in total revenues with a cap on the amount of sound recordings streamed), and webcasters providing bundled, syndicated, or subscription services.[20]

Table 2.22 Mechanical Royalty Rates (Songwriters and Music Publishers)

Type	Rate	Per Minute
Physical records	$0.091	$0.0175
Digital downloads	$0.091	$0.0175
Ring tones	$0.24	–

Table 2.23 Selected Webcaster Performance Royalty Rates, 2009, for Sound Recordings

Year	Large Comm. Webcasters Rate/Performance*	Webcasters Bundling Rate/Performance	Small Webcasters (2009–2014 Only)
2009	$0.00093	$0.0015	12% of first $ 250,000 in Revenue
2010	0.00097	0.0016	and
2011	0.00102	0.0017	14% of revenue above $250,000
2012	0.00110	0.0020	or
2013	0.00120	0.0022	7% of Expenses
2014	0.00130	0.0023	
2015	0.00140	0.0025	–

*Or 25% of gross revenue whichever is greater.
Source: www.soundexchange.com.

Some of these legal issues have yet to be resolved to make the licensing process more effective and the new royalty rates described above are already coming under attack. In a September 1, 2009 article, *Billboard* magazine reports that Internet radio provider Live365, one of the few webcasters to reject the recent SoundExchange compromise agreement for streaming royalty rates, is challenging the constitutionality of Copyright Right Board. The basis for this challenge is a recent opinion of the US Court of Appeals in the District of Columbia, where one of the judges said the CRB "raised a serious Constitutional issue." Furthermore, the article said that Live365 has also filed a federal lawsuit in the US District Court for the District of Columbia seeking an injunction against all further CRB proceedings until the constitutionality of the entity is resolved.[21] The battle over music royalties in the nascent streaming industry that has yet to show that it may be viable in the long run further threatens to derail the industry. In the recession climate of 2009 with shrinking advertising dollars, even large companies might eliminate some forms of web radio as the costs of streaming due to rights fees increase.

2.4 Broadcast, Cable, and Satellite Television

Throughout the 1970s and well into the 1980s–NBC, CBS, and ABC (the big three as they were known) were the dominant broadcast television networks in the US. These television networks were created as the divisions of major radio networks, and television and radio manufacturers. These networks remain unchallenged until the 1980s, when a pay television segment called cable and, a fourth new broadcast network, Fox Broadcasting became serious rivals that challenged the big three for viewers and advertising revenue. Cable gets it name from the coaxial cable used to transmit transponder signals from the cable operators' 'head-end' or local central office into their customers' homes after the signals were received from orbiting satellites.

As cable system deployment expanded beyond the re-transmission of broadcast signals in rural areas, the ownership structure of the industry and viewership changed. Once characterized by privately owned small cable systems scattered in non-contiguous areas of the US, the cable industry was soon transformed into large media companies in which several systems were combined to form large multiple system operators (MSOs). Several of these MSOs also invested in the development of cable networks as well, while providing both content and a cable pipe into the home that would later lead to voice, video, and data applications, the so-called 'triple play.'

The television industry segments soon became broadcast, cable, and satellite (an important competitor to cable) each with its own business and pricing models. Cable and satellite are subscription and advertising services that involve a monthly flat fee for a basic level of service while premium channels such as HBO and elective services such as pay-per-view (PPV) can cost extra fees. Until the switch over to digital from analog broadcasting requiring a set-top box in June 2009, terrestrial broadcast signals were received by anyone within a certain geographic range with an indoor or outdoor antenna. Cable, initially designed for hard-to-reach rural areas with broadcast reception problems, has evolved and can now be found in densely populated areas where there is little restriction on the laying of coaxial or fiber optics cable.

In 1981, a new cable music channel called MTV was started and would soon change the way in which music was performed and distributed. The broadcast and cable industries were transformed in the late 1990s with one of the most important technological changes in broadcasting: The switch from analog to digital transmission of terrestrial and satellite television signals. Satellite television subscription service got its start in the 1980s, and focused mostly on subscribers in rural areas where over-the-air broadcast signals and cable systems were problematic.

Tables 2.24 and 2.25 show that local and network broadcast revenues have been declining since 2007, while national cable television advertising revenue has been growing.

Table 2.24 Broadcast and Cable Networks Advertising Revenue (in $millions)

Media	2005	2006	2007	2008	2009E	2010E
Local Broadcast TV[c]	17, 485	16, 170	17, 614	14, 817	11, 674	11, 483
Network Broadcast TV[a,b]—Engl.	14, 617	14, 522	14, 433	13, 614	12, 816	13, 249
National Cable TV[a]	15, 291	15, 972	17, 053	17, 886	17, 600	19, 195
Local Cable TV[c]	3, 322	3, 346	3, 713	3, 337	2, 810	2, 862
National Syndication	2, 152	1, 969	1, 974	1, 935	1, 817	1, 774
Network Broadcast TV—Span.	912	980	1, 082	1, 063	1, 035	1, 119
Total	53, 779	52, 959	55, 870	52, 652	47, 752	49, 681

E = Estimated

[a] Excludes online advertising revenues.

[b] Excludes incremental Olympic advertising revenues.

[c] Excludes local political advertising revenues.

Source: Based on data from B. Wieser, www.magnaglobal.com.

Table 2.25 Share of Broadcast and Cable Networks Advertising Revenue (%)

Media	2005	2006	2007	2008	2009E	2010E
Local Broadcast TV	32.52	30.53	31.53	28.14	24.45	23.11
Network Broadcast TV - Engl.	27.18	27.42	25.83	25.86	26.84	26.67
National Cable TV	28.43	30.16	30.52	33.97	36.86	38.64
Local Cable TV	6.18	6.32	6.65	6.34	5.89	5.76
National Syndication	4.00	3.72	3.53	3.67	3.80	3.57
Network Broadcast TV - Span.	1.70	1.85	1.94	2.02	2.17	2.25

E = Estimated

Source: Based on data from B. Wieser, www.magnaglobal.com.

In 1994 Direct Broadcast Satellite (DBS) was first introduced and soon became widespread due to many technological advantages over cable. Satellite service operators can establish a broad geographic reach without the need for headends and multiple cable systems dispersed over a broad non-contiguous area. DBS's technical advantages included fully digital systems, compared to cable's older analog technology. DBS's fully digital capabilities at the time would soon be exploited in the way in which video signals when 'compressed' could provide the satellite capacity for hundreds of new digital channels on a nationwide basis.

Many new digital channels began to appear, often just the digital offering of the analog channel on cable systems. From a music use perspective, the most important consideration is the amount of revenue generated by broadcasters and cable networks from their advertising and subscription fees. In turn, corporate profits determine the amount of money spent to advertise on broadcast and cable TV, radio, and the Internet. Broader macroeconomic problems such as declining aggregate demand and cyclical problems such as a recession will in turn affect corporate profits and advertising revenue.

2.5 Internet Media

The older information retrieval and search services that initially supplied textual, numeric, and graphic data to the scientific and business communities were soon replaced with a new technology, the 1995 introduction of Netscape, the first popular web browser. Netscape would transform web search into an interactive multimedia environment with the integration of voice, video, audio, text, and images in a end-user controlled setting.

As the adoption rates of broadband bandwidth increased dramatically, and more Americans had high-speed access to the Internet both at home and at work, there was significant growth in the number of online music performances. These 'portals' now offered online radio (discussed above) and streaming video programming that only once appeared on television. The Internet made listening to music or viewing a video clip more interactive and selective, as users could now see and hear their favorite songs, recording artists, and videos at the time and place of their choosing.

Several Internet 'search engine' companies or 'portals' soon sprang up with new business models for access to content on the Internet. One such business model was the so-called search-related advertising model that demonstrated that search when paired with advertising could be monetized. And the other model was a subscription model in which users purchased content on a one-time basis or for a fixed monthly recurring charge.

Google, Yahoo, Microsoft, Ask, and AOL, the so-called Internet media companies, are some of the large competitors left standing after the brutal shakeout following the dot.com bubble implosion in 2001. In 2009, Google accounted for more than 65 percent of the online search market as shown in Table 2.26.

Table 2.26 Online Search Share (November–December 2009)

Website	Nov-09 (%)	Dec-09 (%)	Change	% Change
Google Sites	65.6	65.7	0.1	0.15
Yahoo Sites	17.5	17.3	−0.2	−1.14
Microsoft Sites	10.3	10.7	0.4	3.88
Ask Network	3.8	3.7	−0.1	−2.63
AOL LLC Network	2.8	2.6	−0.2	−7.14

Source: Based on comScore.com data.

Table 2.27 Sources of Online Search Revenue ($mil.) (2Q-2008)

Advertising Format	2Q 2008 Revenue($)	% Share
Search	$2, 508	44.00
Banner Ads	1, 197	21.00
Classifieds	798	14.00
Rich Media (audio/video)	399	7.00
Lead Generation	399	7.00
Digital Video	171	3.00
Sponsorship	114	2.00
Email	114	2.00
Total	5, 700	

Source: IAB Internet Advertising Revenue Report, October 2008, p. 8.

Social networking sites such as youTube, Facebook.com, and MySpace.com would soon emerge to compete with the established Internet media companies. These portals generated revenue through the various forms of advertising when users conducted a search, viewed display banner ads, opened an email, or watched a video. For example, as shown in Table 2.27, in the second quarter of 2008, the Interactive Advertising Bureau (IAB) estimated online revenue in the $5.7 billion range with search revenue accounting for 44 percent of online revenue.

Advertisers paid the portals based on the number of times a webuser viewed the page containing the advertiser's ad, and perhaps 'clicked-through' to the advertisers own website for additional content. As advertising dollars flowed to the Internet portals, advertisers demanded objective measurements of such things as the number of unique visitors, total time spent on Internet sites, audience demographics, search activities, buying habits and reach, the percentage of the total Internet population that visited a particular site at a given time. Just like terrestrial radio stations that rely on Arbitron and television stations rely on Nielsen for rankings and ratings data, online companies rely on Nielsen and comScore for Internet traffic and usage data.

The number of unique visitors, views or 'impressions,' and 'click-throughs' would later become common metrics used for measuring music content in the industry. Each year, Google, Yahoo, Microsoft, and AOL attract hundred of millions of unique visitors to their various websites. Selected month-over-month growth in unique visitors and page view metrics for the Internet media companies Google, Yahoo, Microsoft, and AOL from comScore are shown in Tables 2.28 and 2.29.

Table 2.28 Selected M/M Growth in Unique Visitors (000)

Company	Dec. 2008	Jan. 2009	Change	% Change
Google	149, 027	151, 010	1,983	1.33%
Yahoo	145, 708	146, 131	423	0.29
Microsoft	125, 351	125, 568	217	0.17
AOL	109, 879	108, 441	(1,438)	−1.31

Source: Based on licensed data from comScore.

Table 2.29 Selected M/M Growth in Page Views (mil.)

Company	Dec. 2008	Jan. 2009	Change	% Change
Google	31, 302	34, 318	3, 016	9.64
Yahoo	38, 007	42, 586	4, 579	12.05
Microsoft	16, 732	17, 641	909	5.43
AOL	18, 761	19, 898	1, 137	6.06

Source: Based on licensed data from comScore.

PROs would sometimes use a music adjustment factor to make adjustments for cases in which there is a dispute to the amount of music intensity usage by various music users. The music adjustment factor is usually a variation of the ratio of total music hours (amount of time users spent streaming audio and video, etc.) divided by total site hours (total amount of time spent at a website, etc.). Some PROs rely on these companies to provide the independent data for its computation. As you can imagine, companies can both use different methodologies and reach different and controversial conclusions, which can have a direct impact on royalty licensing fees. The end result of this controversy is often the subject of litigation. We will not cover any of these legal disputes. Our focus is primarily on academic economists who are interested in the economics of art and culture.

2.6 General Licensing and Other Types of Music Users

PRO's general licensing of public performance venues can include bars, music clubs, restaurants, hotels, amusement parks, retail shops, symphonic concert halls, gyms, sports stadiums, colleges, universities, and many others. Non-dramatic music performances can occur on music channels on an airplane, music at a convention, or music on hold on a telephone. Jukebox music users are also required to have a license. The cost of a blanket license for these establishments depends on the type of business, the manner in which music is performed (live, recorded, or audio only or audio/visual), the size of the establishment or potential audience for the music, the number of nights per week music is offered, whether admission is charged, and several other factors.

Concert rates are based on the ticket revenue and seating capacity of the facility. Rates for music used by corporations ('Music In Business') are based upon the number of employees. College and university rates are based upon the number of full time students; retail store rates depend on the number of speakers and square footage. Hotel rates are based on a percentage of entertainment expenses for live music and an additional charge if recorded music is used.[22]

2.7 Performance Census and Sample Surveys

In order to pay royalties to songwriters and composers, the *Second Amended Final Judgment*, AFJ2 (2001), requires that where,

> feasible ASCAP shall conduct, or cause to have conducted, a census or a scientific, randomly selected sample of the performances of the works of its members. Such census or sample shall be designed to reflect accurately the number and identification of performances and the revenue attributed to those performances, made in accordance with a design made and periodically reviewed by an independent and qualified person.

It is worth noting here that under the traditional blanket licenses issued by ASCAP and BMI, it is ASCAP's and BMI's responsibility to keep track of music performances and usage, not the broadcasters. ASCAP uses both a Census and a Sample survey to quantify musical performances. It is only under the per-program license (which is still a blanket license for music used in certain programs or segments) in which broadcasters are required to report music usage for fee calculation purposes.

Whenever it is economically sensible, ASCAP will conduct a *Census Survey*, or a complete count of performances in a medium. Where a Census Survey is impractical, ASCAP conducts a *Sample Survey* designed to be a statistically accurate representation of performances in a medium. All times of the day, all days of the year, every region of the country, and all types and sizes of stations are represented in the ASCAP sample surveys.[23]

The Census Survey consists of a complete count of all performances, including commercial, promotional and public service announcements, on network television such as ABC, NBC, and CBS. For other networks such as Fox, UPN, and WB, the count would include all programs and promotional announcements, while for the Univision and ION networks, the count would include all programs. Local television, cable television, PBS, live concerts, Internet, background and foreground music services, and other media such as theme parks, circuses, and digital jukeboxes would be counted using various factors.[24]

The Sample Survey includes commercial radio stations, National Public Radio, college radio stations, and satellite radio, airlines and other areas where the Census Survey is not practical. The greater the fee a licensee pays, the more often that licensee is sampled by ASCAP. The Sample Survey would consist of hundreds of thousands of hours of non-dramatic performances or detected airplay data from Mediaguide, station logs, 6-hour sample tapes and cue sheets, program guides and other electronic data from radio, television, cable, and other general licensing music users.[25] Table 2.30 takes a selected look at some of the variables involved in a typical radio performance Sample Survey conducted by ASCAP and its partners.

Table 2.30 Selected ASCAP Radio Performances Survey Variables

Variable	Measurement type
Station	Commercial, Non-Commercial, Satellite
Radio Band	AM vs. FM
License Type	Blanket vs. Per Program
Region	West, Midwest, South & Northeast
Genre	Pop, Spanish Language, Sport/News/Talk, Urban Contemporary, Country, Religious, Jazz, Classical and Ethnic

As shown in Table 2.30, the Sample Survey would take into account large, medium, and small markets and it might also involve weighting FM stations higher than AM stations given the ratio of FM to AM stations in various regions and markets. Data from Mediaguide would also include the number of detected airplay of copyrighted compositions on hundreds of radio stations in many different ranked markets across the nation at different time period intervals.

2.8 Performances and Airplay

Every year billions of musical performances are licensed, and billions of dollars are collected by performing rights societies from various music users around the world on behalf of copyright holders. The licensing fees collected must then be distributed in a fair, accurate and efficient manner to the copyright holders when their copyrighted music is used in a variety of mediums. In order to accomplish this goal, the music must first be tracked on radio, television, the Internet, live venues, and other media and a determination made to as which music has been performed before the appropriate copyright holders can be paid. The PROs may all have different distribution options and payment formulas that can include premium payments for hit songs, payment schedules, and dedicated resources for collecting performance rights licensing fees.[26]

Ring tones and ring-back tones, the music heard and played on cell phones, represent an entirely new market in transmission technology. The cell phone is now a receiving and playing device for copyrighted musical compositions. Mechanical royalty fees, as established by the CRB, are collected and artists are compensated based on the number of ring tones downloaded from the Internet.

Tables 2.31, 2.32 and 2.33, based on data from NARM, show the 2008 top 10 radio broadcast streamed performances and the number of ring tones sales data, respectively, by song title collected by Nielsen's Broadcast Data Systems (BDS) at year-end 2008. For example, the song title *Bleeding Love* was the number one most played and most streamed song, and number six in ring tones sales in 2008. Based on these performances and ring tone downloads, the copyright holders are paid accordingly.[27]

Upon title registration, royalty income to songwriters, composers, and music publishing royalty based on established payment methods by the PROs would then

Table 2.31 Top 10 Most Played Songs on Radio Year-End 2008

Rank	Title	Artist	Detections	% Share
1	*Bleeding Love*	Leona Lewis	468, 000	12.31
2	*Low*	Flo Rida/ T-Pain	410, 000	10.78
3	*Love Song*	Sara Bareilles	398, 000	10.47
4	*Apologize*	Timbaland/ One Republic	383, 000	10.07
5	*With You*	Chris Brown	369, 000	9.71
6	*No Air*	Jordin Sparks/Chris Brown	365, 000	9.60
7	*Love In This Club*	Usher/Young Jeezy	364, 000	9.57
8	*No One*	Alicia Keys	362, 000	9.52
9	*Lollipop*	Lil Wayne/Static Major	342, 000	9.00
10	*Sexy Can I*	Ray J./Yung Berg	341, 000	8.97
	Total		3, 802, 000	

Source: Based on data from http://www.narm.com/Nielsen/NielsenMusic2008.pdf.

Table 2.32 Top 10 Internet Streamed Songs Year-End 2008

Rank	Title	Artist	Streams	% Share
1	*Bleeding Love*	Leona Lewis	10, 699, 000	11.58
2	*Love Song*	Sara Bareilles	10, 558, 000	11.42
3	*Low*	Flo Rida/T-Pain	9, 837, 000	10.64
4	*No One*	Alicia Keys	9, 680, 000	10.47
5	*With You*	Chris Brown	8, 971, 000	9.71
6	*Sorry*	Buckcherry	8, 940, 000	9.67
7	*Love In This Club*	Usher/Young Jeezy	8, 892, 000	9.62
8	*Touch My Body*	Mariah Carey	8, 675, 000	9.39
9	*No Air*	Jordin Sparks/Chris Brown	8, 160, 000	8.83
10	*Stop and Stare*	One Republic	8, 004, 000	8.66
	Total		92, 416, 000	

Source: Based on data from http://www.narm.com/Nielsen/NielsenMusic2008.pdf.

Table 2.33 Top 10 Mastertones Year-End 2008

Rank	Title	Artist	Sales	% Share
1	*Lollipop*	Lil Wayne	2, 365, 000	19.46
2	*Whatever You Like*	T.I.	1, 627, 000	13.39
3	*Low*	Flo Rida	1, 607, 000	13.23
4	*I Kissed A Girl*	Katy Perry	1, 138, 000	9.37
5	*Love In This Club*	Usher/Young Jeezy	1, 013, 000	8.34
6	*Bleeding Love*	Leona Lewis	922, 000	7.59
7	*With You*	Chris Brown	892, 000	7.34
8	*Bust It Baby*	Plies	891, 000	7.33
9	*Sexy Can I*	Ray J.	852, 000	7.01
10	*Take A Bow*	Rihanna	844, 000	6.95
	Total		12, 151, 000	

Source: Based on data from http://www.narm.com/Nielsen/NielsenMusic2008.pdf.

be made on the basis of these non-dramatic performances or airplay of the copy-righted musical compositions when used on television, radio, the Internet, on cell phones, and other licensing areas.

2.9 Selected Types of Performances and Airplay

A copyrighted musical composition can be used in its entirety when played as a full featured song on the radio. The song or parts of the same song can be used on tele-vision for musical and other talent type shows. Another part of a song could be used in a jingle to help sell products or services on television. Table 2.34 shows a selected view on how licensed music works for which the PROs have the right to license for public performances are used by the music users in a variety of *performance types* or airplay such as features, theme music, jingles, underscores, ring tones, or network station promos.

Different types of performances (radio and television airplay) such as features, themes, jingles, background/foreground music and network promos as classified by PROs are weighted differently and earn different royalty amounts. Performances reaching or bypassing a certain airplay threshold are sometimes paid a premium or bonus amount.

Feature performance: A feature performance is the performance of a song that is used whether in part or in whole and is a principal focus of audience attention at the time of the broadcast. The musical work can be performed live or by means of a recording. These works are indicated on a cue sheet with the following codes: Visual Vocal *(VV)* is used when the vocalist appears on camera singing a song. Visual Instrumental *(VI)* is used when the instrumentalist appears on camera performing a song. Background Vocal *(BV)* is used when a song is audible to the listening audience, even though there is dialogue and other action in the foreground scene. A medley is considered a type of feature in which several whole songs or parts of songs are used in a compilation.

Theme performance: Theme music is the performance of a work used to open or close a program, typically on television. It is the music that listeners might recognize as the theme of their favorite show with multiple episodes.

Table 2.34 Selected Medium and Performance Type

Music User	Performance/Airplay Type
Local Radio	Features of Variable Lengths
Local TV	Opening/Closing Theme Music
Network TV	Background or Underscore Music
Basic & Premium Cable	Jingles
Internet	Network TV Promos
Background Music	Ring Tones
Others, Concerts etc.	Ring-Back Tones

Background and Foreground performance: Background/foreground music is the performance of a work that when used in a television show is neither the recognized opening/closing theme nor a feature and used as underscore or background music in a show to create a certain mood or atmosphere that is normally not the focus of audience attention. On a cue sheet, the code *BI* would designate works that are background instrumental in nature.

Jingle performance: A jingle is the performance of a work in which a memorable melody with or without lyrics is used to brand an advertiser's product on radio or television so that the product remains in the minds of consumers. The jingle can also include a musical work written for other purposes but with the lyrics changed for commercial or promotional advertising.

Promotional announcement performance: Network or station 'promos' are music performances that announces an upcoming television or radio program. It can also include the station identification music used for tune-in.

2.10 Performances or Airplay Data Collection: Radio and Internet

Mediaguide,[28] one of several radio performance data collection companies in the industry,

> monitors music, advertising, copyright compliance and other functions on over 2,700 college, non-commercial and commercial radio stations in 150 US markets; and over 3,500 Internet stations in real-time, 24 hours per day, 7 days per week.
>
> Mediaguide was formed to meet ASCAP's exacting requirements for knowledge of broadcast airplay information to accurately pay songwriters. In order to meet those standards, Mediaguide developed a robust digital fingerprinting technology.
>
> Mediaguide compiles a database of songs played on the radio and other media broken by many factors including, song titles, recording artists, record labels, genre, radio station, region, market, rankings and so on using its digital fingerprinting content recognition technology that can identify audio or video in online or offline environments.
>
> Using a compact representation of audio or video content ('fingerprint'), Mediaguide technology identifies an unknown media by matching it to a database of the fingerprints of registered works.

Table 2.35 gives a sample of the radio performances data collected by Mediaguide for the week of 08/03/09–08/09/09 broken down by song title, artist, record label, and rankings.

For example, Mediaguide in a genre called CHR/Pop, recorded 7,306 total plays for the week of 08/03/09–08/09/09, an increase of 849 plays from the previous week, for the song *I Gotta Feeling* by the recording group 'Black Eyed Peas' and the record label was Interscope. The song was ranked number one for that week, and in the previous week it was ranked number two. The song has been on the charts for 10 consecutive and peaked at number one. Table 2.36 shows a selection of the 105 radio stations in 89 markets that were electronically monitored by Mediaguide to provide the airplay data shown in Table 2.35.

Table 2.35 Selected Example of CHR*/Pop Radio Performances (Airplay) Data Week of 08/03/09–08/09/09

LW	TW	Title	Artist	Label	Plays	Gains(+/−)	Weeks	Peak
2	1	*I Gotta Feeling*	Black Eyed Peas	Interscope	7,306	849	10	1
1	2	*Waking Up In Vegas*	Katy Perry	Capitol	6,793	−12	17	1
4	3	*You Belong With Me*	Taylor Swift	Big Machine	6,281	301	15	3
5	4	*Knock You Down (w/Ne-Yo & K. West)*	Keri Hilson	Mosely/Zone/4 Interscope	5,784	92	16	4
3	5	*LoveGame*	Lady Gaga	Streamline/Interscope	5,562	−541	17	1
10	6	*Good Girls Go Bad (w/L. Meester)*	Cobra Starship	Fueled By Ramen/ Atlantic	4,372	226	11	6
7	7	*Fire Burning/Dance Floor*	Sean Kingston	E1/Beluga Hgts./Epic	4,280	−338	15	7
11	8	*Battlefield*	Jordin Sparks	Jive	4,158	84	12	8
12	9	*Use Somebody*	Kings Of Leon	RCA	4,103	488	11	9
6	10	*I Know You Want Me*	Pitbull	Ultra	3,885	−886	24	4

*CHR = Contemporary Hit Radio Music.

TW = this week's rank.

LW = last week's rank.

Plays = total plays for the week.

Gains +/− = change in total plays from the previous week.

Weeks = number of consecutive weeks on the chart.

Peak = peak position achieved on the chart.

Weeks at #1 = consecutive (not cumulative) weeks at #1.

Resets after song/release is replaced by new #1 entry.

Source: Based on licensed data from http://charts.mediaguide.com/format/CHR_Pop_single.html, Mediaguide, Inc., © 2009.

Table 2.36 Mediaguide Electronically Monitored Radio Stations

Station	Frequency	Market	Market Rank
WHTZ	100.3	New York, NY	1
KIIS	102.7	Los Angeles, CA	2
WKSC	103.5	Chicago, IL	3
KHKS	106.1	Dallas/Ft. Worth, TX	5
KRBE	104.1	Houston/Galveston, TX	6
WSTR	94.1	Atlanta, GA	7
WIOQ	102.1	Philadelphia, PA	8
WIHT	99.5	Washington, DC	9
WXKS	107.9	Boston, MA	10
WHYI	100.7	Miami/Ft. Lauderdale/Hollywood, FL	12
KBKS	106.1	Seattle/Tacoma, WA	13
KZZP	104.7	Phoenix, AZ	15
KDWB	101.3	Minneapolis/St. Paul, MN	16
KHTS	93.3	San Diego, CA	17
WFLZ	93.3	Tampa/St. Petersburg/Clearwater, FL	18
KSLZ	107.7	St. Louis, MO	20
WXAJ	99.7	St. Louis, MO	20
KKRZ	100.3	Portland, OR	23
WNKS	95.1	Charlotte/Gastonia, NC/Rock Hill, SC	25
KDND	107.9	Sacramento, CA	27
WKFS	107.1	Cincinnati, OH	28
WAKS	96.5	Cleveland, OH	29
KVFX	94.5	Salt Lake City/Ogden/Provo, UT	30
KZHT	97.1	Salt Lake City/Ogden/Provo, UT	30
KXXM	96.1	San Antonio, TX	31
KMXV	93.3	Kansas City, MO-KS	32
WXXL	106.7	Orlando, FL	34
WNCI	97.9	Columbus, OH	36
WXSS	103.7	Milwaukee - Racine, WI	37
KHFI	96.7	Austin, TX	39
WPRO	92.3	Providence/Warwick/Pawtucket, RI	41
WRVW	107.5	Nashville, TN	44
WDCG	105.1	Greensboro/Winston-Salem/High Point, NC	45
WKZL	107.5	Greensboro/Winston-Salem/High Point, NC	45
WAPE	95.1	Jacksonville, FL	46
WFKS	97.9	Jacksonville, FL	46
WLDI	95.5	West Palm Beach/Boca Raton, FL	47
KJYO	102.7	Oklahoma City, OK	48
WHBQ	107.5	Memphis, TN	49
CKEY	101.1	Buffalo/Niagara Falls, NY	52
WKSE	98.5	Buffalo/Niagara Falls, NY	52
WDJX	99.7	Louisville, KY	53
WZKF	98.9	Louisville, KY	53
WRVQ	94.5	Richmond, VA	54
WEZB	97.1	New Orleans, LA	55
WKGS	106.7	Rochester, NY	56
WPXY	97.9	Rochester, NY	56
WQEN	103.7	Birmingham, AL	57
WFBC	93.7	Greenville/Spartanburg, SC	59
KRQQ	93.7	Tucson, AZ	60
WFLY	92.3	Albany/Schenectady/Troy, NY	63

Table 2.36 (continued)

Station	Frequency	Market	Market Rank
WKKF	102.3	Albany/Schenectady/Troy, NY	63
KHTT	106.9	Tulsa, OK	65
WBHT	97.1	Wilkes Barre/Scranton, PA	70
WKRZ	98.5	Wilkes Barre/Scranton, PA	70
WWST	102.1	Knoxville, TN	71
KQCH	94.1	Omaha, NE/Council Bluffs, IA	72
WSTW	93.7	Wilmington, DE	77
WFMF	102.5	Baton Rouge, LA	78
WHKF	99.3	Harrisburg/Lebanon/Carlisle, PA	79
KHOP	95.1	Stockton, CA	80
WYKS	105.3	Gainesville/Ocala, FL	81
WIHB	92.5	Charleston, SC	84
WSSX	95.1	Charleston, SC	84
KLAL	107.7	Little Rock, AR	85
WERO	93.3	Greenville/New Bern/Jacksonville, NC	87
WNOK	104.7	Columbia, SC	89
KKDM	107.5	Des Moines, IA	90
WTWR	98.3	Toledo, OH	91
WVKS	92.5	Toledo, OH	91
KQQB	104.5	Spokane, WA	92
KZZU	92.9	Spokane, WA	92
KKMG	98.9	Colorado Springs, CO	94
WABB	97.5	Mobile, AL	96
WJLQ	100.7	Mobile, AL	96
WAOA	107.1	Melbourne/Titusville/Cocoa, FL	97
WZEE	104.1	Madison, WI	98
KZCH	96.3	Wichita, KS	99
KSAS	103.3	Boise, ID	100
KZMG	93.1	Boise, ID	100
WAEZ	94.9	Johnson City/Kingsport, TN/Bristol, VA	102
WLKT	104.5	Lexington/Fayette, KY	104
KSMB	94.5	Lafayette, LA	105
WZYP	104.3	Huntsville, AL	108
WXLK	92.3	Roanoke/Lynchburg, VA	111
WLAN	96.9	Lancaster, PA	112
KSME	96.1	Ft. Collins/Greeley, CO	120
WYOY	101.7	Jackson, MS	121
WIOG	102.5	Lansing/East Lansing, MI	125
WJSZ	92.5	Lansing/East Lansing, MI	125
WWCK	105.5	Flint, MI	127
WDJQ	92.5	Canton, OH	129
KRUF	94.5	Shreveport, LA	133
KSPW	96.5	Springfield, MO	136
WXXX	95.5	Burlington, VT/Plattsburgh, NY	138
WAYV	95.1	Atlantic City/Cape May, NJ	141
WPST	94.5	Trenton, NJ	142
KBEA	99.7	Quad Cities (Davenport, Bettendorf, IA/ Rock Island, Moline, IL)	146
KDUK	104.7	Eugene - Springfield, OR	147
WPIA	98.5	Peoria, IL	152
WIXX	101.1	Green Bay, WI	187

Table 2.36 (continued)

Station	Frequency	Market	Market Rank
WKSZ	95.9	Green Bay, WI	187
WQKX	94.1	Sunbury/Selinsgrove/Lewisburg, PA	219
WZNS	96.5	Ft. Walton Beach, FL	227
WBNQ	101.5	Bloomington, IL	241

Source: Based on licensed data from www.http://charts.mediaguide.com/panels/CHR_Pop. html, Mediaguide, Inc., © 2009 Week of 08/03/09–08/09/09 for data in Table 2.35.

2.11 Performances or Airplay Data Collection: Television

Broadcast television and cable network performances are measured using data from station or network logs, tapes, cue sheets, play lists, program guides, schedules, and other means. A cue sheet is a document, now in electronic format, that lists all of the musical compositions contained in television programs—including infomercials and commercials—made for television movies or theatrical movies that will be broadcast on television.

ASCAP and BMI use cue sheets provided by audio/visual production companies to determine how the music is used in a musical composition such as a feature, theme, background music, or in opening/closing credits, the owners' share of the copyrighted musical composition, their PRO affiliation, and so on in order to distribute royalty payments for the works.

ASCAP and BMI, along with CBS, NBC, Disney, Fox, Sony, Paramount, and others use a system called 'RapidCue,' a state-of-the-art web-based application that allows production companies to enter, manage, and electronically submit cue sheet data to ASCAP and BMI. The tens of thousands of cue sheets received each year by the PROS are then matched to television broadcast schedules to determine the number of performances; songwriters and composers are then paid accordingly for their works used.

The composer, music editor, or music supervisor is, generally, tasked with collecting the relevant information included on a cue sheet. The cue sheet information is then sent to the production company for verification of accuracy and the inclusion of additional information, such as the proper copyright information for licensed music or other publishing-related information. The production company then distributes the finished cue sheet to all interested parties, such as publishers, composers, attorneys, and performing rights organizations like ASCAP.[29]

Table 2.37 gives an illustration of a partial example of a cue sheet provided by the production company, Urban Skies for an episodic television series called *Urban Skies* after the final version had been edited and the show aired on the Showtime cable network. The cue sheet lists all the musical compositions; their various uses such as main title or background instrumental; the number of times that each composition was used in the hour-long program and the associated performing rights affiliation of the songwriters and publishers. Notice that the production company established a music publishing company called Urban Skies Music to collect the publisher's share of performance royalties. The songwriters, composers, and

Table 2.37 Partial Example of a Music Cue Sheet

Series/Film Title: *Urban Skies*
Episode Title/Number: *Grape Soda (#12)*
Estimated Airdate: 1-12-99
Program Length: 60 minutes
Program Type: Comedy series

Company Name: Urban Skies Productions
Address: 7920 Sunset Blvd., L.A., CA 90027
Phone: 1-800-662-4490
Contact: Chris Moll
Network Station: Showtime

Cue No.	Cue Title	Use*	Timing	Composer(s)/Affiliation %	Publisher(s)/Affiliation %
1	Urban Skies Theme	MT	0:16	Rhonda Sims (ASCAP) 100%	Urban Skies Music (ASCAP) 100%
2	Running Home	BI	0:08	Rhonda Sims (ASCAP) 100%	Urban Skies Music (ASCAP) 100%
3	Backwards Love	BI	0:13	Rhonda Sims (ASCAP) 100%	Urban Skies Music (ASCAP) 100%
4	Uptown	BI	0:09	Rhonda Sims (ASCAP) 100%	Urban Skies Music (ASCAP) 100%
5	Skies the Limit	BV	1:03	Terry Oakley (ASCAP) $33\frac{1}{3}$%	Terrycotta (ASCAP) $33\frac{1}{3}$%
				Larry Joyce (PRS) $33\frac{1}{3}$%	Larry Joyce Music (PRS/ASCAP) $33\frac{1}{3}$%
				Ennio Blake (APRA) $33\frac{1}{3}$%	Ennio B. Music (APRA/ASCAP) $33\frac{1}{3}$%
6	Synthroid	BI	0:05	Rhonda Sims (ASCAP) 100%	Urban Skies Music (ASCAP) 100%
7	Coffee In Bed	BI	0:32	Rhonda Sims (ASCAP) 100%	Urban Skies Music (ASCAP) 100%
8	Roll With It	BI	0:15	Rhonda Sims (ASCAP) 100%	Urban Skies Music (ASCAP) 100%
9	Knock Me Down	BI	0:01	Rhonda Sims (ASCAP) 100%	Urban Skies Music (ASCAP) 100%
10	Spinach and Ham	BI	0:16	Rhonda Sims (ASCAP) 100%	Urban Skies Music (ASCAP) 100%
11	Swing to Live	VV	0:34	Jerry Fin (ASCAP) 100%	Fins Alive Publishing (ASCAP) 100%
12	Good Luck	BI	0:11	Rhonda Sims (ASCAP) 100%	Urban Skies Music (ASCAP) 100%
13	Hot Water Beaches	BI	0:36	Rhonda Sims (ASCAP) 100%	Urban Skies Music (ASCAP) 100%
14	Polar Opposites	BI	0:02	Rhonda Sims (ASCAP) 100%	Urban Skies Music (ASCAP) 100%
15	No Way Jose	BI	0:01	Rhonda Sims (ASCAP) 100%	Urban Skies Music (ASCAP) 100%

*Use Codes: MT = Main Title, VI = Visual Instrumental, BV = Background Vocal, VV = Visual Vocal, ET = End Title, BI = Background Instrumental, and T = Theme

Source: http://www.ascap.com/musicbiz/cue_sheet_corner/pdf/SampleCueSheet.pdf.

publishers will be paid directly and separately by the PROs, there is no co-mingling of royalty income.

Logs, program guides, lists, tapes, or other measures are used to determine airlines, live concerts, circuses, concert halls, theme parks, and jukeboxes performances.

2.12 Computing Royalty Payments for Writers and Publishers

The payment method and rules for ASCAP and BMI vary by medium licensed (radio, television, Internet, etc.) as well as type of performance (theme songs, underscore, feature performances, jingles, logos, etc.). A successful writer could be receiving payments based on the numbers of performances for a musical composition that was played on network television or cable (or both) in a full feature format (such as being sung on a musical show), parts of the songs could have been used in a network promo/tune-in, a jingle or a commercial. The same song could have been played on the radio or streamed from a website. The royalty payments made to writers and publishers are typically referred to as 'distributions.'

It is beyond the scope of this monograph to go into the often complicated weighting rules, weighting formulas, various distribution plans for members, and survey methods used in computing PROs distributions (royalty payments) to songwriters, composers, and music publishers.

Each PRO has a different method for computing these factors and from time to time new rules are added or old ones changed. The reader interested in further details and documents that govern ASCAP and its relationship with its membership can research the following documents available at http://www.ascap.com/reference. There you will find several helpful documents:

- *Articles of Association*: The basic document that sets out ASCAP's structure and governs its relationship with its members, as amended through May 2002.
- *Membership Application and Agreement*: The documents that all members sign when they join ASCAP.
- *Distribution Resource Documents*: The rules and regulations governing distribution of royalties to members, including the Writers' Distribution Plans, the Writers' and Publishers' Distribution Formulas, the Weighting Rules and Weighting Formula.
- *Second Amended Final Judgment entered in United States v. ASCAP*: ASCAP's Consent Decree with the United States government that largely governs ASCAP's licensing activities.

For information on the methods by which BMI royalties are calculated and distributed, you can find that information at http://www.bmi.com/creators/royalty/533113.

PROs pay their songwriters and publishers for US performances approximately 6 months after the end of each-month performance period. In ASCAP's weighting rules, as described in its *Distribution Resource Documents*, performance credits are used as units of measure based on the results from its survey of music performances. For example, a feature performance may be awarded one use credit. Fractional use credits may be awarded for compositions performed as a theme, jingle or as a background, cue, or bridge music.[30]

A broadcast network royalty payment example as shown in Table 2.38 might be a helpful illustration. The broadcast network distribution payments would take into account the *weight* of the broadcast station based on ratings, the *use weight* for the type of performance, the *strata* multiplier for the medium in which the performance takes place, the feature multiplier add-on to all television performances and time of day.

Table 2.38 Example of ASCAP's Network Royalty Payment Formula

Strata	Use Wgt.	Stat. Wgt.	Credits	Credit value	Dollar value
150	.60 (Underscore)	1	90	$6.43	$578.70
150	.60 (Theme)	1	90	$6.43	$578.70
150	.03 (Jingle)	1	4.5	$6.43	$28.94

Source: Brabec and Brabec (2008, p. 307).

The result of all of these factors is the total number of credits generated for a performance that is later translated into dollar amounts. A credit value in dollar amounts is then computed separately by dividing the total amount of license fees available for distribution (less the cost of administration) by the total number of performance credits.[31]

2.13 Foreign Royalties Collection

The PROs have reciprocal agreements with performing rights organizations throughout the world. These agreements allow those foreign PROs to license the works of the US PROs and collect licensing fees on their behalf when the music is performed outside the United States. The CISAC, the International Confederation of Societies of Authors and Composers, organization works toward increased recognition and protection of creators rights worldwide. As of June 2008, CISAC numbers 225 authors societies from 118 countries and indirectly represents more than 2.5 million creators within all the artistic repertoires: music, drama, literature, audio-visual, graphic, and visual arts.[32] CISAC at their website says their main activities and member services are to:

- to strengthen and develop the international network of copyright societies;
- to secure a position for creators and their collective management organizations in the international scene;
- to adopt and implement quality and technical efficiency criteria to increase copyright societies interoperability;

- to support societies strategic development in each region and in each repertoire;
- to retain a central database allowing societies to exchange information efficiently;
- to participate in improving national and international copyright laws and practices.

Notes

1. Coen (2008).
2. See www.magnaglobal.com. Magna is a unit of Interpublic. McCann Erickson is now part of the McCann WorldGroup and one of Interpublic's operating entities.
3. McBride (2009).
4. See GAO (2007) Report No. GAO-08-330R.
5. Based on B. Wieser's, January 2010 Advertising Revenue Forecast, www.magnaglobal.com.
6. See Fabrikant (2009).
7. See *Citadel Files for Bankruptcy Amid Harsh Radio Climate*, *Wall Street Journal*, 12/21/2009, p. B3.
8. GAO (2007).
9. See http://www.ibiquity.com/hd_radio.
10. Brabec and Brabec (2008, p. 16).
11. See GAO (2004) Report No. GAO-04-700.
12. See GAO (2004).
13. See GAO (2004).
14. See http://www.soundexchange.com.
15. We will not go into the details of the many lawsuits discussed and analyzed elsewhere. The reader can do an Internet search using the United States District Court: Civil Action No. 41-1395 for cases related to ASCAP or visit the Copyright Right Board at www.loc.gov/crb for the relevant proceedings.
16. See Dertouzos (2008).
17. See Table 3.1: *Why Cultural Goods Are Not Like Ordinary Commodities* in Grant and Wood (2004, pp. 42–60).
18. See www.loc.gov/crb/proceedings/2005-1/rates-terms2005-1.pdf.
19. See http://www.loc.gov/crb/proceedings/2006-3/dpra-public-final-rate-terms.pdf.
20. See www.SoundExchange for further details not reported here.
21. See the September, 1, 2009, *Digital Briefs: Live365, CRB, Napster, Live Nation* by Anthony Bruno, www.billboard.biz.
22. See http://www.ascap.com/licensing/licensingfaq.html.
23. Sampling methods, music weights, and survey coverage described here may vary among PROs. Not everyone follows the same exact procedures in place at ASCAP.
24. See http://www.ascap.com/about/payment/surveys.html for detailed information on both the Census Survey and the Sample Survey.
25. BMI uses Landmark Digital Services LLC, its wholly owned subsidiary, for some radio performance survey data.
26. It is beyond the scope of this monograph to go into the distinguishing distribution and payment methods of each PRO. See Brabec and Brabec (2008) for a more extensive overview.
27. NARM is the National Association of Recording Merchandisers, www.narm.com.
28. See www.mediaguide.com for more information on Mediaguide. Competitors to Mediaguide include Landmark Digital Services LLC, a wholly owned subsidiary of BMI, and Nielsen Broadcast Data Systems (BDS).
29. See http://www.ascap.com/playback/2005/winter/features/cuesheets.aspx.
30. See *ASCAP's Distribution Resource Documents*, pp. 1–30 available at http://www.ascap.com/reference.

31. See, for example, http://www.ascap.com/about/payment/royalties.html for ASCAP's royalty calculation method.
32. See the International Confederation of Societies of Authors and Composers, www.cisac.org.

References

AFJ2 (2001). Second Amended Final Judgment, USA vs ASCAP, Civil Action No. 41 − 1395. United States District Court, S.D.N.Y. (White Plains), pp. 1–19.

Brabec, J. and Brabec, T. (2008). *Music Money and Success: The Insiders Guide to Making Money in the Music Industry*. Schirmer Trade Books-Music Sales, New York, NY, 6th edition.

Coen, R. (2008). Insider's Report: Advertising Expenditures, December 2008. *MAGNA Insights*.

Dertouzos, J. (2008). *Radio Airplay and the Record Industry: An Economic Analysis*. National Association of Broadcasters. Unpublished.

Fabrikant, G. (2009). 'Radio Giant Faces Crisis in Cash Flow'. www.nytimes.com. April 29.

GAO (2004). *Intellectual Property: Economic Arrangements Among Small Webcasters and Third Parties and Their Effect on Royalty*. United States Government Accountability Office. Report No. GAO-04-700.

GAO (2007). *Telecommunications: Preliminary Information on Media Ownership*. United States Government Accountability Office. Report No. GAO-08-330R.

Grant, P. and Wood, C. (2004). *Blockbusters and Trade Wars: Popular Culture in a Globalized World*. Douglas and McIntyre, Vancouver, BC.

McBride, S. (2009). Commercial Radio Stations Beg For Cash. *Wall Street Journal*. April 30, p. B3.

Chapter 3
Economic Analysis of Music Copyright: Music Publishers

Abstract In this chapter we look at the economics of performing rights organizations from the perspective of the music publishers, one of the suppliers of music. One of the most important aspects of the music publishing business is the exploitation of the music copyrights in their catalogs in order to increase record sales and maximize revenue. We will examine the various ways music is licensed, sources of income for music publishers, and the royalty collection agencies involved in music licensing. The publisher's focus is not just on managing both domestic and international master recording rights of the songwriter, but can also include licensing the image and likeness of the recording artist for merchandising as well.

3.1 Introduction

Music publishers are often described as *music content* companies. Most of their content (which is treated as an asset) is derived from their recorded music libraries which include their catalogs of best-selling single records and albums, and a roster of established and emerging songwriters and composers spanning all musical genres and time periods. In essence, the songwriters and composers create the content, the musical compositions, and the publisher and record label are responsible for distribution and marketing, among other things.

The content of music catalogs have a unique set of characteristics that are common in the music industry. The majority of the cost of creating the content is usually upfront, sunk at the beginning and borne by the publisher or record label. The subsequent costs of duplication and distribution are minor in comparison. The second characteristic of the music industry is that a small number of titles generate most of the revenue from record sales and royalty payments from public performances. These small number of revenue generating titles will then offset the losses of the vast majority of titles released by the publisher.

The typical music publishing company used to classify its business model into two segments: Recorded Music and Music Publishing. The Recorded Music segment produces revenue through the sale of music in various channels and the

I.L. Pitt, *Economic Analysis of Music Copyright*,
DOI 10.1007/978-1-4419-6318-5_3, © Springer Science+Business Media, LLC 2010

licensing of recorded music in various formats. The Music Publishing segment acquires the rights to musical compositions from songwriters and composers, and receives revenue in the form of royalties payments or fees for their use by music users in the United States and abroad.

The music publisher will exploit the many ways in which songwriters and composers can benefit from other types of licensing such as the use of the artist's name, image, and likeness for things like perfumes, clothing, and beverage advertising. The role of the music publisher has now been enhanced to that of a marketer, agent, manager, lawyer, and business advisor to the songwriter, and there is now a lot of overlap with the creative services normally handled by a manager.[1]

Song or title registration of new compositions; catalog licensing of existing songs; performance, mechanical, and synchronization royalty collection; and creative marketing are just four areas of responsibility of music publishers in the publisher/songwriter relationship as shown in Table 3.1. These four areas of responsibilities will vary depending on whether the publisher is one of the major publishing companies that can offer all four, or an independent music publisher, sub-publisher, record label, or copyright administrator with fewer responsibilities.

Table 3.1 Selected Roles of Publishers, Record Labels and Producers (Majors and Independents)

Entity	Functions
Publisher	Register new works or titles, License mechanical, performance & synchronization copyrights, Evaluate and market new artists.
Record label	Sign new artists with commercial potential, including touring and merchandising, Finance, distribute, promote, market, and sell Music CDs, DVDs, etc.—through retailer relationships and on TV and radio, Perform artist development, May also perform some of the functions of publishers, and Handles the sound recording copyrights.
Record producer	Produce the final record or arrangement (tracks)—including working with instrumentalists and vocalists, Interface with record labels, Develop new artists for records labels, and Co-write songs.
Copyright administrator	Performs some of the duties of publisher on behalf of a copyright owner(s), Collects performance, mechanical, synchronization, print—and foreign income for a commission, All rights, including creative exploitation, remain with the copyright owner(s).

The independent record label, sometimes referred to as an 'indie label,' will also differ in their ability to offer artists large up-front advances as an offset to future royalty income. An 'indie label' may also be affiliated with a major music publisher. The music publisher sees to it that the rights of the songwriters are protected from infringement under Federal Copyright Laws statutory requirements by making sure that their music is registered through a performing rights organizations.

In the normal course of action, a music publisher or administrator will establish a publishing agreement and register the song with the PRO once the appropriate copyright ownership between the songwriter and the publisher has been tabulated. A signed agreement details the contractual relationship between publishers and the performing right organizations as to how to pay all or part of the performance rights royalties to various parties, entities, sub-publishers, or foreign affiliates designated in the agreement. The registration agreements are designated for a fixed term and the territories such as the US and its possessions and other foreign countries covered under the agreement are documented.

There are several types of registration agreements, two of the most important ones are the General Catalog Agreement and the Specific Catalog Agreement. In the General Catalog Agreement, the publisher or a designated entitled party, sometimes called a collector, receives performance royalties for all titles or works in the publishers catalog registered with the PRO, while only a defined set of works are covered under the Specific Catalog Agreement.

The primary role of record label, sometimes a subsidiary of a major publisher and housed under one roof, is to arrange for the financing and manufacture of the physical product such as CDs, DVDs, cassette tapes, and the distribution of a songwriter's song in as many domestic distribution channels as possible such as music stores, greeting cards stores, big-box retailers, radio, broadcast television, cable television, motion pictures, the Broadway theater, the Internet (downloads), cell phones (ring tones), and foreign markets. Some labels may also combine other services such as record production, marketing promotions, and artist management and development under a single roof.

In general, the music publisher handles some or all aspects of the performance rights (as licensed through ASCAP, BMI, and SESAC) and print rights (through the Harry Fox Agency or others) of their copyrighted songs, while the record labels handle the sound and audio recording rights (through SoundExchange). A single song could have multiple songwriters and co-publishers as copyright holders, and multiple agencies involved in performance, mechanical, and synchronization copyright clearance depending on how the song is used. There is no 'one-stop' shop in the United States to obtain all the licenses required before a copyrighted song can be used.

The record producer's primary role is to select the material suitable for the performing artist, direct the studio musicians on what to play to support the artist, and interface with the record label. The producer may also help to develop artists with commercial potential for record labels, or they may co-write songs for artists who do not write their own. It is not uncommon to have songwriters produce their own songs and own the record label as well.

3.2 Structure of the Music Publishing Industry

The top 4 major music publishers, at the time of writing, were EMI, Sony, Universal, and Warner Music in various order with an independent label rounding out the top 5. Even though Universal held the overall top ranking in the fourth quarter of 2008, EMI replaced Universal as the leader by first quarter of 2009 as shown in Tables 3.2 and 3.3.[2] For example, as shown in Table 3.3, the top 4 publishers in the music industry are based on market share. EMI was ranked number one in terms of the largest market share based on airplay by having had shares of 34 songs that finished in the top 100 for the quarter.[3]

The top 10 major music publishers in the fourth quarter of 2008 accounted for 75.75 percent of the airplay of the top 100 songs monitored by Nielsen and the Harry Fox Agency. By the first quarter of 2009, the top 10 publishers accounted for 78.02 percent of the featured songs monitored by Nielsen. Publishers can be

Table 3.2 Major Publishers Airplay Chart Q4 2008

Rank	Publisher	Songs/share in Top 100	Industry % share	Top 10 only % share
1	Universal Music Group	32	17.25	22.77
2	EMI Music	35	16.72	22.07
3	SONY/ATV Music	31	16.26	21.47
4	Warner/Chappell	22	11.22	14.81
5	Kobalt Music	6	4.99	6.59
6	Goo Eyed Music	1	2.26	2.98
7	Wixen Music	2	2.07	2.73
8	Bug Music/Windswept	7	1.97	2.60
9	Word & Music Copyright	3	1.69	2.23
10	Cherry Lane Music	3	1.32	1.74
	Industry Share %		75.75	100.00

Source: Based on Christman (2009a), *Billboard* magazine, 2/21/2009 issue. Used with permission of e5 Global Media.

Table 3.3 Major Publishers Airplay Chart Q1 2009

Rank	Publisher	Songs/share in Top 100	Industry % share	Top 10 only % share
1	EMI Music	34	17.69	22.67
2	SONY/ATV Music	26	16.88	21.64
3	Universal Music Group	31	14.87	19.06
4	Warner/Chappell	39	12.64	16.20
5	Kobalt Music	10	5.45	6.99
6	Bug Music/Windswept	9	2.82	3.61
7	Word & Music Copyright	3	2.19	2.81
8	Peer Music	4	1.92	2.46
9	Goo Eyed Music	1	1.90	2.44
10	Wixen Music	2	1.66	2.13
	Industry Share %		78.02	100.00

Source: Based on Christman (2009b), *Billboard* magazine, 5/16/2009 issue. Used with permission of e5 Global Media.

displaced when the rankings are broken down by genres such as rock publisher or country publisher. This variation in rankings can be caused by the number of recent acquisitions to their catalogs, or on the number of 'hits' as tabulated and published by *Billboard* magazine.

In a typical publisher/songwriter arrangement, the songwriter, lyricist, or composer creates a song and then assigns the copyright to a publisher. The song is added to the publisher's catalog of existing songs and made available for licensing to music users. The publisher, composer, and songwriter will then earn royalty income from record sales and public performances of the music as described in Table 3.4.

Table 3.4 Selected Publisher and Songwriter/Composer Sources of Income For Copyrighted Musical Compositions and Signed Agreements

Music composition	Type	Payment	Terms
Used on Radio, TV, Internet, etc.	Performance	Varies	Songwriters, performers, and publishers paid separately and directly by ASCAP, BMI, & SESAC
Sheet Music	Print	$0.05 to $0.15	Writer's receipts for individual pieces of a song sheet
		plus 50%	Of publisher's receipts from such use
Christian Sheet Music	Print	10%–20%	Publisher receipts from retail prices of hymnals, etc.
			Writer receives a pro-rata share of publisher's receipts
Folios	Print	10%–15%	Writer's share based on wholesale selling price, number of songs and writers in the folios
		12%–20%	If songs are designed around a particular writer/team
		plus 50%	Of publisher's receipts from such use
CD, Tapes, Records, Downloads, & Ringtones	Mechanical	50%	Writer's share of publisher receipts in the US
TV & Movie	Synchronization	50%	Writer's share of publisher receipts from songs used in theatrical films and television programs
Commercials	Synchronization	50%	Writer receives share of publisher receipts from songs used in radio, television, Internet ads.
Home & Video Games	Synchronization	50%	Writer's share of all monies received by the publisher
Foreign Exploitation	Foreign	50%	Writer's share of all monies received in the US for sheet music, CDs. television, etc.
Merchandise	Other	Varies	Writer and publisher shares depend on '360' deal signed.

Source: Based on Brabec and Brabec (2006), pp. 15–16 and Keen (2007), US and Canada.

3.3 Sources of Income for the Music Publisher

The primary sources of income for the music publisher come from the commercial exploitation of the copyrights based on a musical composition. These sources of income include performance rights, mechanical licenses, synchronization licenses, print rights, and foreign exploitation. The record label source of income will include the sound and audio recording rights for certain digital transmissions. Music publishers will often license their copyright musical works to music users in television, radio, Internet, films, videos, records, tapes, CDs, sheet music, advertising, and other forms of creative marketing.

The financial terms of the contract between a songwriter and a publisher will determine how the publishing income will be shared between them. Usually, the share is 50 percent to the publishers and 50 percent to the songwriter/composer for mechanical and synchronization rights. Print music income is determined by the numbers of songs and other factors. Performance royalties are paid directly to the publishers and songwriters/composers by ASCAP, BMI, and SESAC.[4]

For example, a songwriter might be paid anywhere from 5¢ to 15¢ for individual pieces of single song-sheet music sold in the United States and Canada (with many contracts guaranteeing the songwriter 50 percent of the publishers' receipts from such uses). The writer can also expect 50 percent of the publisher's receipts for CDs, tapes, records, commercials, video games, ring tones, synchronization, and foreign exploitation.[5] Some songwriters/composers with his or her own publishing company would sometimes enter into agreements with music publishers to handle certain aspects of licensing such as print or sheet music licensing, foreign licensing, and other copyright administration functions for a commission, fee or share of revenue.

3.4 Restructuring and Bypassing the Record Label

The recording music industry is now considered a mature industry when such factors as declining CD sales, the way in which superstars are bypassing the records labels, the use of the Internet to distribute their music, direct-to-retail using exclusive deal with Wal-Mart, or performers partnering with concert promoters such as Live Nation are considered.

We will highlight some of the recent controversial changes that are reshaping the entire economics of the industry and left music publishers searching for a new business models. Today, the record labels' ability to control an artist, retail distribution channels, access to radio play, and the ability to introduce new artists are slowly evaporating.

Several technological advances such as the CD burner, iPod, and the Internet, (with its innovations as a cost saving, user-friendly digital marketing, and distribution channel) are helping new acts as well as established artists circumvent the traditional music publishing industry business model, a mature business.

Many well-established songwriters now have the capability to self-publish their own music while retaining complete ownership of the copyrights, and there is no need to sign away all the rights to their songs to a publisher or record label. It has now become a negotiated arrangement with benefits flowing to the songwriters. Many unknown artists are becoming savvy enough to have websites with MP3 samples of their music and merchandise for sale bypassing the usual record label and publisher. This has had a pronounced effect on the economics in the music industry in which the power is shifting to the recording artist and their managers (or management companies).

These changes are enhancing the clout of concert promoters, managers, and the artists themselves at the expense of the traditional record label. All of these changes are revolutionizing the economics of the music industry in the way in which music is consumed and sold. Music pricing models and the cost of marketing and distribution have changed dramatically. *Billboard* magazine reports on how the balance of power is shifting from record labels to artists and therefore the managers, and in some case managers are supplanting labels all together as we shall see in the Live Nation/Madonna example discussed below. Terry McBride, founder/CEO of Nettwerk Music Group, supports the notion of the super-manager with his observation that 'the intellectual property part of it—the publishing and record label part—at most with any successful artist represents 25–30 percent of their income. The other 70–75 percent is elsewhere, not with the labels or publishers. All of the other revenue sources are basically run by the manager.'[6]

The *Wall Street Journal* reported that a seismic shift in the recording industry occurred in October 2007 when the recording artist known as 'Madonna' abandoned music publisher Warner Music for 'Live Nation,' the world's largest concert promoter after years of record label investment in her career. Live Nation, in addition to being the concert promoter for Madonna is also going to be a merchandiser as well. In examining certain aspects of the reported $120 million multi-media Madonna/Live Nation deal taken at face value with all the usual marketing and public relations hype as shown in Table 3.5, the *Wall Street Journal* reported that 'even as her album sales have steadily diminished, her protean persona has kept her in the news, and maintained her clout as a music draw.' The Irish rock band 'U2' and

Table 3.5 Madonna's $120 Million 10-Year Deal with Live Nation (October 2007)

Terms	
Signing Bonus/Advance	$17.5m
Advance Payment for 3 Albums	$50–$60m
Right to Promote Concert Tours	$50m cash & stock
Concert Tour Split	90% Madonna 10% Live Nation
Income From Licensing Artist's Image	50/50 Split
Risks	
Depending on price, would need to sell 45 million albums to recoup investment/costs.	

Source: Based on Smith (2007), *Wall Street Journal*.

artists such as 'Jay-Z,' 'Nickelback,' and 'Shakira' are also reported to have signed similar deals with Live Nation.'[7]

Concert promoters make money by booking artists and venues for concerts with up to 90 percent of ticket sales going to the performing artist in certain cases (after certain expenses are deducted) and the concert promoter retaining 10 percent plus the revenue from parking and service fees and concession sales.[8]

In the Madonna deal, Warner Music will retain the rights to Madonna's catalog of albums dating back 20 years, and a new album that was due in 2008. Presumably Warner Music has already recovered the investment it made in Madonna's career over the years, or is hoping to recover more from her catalog of past output of song titles. Live Nation is hoping to recoup its investment of cash and stock in exchange for the right to sell three studio albums, promote concert tours, sell promotional merchandise such as tour program guides, T-shirts and mouse pads, and license Madonna's name and image for use in advertising.

The *Wall Street Journal* reports the Madonna deal carries significant risks for Live Nation (a publicly traded company at the time of this writing) as investors have become wary of Live Nation's costly deals with top talent. People in the music industry estimates that Live Nation would have to sell about 45 million copies in the 3-album deal to recoup its investment without the rights to Madonna's catalog of old songs to hedge any risks, but with prices of CDs and downloads alike falling that number could increase.[9]

Madonna may have also have gambled that live concerts would be a better way to boost her income to offset declining album sales, if she can keep up with a rigorous touring schedule year after year. One factor playing a major role in this new type of concert promoter/performing artist business model has been the declining revenue and income from the sales of compact discs and albums that have not been offset by increased sales in digital downloads.

Many established artists are now looking for other sources of income from live concerts, merchandising, and the use of their image in advertising and corporate sponsorships.[10] Revenue from live concert ticket sales can be very lucrative for the performing artist as shown in Table 3.6. The top 25 touring acts alone in 2008 earned close to $1.8 billion in total gross ticket sales with 20,716,811 concert tickets being sold. These artists performed 1,405 times with sell-out crowds occurring 993 times or 71 percent of the time. The top performer was Bon Jovi with close to $211 million in ticket sales, or 11.9 percent of the gross share, where attendance at all 99 of their sold-out shows reached 2,157,675. At the end of 2008, Madonna was the third ranking touring performer with total gross receipts of $186 million or a 10.49 percent of the total gross. Madonna sold-out 38 of her 39 concerts that year with attendance reaching 1,369,452 concertgoers. This is indeed a rather large fan base in which to sell her records and other merchandize such as T-shirts and program guides. It is not hard to see why the concerns raised above about Live Nation, Madonna, and other deals might be accurate.

For example, if following the industry practice of giving the performing artist 90 percent of the gross receipts from ticket sales, Madonna' cut from her 2008 tour would total $167.13 million. That would leave Live Nation with a razor thin

Table 3.6 Selected Live Concert Gross Receipts by Artist (November 2007–November 2008)

Rank	Gross	Share	Artist	Attendance	Capacity	No. of shows	No. of sellouts
1	$210,650,974	11.90%	Bon Jovi	2,157,675	2,157,675	99	99
2	$204,513,630	11.56%	Bruce Springsteen	2,094,851	2,181,839	82	46
3	$185,696,018	10.49%	Madonna	1,357,906	1,369,452	39	38
4	$149,623,800	8.45%	The Police	1,468,705	1,492,947	78	71
5	$91,006,221	5.14%	Celine Dion	738,947	755,710	44	36
6	$86,306,618	4.88%	Kenny Chesney	1,187,622	1,252,227	46	25
7	$81,206,383	4.59%	Neil Diamond	834,689	834,689	61	61
8	$70,123,272	3.96%	Spice Girls	581,066	595,220	45	34
9	$56,625,336	3.20%	Eagles	427,231	436,075	34	27
10	$55,863,364	3.16%	Rascal Flatts	941,827	967,726	65	58
11	$49,017,853	2.77%	Van Halen	462,349	470,536	44	41
12	$47,382,901	2.68%	Trans-Siberian Orchestra	1,103,256	1,229,524	120	67
13	$46,333,163	2.62%	Michael Bublé	640,674	646,889	85	67
14	$45,376,189	2.56%	Hannah Montana/Miley Cyrus	816,421	816,421	57	57
15	$41,133,051	2.32%	Billy Joel	424,984	430,548	29	25
16	$40,080,352	2.26%	Jonas Brothers	940,224	978,029	85	56
17	$39,583,329	2.24%	Dave Matthews Band	763,163	842,082	44	19
18	$39,138,280	2.21%	Tom Petty & Heartbreakers	594,224	609,356	36	29
19	$36,346,675	2.05%	Leonard Cohen	338,749	459,670	65	30
20	$35,695,481	2.02%	Journey	695,397	783,617	57	30
21	$34,547,053	1.95%	Jay-Z, Mary J. Blige	309,143	346,560	27	12
22	$32,451,800	1.83%	Take That	390,450	390,450	30	30
23	$31,699,677	1.79%	Toby Keith	696,192	842,146	56	7
24	$29,906,507	1.69%	American Idols Live	493,296	579,548	53	9
25	$29,432,421	1.66%	Elton John	257,770	261,111	24	19
Total	$1,769,740,348			20,716,811	21,730,047	1,405	993

Source: Based on data from http://www.billboard.com/bbcom/yearend/2008/charts/top25-tours.html. Used with permission of e5 Global Media.

margin of just $18.57 million which it had to recoup from the sale of cheaper tickets, service fees, concession sales, and parking fees. Regardless of the price of admission to the concert, concession and parking fees would be dependent on size of the venue, concert attendance and things people purchase such as food, beverages, and T-shirts on the day of the concert. While ticket prices can be raised to increase the gross receipts and income of the top performers, the net impact can be fewer tickets purchased and declining attendance that may hurt the profitability of tour promoters like Live Nation, a publicly traded company. Higher ticket prices, the recession, shrinking disposable income, and slower consumer spending could also force concert attendees to spend less per capita on concessions.

In another music industry experiment in October 2007, the rock band, 'Radiohead,' launched and distributed their new album called *In Rainbows* over the Internet without their previous record label, EMI. The Internet enabled the band to get their new album out to their fans more quickly cutting down on the usual 3–6 month lead time needed by record labels for marketing a new album. In a twist, the digital version of the album did not have a fixed price, and customers were asked to name their own price for downloads, free for some if they wanted it. The physical version consisting of CDs, lyrics, and other bonus material was priced at around US $80 and available for purchase only at a website.

In yet another business model, the rock bands 'The Eagles' and then 'Journey' signed direct-to-retail sponsorship deals with Wal-Mart, the largest US retailer in 2007. The deals included preferred product placement of new albums in Wal-Mart stores, exclusive audio and video releases. The Eagles' *Long Road Out of Eden* was the third best-selling album of 2007 using Wal-Mart as the exclusive retailer and without the help from a record label. In August of 2008, 'AC/DC,' another rock group, made an arrangement to replicate the successful strategy recently used by the Eagles and Journey, both of whom in recent months have sold new albums exclusively at Wal-Mart.

The AC/DC business model is more of a hybrid one. 'Unlike the Eagles or Journey, AC/DC is under contract to a major record label, Sony BMG's Columbia Records, which brokered the pact with Wal-Mart and will also benefit from sales there. Columbia's decision to sell a major new release at only one chain has the potential to alienate retailers left out. One competitor unlikely to complain is Apple Inc.'s digital iTunes store, where AC/DC has never made its music available.'[11]

On February 4, 2009, it was reported in the *Wall Street Journal* that Live Nation and Ticketmaster would merge by combining the world's biggest concert promoter and the world's dominant ticketing and artist management company into one vertically integrated company. Live Nation is America's biggest concert producer, owners of dozens of amphitheatres and has inked 360 deals with artists like Madonna and Jay-Z, while Ticketmaster is the nation's biggest ticketing service, owners of Front Line Management and secondary ticketing site TicketsNow. In an interview, Live Nation Chief Executive Michael Rapino, who is to be CEO of the new entity, called the merger an attempt to create 'the company of the future that can serve the evolving needs of the artist and fans.' This merger is said to have vastly diminished the major record labels' clout, and enhanced the power of concert promoters and artists' managers alike.[12]

The issue of whether the Live Nation/Ticketmaster merger was likely to substantially create or reduce competition in the concert ticketing and promotion markets became moot when the US Justice Department approved the merger on January 25, 2010 after a year-long review, while imposing several significant conditions on the deal. One concern about the merger is that it could 'marginalize the four major record labels. As CD sales dwindle, most of the action in the music industry is now centered around concert tours, a business that excludes the labels.'[13]

Prior to the recession in 2009, live concerts and the merchandising side of the music business were said to be booming as recording artists looked to tap into these revenue streams, while the industry struggled with effects of declining sales of CDs. More recent data show that the demand for tickets are still high and performing artists like 'The Dead' and Kenny Chesney are still playing to sell out crowds in a snapshot of March–May 2009 touring data shown in Table 3.7. Live Nation is the concert promoter for 'The Dead' where the price per ticket varies from $39.50 to $95 depending on the size of the market and arena. The most expensive ticket in the United States costing $148.50 was for a 'Fleetwood Mac's concert at Amway Arena in Florida that failed to sell out. The music industry has had a difficult time monetizing its digital distribution strategy.

Smith (2009c) reports that music labels eager to find alternative online business models are turning to such strategies as selling ads alongside free streamed music or videos, creating online music services that generate revenue by presenting music to the public rather than through middlemen such as Apple's iTunes store, investing in digital music startups, establishing joints ventures with MySpace, or extracting large upfront fees from, or even ownership stakes, in new technology companies seeking licenses to use their music.

During the recession of 2009, many music retail outlets, such as Circuit City, went out of business, while others have reduced shelf space devoted to music. This has turned into a vicious cycle for music publishers. As compact disc sales declined, music retailers cut shelf space devoted to music and/or divert existing shelf space to other products, further reducing the amount of inventory devoted to music sales and accelerating the decline in CD sales and revenue. Whether it is record labels left scrambling to regain control of the process with new Internet business models, store closings, consumers migration to digital music, or recording artists giving away their music for free or artists abandoning record labels, all these economic factors will continue to harm record sales.

And despite all of the changes mentioned above, competition has been increasing for music publishing catalogs as investors view the catalogs as a 'conservative investment,' not necessarily from a huge return on investment (ROI) perspective, but from some cash flow value protected against inflation generated from performance and synchronization royalties. According to one report, the owners of the catalogs can expect to earn cash returns of 7 percent to 20 percent or more a year, depending on the songs and how they are marketed.[14]

Table 3.7 Selected Live Concert Gross Receipts by Promoter (March–May 2009)

Rank	Artist(s)	Venue	Attendance	Capacity	Ticket Price Range*	Gross Receipts	Avg. Price	Promoter
1	The Dead	Allstate, IL	28,469	34,942	$50–$90	$2,298,385	$80.73	Live Nation
2	The Dead	Forum, CA	16,920	Sellout	$49.50–$85	$1,337,522	$79.05	Live Nation
3	The Dead	Pepsi Ctr., CO	16,091	Sellout	$39.50–$94.50	$1,269,200	$78.88	Live Nation
4	K. Chesney, M. Lambert, L. Antebellum	Sprint Ctr., MO	13,922	Sellout	$21–$90.50	$998,116	$71.69	Messina Group, AEG Live
5	K. Chesney, M. Lambert L. Antebellum	Qwest Ctr., NB	14,270	Sellout	$20–$91.50	$919,296	$64.42	Messina Group, AEG Live
6	Fleetwood Mac	Amway Arena, FL	7,668	10,688	$34–$148.50	$756,311	$98.63	Live Nation
7	Steve Harvey, Nephew Tommy, D. Clay	Radio City, NY	11,971	2 Sellouts	$51–$65	$691,408	$57.76	Nu-Opp Chugg Ent.,
8	Brooks & Dunn, Dierks Bentley, A. Harvey	Acer Arena, Aust.	6,419	6,520	$73.46–$184.76	$685,908	$106.86	Robert Potts
9	The Dead	Wachovia Arena, PA	6,526	8,275	$65–$95	$606,190	$92.89	Live Nation
10	K. Chesney, M. Lambert L. Antebellum	Wells Fargo Arena, IA	11,183	Sellout	$21–$99	$601,596	$53.80	Mischell Productions, Messina Group, AEG Live

Table 3.7 (continued)

Rank	Artist(s)	Venue	Attendance	Capacity	Ticket Price Range*	Gross Receipts	Avg. Price	Promoter
11	Metallica, Machine Head, The Sword	Trent FM Arena, Eng.	10, 223	13,164	$58.01	$593, 004	$58.01	Kilimanjaro Live
12	Metallica, Machine Head, The Sword	S.E.C.C. Scotland	9, 935	Sellout	$58.84	$581, 563	$58.54	Kilimanjaro Live
13	IL Divo	Arena Beograd, Serbia	7, 082	7,627	$32–$156.26	$577, 801	$81.59	Live Nation, Beograd
14	Lil Wayne, T-Pain, Gym Class Heroes, K. Hilson	Journal Pavilion, NM	13, 881	15,004	$19.50–$125	$576, 125	$41.50	Live Nation Haymon Ent.
15	Simply Red, Valeriya	Sheffield Arena, Eng.	10, 280	10,985	$54.58–$61.86	$561, 130	$54.58	Kilimanjaro Live
Total			184, 840			$13, 053, 555	$70.62	

*These ticket prices may not include service fees.
Source: Based on *Billboard* magazine Boxscore Data, May 23, 2009, p. 8.
Used with permission of e5 Global Media.

Table 3.8 Selected Equity Investors in Music Catalogs (By Year)

Investor	Catalog/Group	Investment ($ mil.) E	Titles	Year
KKR	Crosstown	$70[1]	8,000	Jul-09
Pegasus Capital	Spirit Music Group	$55[1]	15,000	Apr-09
Dutch Pension Fund/ Imagen	Rodgers &II Hamerstein II	$200[1]	200,000[3]	Apr-09
Balderton Capital	Kobalt	$16[2]	250,000[4]	Feb-08
Spectrum Equity	Bug Music	NA	250,000	Jul-06

E = Estimated

Sources: Titles Data: Satariano (2009), www.bloomberg.com.

[1] www.reuters.com/article/privateEquityConsumerGoodsAndRetail/idUSN2339541320090723.

[2] www.venturebeat.com/2008/02/12/music-publishing-kobalt-banks-on-higher-revenues-for-artists.

[3] included other song titles.

[4] 'Modes of revenue streams/music products.'

In contrast, publicly record labels must constantly generate hit songs to meet their profit objectives. Table 3.8 highlights some of the recent deals that sparked private equity and pension fund investors' interest in music publishing. The goal of some of these investors is to create a sizable new entrant in music publishing in order to diversify their portfolios. For example, Pegasus Capital, a $2 billion fund, acquired Spirit Music Group in April 2009 in an estimated $55 million deal. 'Spirit controls a catalog of 15,000 classic and contemporary copyrighted songs that range from the standards of Frank Sinatra and Billie Holiday to the pioneering rock of Elvis Presley, Chubby Checker and Dion; from the seminal blues of Elmore James and Lightnin' Hopkins to the envelope-pushing jazz of Charles Mingus; from the timeless soul of Chaka Khan to the influential work of Lou Reed and The Grateful Dead and massive pop hits by Madonna, Mariah Carey, Janet Jackson and Jay-Z. Spirit Music's collection of works reflects more than 700 charted hit songs, according to a press release announcing the deal.'[15]

While the role of the music publisher and record label is constantly changing, they still remain an important force in the music industry. The goals now appear to find and develop talented songwriters who can be successful in selling music across a broad platform such as in films, television, advertising commercials, video games, merchandising, and Internet streaming services, in a rather difficult environment.

Notes

1. See Brabec and Brabec (2008), Passman (2000), and Walker (2008) for a more detailed discussion on the inner workings of the music publisher–songwriter relationship.
2. Nielsen BDS calculated the publisher ranking and market using the overall top 100 detecting songs from 1,551 radio stations in the fourth quarter of 2008 and 1,608 radio stations in the first quarter of 2009. The Harry Fox Agency researches the publishers' splits for each song in the top 100 to calculate their share of those songs.

3. See Christman (2009a,b).
4. Brabec and Brabec (2008, pp. 15–16).
5. Brabec and Brabec (2008, pp. 15–16).
6. See the article by Waddell (2008, p. 10) for the quote.
7. See Smith (2007, 2008).
8. See Smith (2007, 2009a,b).
9. See Smith (2007, 2009b).
10. See Smith (2007).
11. Kardos and Smith (2008).
12. See Smith (2009a,b).
13. Smith and Catan (2010).
14. See Satariano (2009).
15. See http://news.prnewswire.com/ViewContent.aspx?ACCT=109\&STORY=/www/story/ 04- 08-2009/0005003009\&EDATE=.

References

Brabec, J. and Brabec, T. (2008). *Music Money and Success: The Insiders Guide to Making Money in the Music Industry*. Schirmer Trade Books-Music Sales, New York, NY, 6th edition.

Christman, E. (2009a). 'EMI Prevails'. *Billboard Magazine*. May 16, p. 20.

Christman, E. (2009b). 'Universal Still Tops'. *Billboard Magazine*. February 21, p. 11.

Kardos, D. and Smith, E. (2008). 'AC/DC to Sell New Album Only Through Wal-Mart'. www.online.wsj.com. August 18.

Keen, D. (2007). http://www.ascap.com/musicbiz/christian_music_faq/

Passman, D. (2000). *All You Need to Know About the Music Business*. Simon & Schuster.

Satariano, A. (2009). 'Jackson, Grateful Dead Royalties Sound Sweet to Music Investors'. www.bloomberg.com. August 3.

Smith, E. (2007). 'Madonna Heads for Virgin Territory: Concert Promoter Lures Material Girl from Warner Music with $120 Million'. *Wall Street Journal*. October 11, p. B1.

Smith, E. (2008). 'For U2, Live Nation Deal Rocks'. *Wall Street Journal*. December 18, p. A3.

Smith, E. (2009a). 'Live Nation Agrees to All-Stock Buy of Ticketmaster'. *Wall Street Journal*. February 11, p. B3.

Smith, E. (2009b). 'Ticketmaster, Live Nation Near Merger'. *Wall Street Journal*. February 4, p. A1.

Smith, E. (2009c). 'Universal Music Takes Another Stab Online'. *Wall Street Journal*. May 15, p. B8.

Smith, E. and Catan, T. (2010). 'Concert Deal Wins Antitrust Approval'. *Wall Street Journal*. January 26, p. B1.

Waddell, R. (2008). 'Rise of the Super-Manager'. *Billboard Magazine*. Year-end Double Issue, December, pp. 10–11.

Walker, J. (2008). *This Business of Urban Music: A Practical Guide to Achieving Success in the Industry, From Gospel to Funk to R&B to Hip-Hop*. Billboard Books.

Chapter 4
Economic Analysis of Music Copyright: Songwriters and Composers

Abstract The preceding chapter looked at the publishing side of music from a 'business' perspective and illustrated the many sources of income for both the songwriter and the publisher. In this chapter, we look at the songwriter from the perspective of creative and business processes involved in making music. The creative process for a songwriter starts with the song and will involve many months of intense planning, writing, and rewriting. In the highly competitive music industry, it can be challenging to produce songs that are sufficiently distinctive, original, unique, and inspirational that consumers will love, want to purchase, and the record labels can easily market. The songwriter, composer, or lyricist will be collaborating with many others including other writers, the record labels, music managers, agents, producers, attorneys, sound studio owners, and publishers to produce and market a song. Once a song has been recorded, released, and registered with a PRO, the songwriter/composer then expects a flow of income from the performance rights attached to the composition. In this monograph we sometimes treat the author, composer, and lyricist as a single entity, calling him or her a songwriter; however, the division of labor can be distinct, but in a collaborative fashion.

4.1 Introduction

Lathrop (2003, pp. 5–6) describes some of the traditional music business process model in terms of marketing and promotion for a performing songwriter as follows:

1. Sign a contract with a major record company which handles the marketing and promotion process.
2. Sign with a music publisher which handles the administration and promotion of original music compositions.
3. Affiliate with a performance right organization (such ASCAP, BMI, and SESAC), which tracks radio, TV, and Internet airplay and handles royalties for such use.
4. Market through partnership with an established management agency which oversees all the career decisions of the performing songwriter, and a large

talent and booking agency, which handles the business of touring and live performances.
5. Hire an independent publicity firm to support the record label's publicity efforts (mostly coverage in magazines, newspapers, television, and the Internet).

4.2 Impact of the Internet on Songwriting

The Internet is one way in which the traditional business model has changed in the music world. The Internet has become one of the primary means of listening to music. The Internet, particularly sites such as MySpace and youTube, is an important new way in which many new songwriters and composers are being discovered. The songwriter can now write a song, 'demo' it or produce it in a home-studio, release it on MySpace, and then hope it is seen by a record label representative. Internet sites such as MySpace accounted for 40 percent of the way new songwriters and other acts were discovered in 2008 by music industry talent scouts, the same percentage as professional referrals. Word of mouth now accounted for 15 percent of the way A&R executives found new acts, while radio accounted for a mere 5 percent according to a December 2008 survey in *Music Connection* magazine.[1]

Talent scouts are referred to in music business as A&R executives, and they usually work for a record label. A&R stands for artists & repertoire. The main function of a record label's A&R executive is to help the record label attract, sign, and develop new artists with the potential to sell a large quantity of songs, while helping the record company achieve its financial goals and strategies. As such the A&R executive will keep abreast of all the latest music industry trends including the most popular genres such as pop, rock, urban dance music, or singer/songwriter, a new category; listening preferences of music fans such as which websites have become the primary means of listening to new music, and the type of deals artists are signing with various labels, such as the so-called '360' deal.

The 360 deal is one in which the artists and record labels share not only the income from mechanical, public performances and synchronization royalties, but also other income streams from live concert tours, merchandising, online, and the use of the artist's name and image in advertising with concert promoters. Merchandising deals with the major publishers/labels are setup as upfront advance payments versus royalties, with the bigger artists rating heftiest advances, guarantees, and most favorable royalty rates. Independent merchandising companies usually compete by focusing on bigger back-end earnings and better service for a smaller stable of artists.[2] In the past, merchandising focused on selling items mainly at concert venues on the day of concerts. Today, however, merchandising sales are occurring year-round at big-box retailers such as Wal-Mart, or direct to consumer via the Internet.

Some of the merchandisers involved in these 360 multi-rights deals include the divisions of major concert promoters such as Live Nation; major music publishers such as Sony and Universal, and independents merchandisers such as Cut Merch as

Table 4.1 Selected 360 Merchandising Deals

Merchandiser	Affiliation	Performing artists
Live Nation Merchandise	Live Nation	Madonna, Jay-Z, U2, Shakira & Nickelback
Thread Shop	Sony	Johnny Cash, Miles Davis, T-Pain & Pitbull
Bravado	Universal	Rolling Stones, Michael Jackson, Paul McCartney, Kanye West, Beyoncé, Lady GaGa, Elton John, Guns N' Roses, Metallica & Led Zeppelin.
Cut Merch	Independent	Eric Clapton
Richards and Southern	Independent	Taylor Swift, Kenny Chesney, George Strait & Sugarland

Source: *Billboard* magazine, October 3, 2009, pp. 22–32. Used with permission of e5 Global Media.

shown in Table 4.1. Bravado is Live Nation's closest 'merch' competitor in terms of size, geographic scope, experiences, and financial resources.[3]

The Internet, with its huge cost savings, makes it possible for the A&R executive to research songwriters, hear some of their music and perhaps watch a video performance online without the need for travel to watch an artist perform live. The record label now has a means in which to review acts before time, money, and other resources are expended, even though the quality of some online videos can be mediocre at best. Internet tracking firms, such as comScore, make it possible to track the number of hits an artist attracts online at various websites. The number of hits a songwriter receives online might serve as an indicator of potential future sales of records and that might in turn attract the attention of record labels. The dependence of the record label and the aspiring songwriter to generate demand for record sales in a highly competitive environment can mean that A&R people will only try to sign artists that are already somewhat established and successful on the Internet, making it difficult for an 'unknown' to break through.

Labels are no longer willing to risk resources on 'unknown' artists. The focus is on artists who may have already established a presence in an already tough and competitive environment rather than just someone looking to break through. Today's artists must, therefore, develop a demand for their music using sites such as MySpace, where they can accumulate a fan base of music enthusiasts who are acquainted with their music, and make them want to buy the music after first listening to it. It is only after this process of building up a fan base online, perhaps with a hit song, is first completed that the traditional record label interested in the physical and digital distribution of a song might occur. Building up a fan base becomes a very critical priority necessary to exploit the new areas of income, from live concert tours and merchandising, that have replaced declining compact disc sales.

The new business model in music appears to be that first and foremost an A&R person is looking for a songwriter with a hit song on the Internet, rather than the traditional radio airplay that may be crucial at a later stage. With the declining revenue from the sale of CDs, the live concert tour is another source of income that is being exploited. In the case of the singer/songwriter, this person must possess a powerful stage presence or least write music with such a venue and theatrics in mind.

Merchandising is yet another source of income usually for the performing artist or the front person of the band. It probably would help if that person had some 'star quality,' whatever that may mean to various segments in the music industry since image plays an important part in the success of an artist. Being able to place songs in television movies, theatrical films, advertising commercials, video games, and streaming Internet services are also another source of income for the songwriter. However, *Billboard* magazine reports that clothing apparel emblazoned with the lyrics of songwriters is a new revenue stream for publishers and songwriters. Everything from T-shirts, jeans, scarves, and 'hoodies' are now being sold in specialty boutiques with songwriters' lyrics on them. The songwriter is said to receive a royalty based on the wholesale price of each item sold.[4]

4.3 Two Types of Songwriters and Composers

Songwriters can be broken down into two broad groups: the non-performing songwriter and the performing songwriter. The songwriting division of labor, as will be shown later, can vary within these two groups.

4.3.1 Non-performing Songwriter

Some writers may simply write song material for singers and other performers. Some non-performing songwriters may not be skilled instrumentalists or singers, but they understand melody, lyrics, harmony, and how it can be musically combined to create a hit song. These non-performing songwriters may have the ability to write great songs, but they need someone else to bring it to life through skilled musicianship. A non-performing songwriter will usually approach music publishers for access to performing artists looking for songs, as well as the artists' managers, their producers, and record companies.[5]

Hatfield (2008, p. 6) suggests, on the other hand, 'that many incredibly talented musicians cannot write musical compositions and need someone else to provide them with good songs to perform.' In addition, some non-performing songwriters may simply suffer from stage fright, unable to perform in public, and may not like performing at all. From a comparative advantage, it may make more sense in terms of efficiency if the songwriter spends more time writing songs rather than touring and performing.

There is a long history of music industry where recording artists may also press for writing credit to increase their income from performance royalty. The matter usually ends up in court when the recording artist is sued for copyright right infringement by other songwriters for claiming rights to a song that they may not have written. It is not uncommon for some recording artists to allow only songwriters to work on a particular album, if they (the recording artists) are also given writing credit.

Some songwriters and composers will usually agree to this arrangement if the recording artist has the ability to sell a large quantity of songs in the millions. Novice songwriters just starting out may be exploited by having to offer writing credits to a well-known recording artist whose songwriting contribution to a song would be considered dubious, knowing that if a blockbuster hit should occur, the income generated and career advancement would offset any unethical behavior when it comes to song writing credits. To be taken seriously in the music industry, some performing artists must appear to have written or at least contributed in some meaningful way to their songs in order to increase credibility with their fans base.

4.3.2 Performing Songwriter

'Many of the famous songwriters are also skilled interpreters of their own material. They know how to write music to suit their own particular talents as musicians.'[6] These artists may not need the help of publishers, record labels, or producers to find them suitable singing material.

Looking at *Billboard* magazine's Top 10 songwriters for the period of January 1 through March 31, 2009, in Table 4.2, the top ranking songwriter at the end of the period was the performing songwriter Clifford Joseph 'T.I.' Harris, based on airplay generated by 3 tracks in *Dead and Gone*, *Live Your Life*, and *Whatever You Like*, for which he shared writing credits. Songwriters Clifford Harris, Taylor Swift, and Stefani Germanotta are recognized as well-known performing songwriters given the media coverage in popular music magazines. Harris is an affiliate of BMI with 167 different titles registered, while Aliaune 'Akon' Thiam is a member of ASCAP with 241 listed in their repertory.

Table 4.2 Billboard's Top 10 Songwriters Jan 1–Mar 31, 2009

Rank	Songwriter	PRO Titles Registered
1	Clifford Joseph 'T.I.' Harris Jr.	167
2	James Gregory Scheffer	180
3	David Siegel	69
4	Taylor Swift	69
5	K. V. Washington	6
6	Jason Mraz	103
7	Lukasz Gottwald	178
8	Aliaune 'Akon' Thiam	241
9 (tie)	Nadir 'Redone' Khayat	213
9(tie)	Stefani 'Lady Gaga' Germanotta	63

Sources: PRO Titles Data:http://www.ascap.com/ace/ and http://repertoire.bmi.com/ as of May 28, 2009.
Songwriters: *Billboard* magazine, May 16, 2009, p. 20. Used with permission of e5 Global Media.

4.4 Division of Labor Among Composers, Songwriters, and Lyricists

The division of labor on writing a song can vary depending on the talents of the individual involved. In general, the division of labor among songwriters, composers, and authors can be described as shown in Table 4.3. From an intellectual property perspective, it is the lyrics and melody that are given copyright protection.

Table 4.3 Division of Labor Among Songwriters, Authors and Composers (Performing and Non-performing)

Participant	Activities
Author/Lyricist	Song title and lyrics
Composer A	Solos, riffs and hooks
Composer B	Melody, harmonization, voicing, rhythmic movements, tempo and dynamics
Producer	Directs studio musicians on what to play or co-writes a song

On any given song, a credited writer may just have been the primary word-smith responsible for the song title and lyrics used in the song's verses and choruses. The solos, riffs, hooks, or the signature instrumental part heard at the beginning of a song intended to support the melody and get the listener interested in hearing the rest of the song may be done by another writer. A third writer might be responsible for scoring or composing the melody, harmonization, rhythmic movements, voicing, and dynamics. Yet a fourth credited writer might be the producer directing the studio musicians on what elements of keyboards, strings, horns, guitars, and drums to play. Some writers and composers wear multiple hats such as songwriter/producer, composer/producer, or performer/producer and could be involved in all the above mentioned roles, including being the featured performer.

The issues of the intent to create a joint work, the joint ownership of a work, the independent contributors of a work and who has the right to license a song often become copyright infringement disputes in the music industry. Under US copyright law, a joint author, even one who has only contributed a small amount of work to a song, has the right to license the rights to another party without the permission of the other joint author.[7] The importance of getting signed releases of the song contributors cannot be overstated since it can affect royalty income.

Table 4.4 is another illustration of the difference between the performing and the non-performer songwriter using popular Christmas songs from ASCAP's repertory. For example, Mel Tormé and Robert Wells are the credited writers for the Christmas standard, *Chestnuts Roasting on an Open Fire*, made famous by the singer Nat "King" Cole. Tormé is a known singer in his own right. José Feliciano is both the credited writer and singer for another Christmas classic *Feliz Navidad*.

With income generation and future earnings—which may be independent of previous chart success—being major factors in the music industry, some writers of hit songs can earn more than the recording artist/vocalist over the lifetime of a song

Table 4.4 ASCAP's Top 25 Christmas Titles (Last 5 Years, November 2008)

Rank	Song title	Songwriters(s)	Recording Artist(s)
1	*Winter Wonderland*	F. Bernard & R. B. Smith	Eurythmics
2	*The Christmas Song (Chestnuts Roasting on an Open Fire)*	M. Tormé & R. Wells	Nat "King" Cole
3	*Have Yourself A Merry Little Christmas*	R. Blane & H. Martin	The Pretenders
4	*Sleigh Ride*	L. Anderson & M. Parish	The Ronettes
5	*Santa Claus Is Coming To Town*	F. Coots & H. Gillespie	Frank Sinatra
6	*Let It Snow!*	S. Cahn & J. Styne	Michael BublĆ
7	*White Christmas*	I. Berlin	Bing Crosby
8	*Jingle Bell Rock*	J.C. Beal & J.R. Boothe	Bobby Helms
9	*Rudolph The Red Nosed Reindeer*	J. Marks	Gene Autry
10	*Little Drummer Boy*	K.K. Davis, H. Onorati & H. Simeone	Harry Simeone Chorale
11	*It is the Most Wonderful Time of the Year*	E. Pola & G. Wyle	Andy Williams
12	*Rockin' Around The Christmas Tree*	J. Marks	Brenda Lee
13	*Silver Bells*	J. Livingston & R. Evans	Kenny G
14	*I'll Be Home For Christmas*	W. Kent, K. Gannon & B. Ram	Amy Grant
15	*Feliz Navidad*	J. Feliciano	José Feliciano
16	*Frosty The Snowman*	S. Nelson & W. E. Rollins	The Ronettes
17	*A Holly Jolly Christmas*	J. Marks	Burl Ives
18	*It's Beginning To Look A Lot Like Christmas*	M. Willson	Johnny Mathis
19	*Blue Christmas*	B. Hayes & J.W. Johnson	Elvis Presley
20	*(There's No Place Like) Home For The Holidays*	B. Allen & A. Stillman	Perry Como
21	*I Saw Mommy Kissing Santa Claus*	T. Connor (PRS)	John Mellencamp
22	*Here Comes Santa Claus*	G. Autry & O. Haldeman	Gene Autry
23	*Carol Of The Bells*	P. J. Wilhousky & M. Leontovich	David Foster (instrumental)
24	*Do They Know It's Christmas?*	M. Ure & B. Geldof (PRS)	Band Aid
25	*This Christmas*	D. Hathaway & N. McKinnor	Gloria Estefan

Source: http://www.ascap.com/press/2008/1124_holiday.aspx, November 24, 2008.

as the physical sales of sound recording decline or are no longer available at retail stores. Songwriters, composers, and authors will still earn income from performance royalties collected by ASCAP, BMI, and SESAC when their songs receive airplay on radio, television, the Internet, and other venues. The continued income stream for songwriters, composers, and authors from performance rights long after a sound recording is no longer sold at retail outlets is, in part, what has been fueling the debate behind sound recordings performance rights.

4.5 Song Title Registration

Once a song is written, the sound recording is released, and the musical composition is registered with a performing rights organization such as ASCAP, BMI, or SESAC. The songwriter/composer expects to receive an income stream from the non-dramatic public performance of the song on radio, television or in some other public place such a retail outlet. Other sources of income generated by the song title can include mechanical royalty, audio/sounding recording royalties for certain digital performances from SoundExchange, synchronization royalty income from movies, commercials, and income from touring, merchandising, and other 360 multi-rights deals. Table 4.5 highlights some of the data that is normally collected at registration of new titles with PROs.

Table 4.5 Substantiating a New Title

Performance	Data elements
Commercial recording	Recording artist, date of release & record label
Public performance	Performer, date of performance, venue & location
Audio visual/ Electronic performance	Medium, program name/film name & date of performance
Published sheet music	Title of sheet music & publisher

Although our focus has been on works associated with 'Top 40' type songs (where the bulk of performance royalties are earned) symphonic and orchestral works are also registered as what is known as 'Serious' works. The PROs in their collecting responsibilities also have reciprocal collection agreements with many foreign affiliates and publishers if recordings are to be sold in areas outside the United States and its possessions. In the age of the Internet, independent songwriters can register their own works and may not need a publisher. It is quite common for collaborating songwriters to belong to different PROs in what is known as cross-registration.

In the hypothetical example shown in Table 4.6, the musical composition, a made-up song title called 'Hit Tune,' showing the entitled parties, songwriters,

Table 4.6 Hypothetical Cross Registration Example of Songwriter/Publisher Copyright Shares

Song Title: *Evergreen Hit Tune*

Entitled Parties	Type	Society	% Shares
H. Jones	Writer	ASCAP	50
J. Smith	Writer	ASCAP	40
T. Adele	Writer	BMI	10
Writers' Total			100
Goldcoast Publisher	Publisher	ASCAP	30
A.G. Publishing	Publisher	ASCAP	20
Royal Publishing	Publisher	ASCAP	40
West Coast Publisher	Publisher	BMI	10
Publishers' Total			100

composers, and publishers of the work. Three credited writers, four credited publishers, and with some writers and publishers cross-registered to different performance rights organizations are shown. The shares, based on the agreements among the entitled parties, are the percentage or portion of a work that each party is entitled to collect. Notice that the publishers' and songwriters' shares add up to 200 percent and there is no allocation for a recording artist. Performing rights organizations like ASCAP, BMI, and SESAC are only collecting licensing fees on behalf of songwriters and publishers.

Some PROs will often evenly divide the licensing fees collected (less administrative costs) down the middle with 50 percent of the receipts going to the publishers, and the remaining 50 percent going to the songwriters, composers, and authors. This means that together the total of both the publisher shares and the writer shares must add up to 100 percent. For example, a writer share listed at 50 percent means that entitled party is entitled to receive the full share of the writer's allocated royalties.

However, the accounting rules in the music industry often differ and the songwriters' and publishers' share are sometimes based on a scale of each having 100 percent for a total of 200 percent. Not every PRO follows this '200' percent practice and we are just illustrating the concept. The publishers' share (50 percent when divided evenly between publishers and songwriters) of performance royalty income collected must therefore add up to 100 percent when divided by the entitled publisher copyright holders for each PRO as shown in Table 4.6. Similarly, the same methodology applies to the entitled songwriter copyright holders whose share will add up to 100 percent once evenly divided. For example, 'BMI considers payments to songwriters or composers and to publishers as a single unit equal to 200%. Where there is the usual division of performance royalties between songwriters or composers and publishers, the total writers' shares will be 100% (half of the available 200%), and the total publishers' shares will be the remaining 100%.'[8]

It is worth keeping in mind that 'when a songwriter assigns his or her copyright to a publisher, the publishers usually pays nothing for that right. For in the music publishing business, as in the recording business, the companies do not actually purchase the asset they acquire. In return for advancing the cost of a recording, the artist ends up paying back the cost of recording from his or own share in royalties. But once the advances are recouped out of the writer's share, the portion of the copyrights that the publisher 'acquired' normally belongs to the publisher for the entire duration of the copyright. In other words, the publisher owns a valuable asset that for which it paid only advances for assuming the risk of releasing a recording.'[9]

SoundExchange has a different distribution formula and copyright holders for certain digital performances of sound recordings (not the underlying musical composition) as shown in Table 4.7 where the publishers or record labels still receive 50 percent of royalty payments for public performances (less administration fees), and the remaining 50 percent allocated among the featured (recording) artists (45 percent), non-featured musicians (2.5 percent), and non-featured vocalists (2.5 percent) based on entitled shares. Songwriters and composers may also have other sources

Table 4.7 PRO Division of Royalties Among Copyright Holders (by Percentage and Less Administration Costs)

Copyright Holders	ASCAP	BMI	SESAC	SoundExchange
Songwriters/Composers	50%	50%	50%	–
Publishers	50%	50%	50%	–
Record Labels	–	–	–	50%
Featured Recording Artists	–	–	–	45%
Non-Featured Musicians	–	–	–	2.5%
Non-Featured Vocalists	–	–	–	2.5%
Total	100%	100%	100%	100%

Sources: http://www.ascap.com, www.bmi.com, www.sesac.com and www.soundexchange.com.

Table 4.8 Selected Singer/Songwriters Sources of Income

Source	Use	Agency
Non-dramatic performances	Live or recorded music used on radio, TV, cable, Internet, cellphone, retail outlets, etc.	ASCAP, BMI & SESAC
Mechanical	CDs, ring tones, etc.	Harry Fox
Certain digital performances	Sound recordings on broadcast digital cable, satellite radio, and TV	SoundExchange
Print	Lyrics, sheet music, and folios	Negotiated
Synchronization	Theatrical and TV movies, commercials	Negotiated
Dramatic performances	Music for the Broadway stage	Negotiated
Touring	Live concerts at various venues	Negotiated
Merchandising	Sale of apparel, posters, and other retail goods.	Negotiated
Artist's image	Image/likeness in advertising	Negotiated

of income beside performing rights in musical compositions that are not the focus of this monograph. Income from mechanical, synchronization, and print are shown in Table 4.8.

4.6 Music Genre

Music Connection magazine in its December 2008 issue reported that the record labels were interested in pursuing only rock, pop, urban, dance, singer/songwriter and country musicians, despite the many other music formats and sub segments in the music industry. This is not so surprising when survey data from the RIAA in Table 4.9 shows that rock, rap/hip-hop, r&b/urban, country, and pop have been the most popular music formats preferred by music consumers for the years 2004–2008.[10] The popularity of the various music genres becomes the segmentation choices of radio station programming managers whose analysis of marketing trends, target audiences, advertisers demand, and other demographic factors play a

Table 4.9 RIAA Consumer Music Preferences, 2004–2008 (%)

Genre	2004	2005	2006	2007	2008
Rock	23.9	31.5	34	32.4	31.8
Rap/Hip-hop[1]	12.1	13.3	11.4	10.8	10.7
R&B/Urban[2]	11.3	10.2	11	11.8	10.2
Country	13	12.5	13	11.5	11.9
Pop	10	8.1	7.1	10.7	9.1
Religious[3]	6	5.3	5.5	3.9	6.5
Classical	2	2.4	1.9	2.3	1.9
Jazz	2.7	1.8	2	2.6	1.1
Soundtracks	1.1	0.9	0.8	0.8	0.8
Oldies	1.4	1.1	1.1	0.4	0.7
New	0.5	1	0.4	0.3	0.3
ChildrenŠs	2.8	2.3	2.9	2.9	3
Other[4]	8.9	8.5	7.3	7.1	9.1

[1] 'Rap': Includes Rap and Hip-Hop.

[2] 'R&B': Includes R&B, Blues, Dance, Disco, Funk, Fusion, Motown, Reggae, Soul.

[3] 'Religious': Includes Christian, Gospel, Inspirational, Religious, and Spiritual.

[4] 'Other': Includes Big Band, Broadway Shows, Comedy, Contemporary, Electronic, EMO, Ethnic, Exercise, Folk, Gothic, Grunge, Holiday Music House Music, Humor, Instrumental, Language, Latin, Love Songs, Mix, Mellow, Modern, Ska, Spoken word, Standards, Swing, Top-40 and Trip-Hop.

Source: www.riaa.com.

role in playlist composition, the source of performance income for songwriters and publishers.

Commercial radio stations often rely on a strong selection of hit songs, including the many sub-segments of Top-40 music, in order to attract the listening audience, particularly those aged 18–34 years old, that advertisers would find appealing. A songwriter may also have to think about all the ways a song can be used other than in today's most popular genres, including international listeners and synchronization.

Notes

1. See *Music Connection* magazine, December 2008, A&R Survey 2008, pp. 38–39.
2. *Billboard* magazine, October 3, 2009, pp. 25–26.
3. *Billboard* magazine, October 3, 2009, p. 26.
4. Donahue (2009).
5. Hatfield (2008, p. 6).
6. Hatfield (2008, p. 6).
7. See www.copyright.gov/title17/circ92.pdf, Section 201(a).
8. See http://www.bmi.com/creators/royalty/533114.
9. Thall (2006, p. 219).
10. See Recording Industry Association of America Website: www.riaa.com.

References

Donahue, A. (2009). 'Big Idea: Words Up'. *Billboard* magazine. May 16, p. 26.
Hatfield, G., editor (2008). *Songwriter's Market 2009*. Writer's Digest Books.
Lathrop, T. (2003). *This Business of Music Marketing and Promotion*. Billboard Books.
Thall, P. (2006). *What They Will Never Tell You About the Music Business: The Myths, the Secrets, and the Lies (& a Few Truths)*. Billboard Books.

Part II
Econometric Analysis

Chapter 5
Theory Review

Abstract In modeling data in the performing arts, the presence of highly paid 'superstars'—earning the lion's share of performance royalty for musical compositions or receipts from live concerts—causes the earnings distribution to be highly skewed. Incorrect probability judgments can be made in the analysis of economic data when normality is assumed, but asymmetry is present. The purpose of this chapter is to review the skew-normal and skew-t statistical distributions theory and present a model that can be used to estimate regression models when the distribution is highly skewed. To correct for asymmetrical forms in econometric data modeling, flexible forms of both the univariate and multivariate skew-normal and skew-t distributions have been developed. Walls (2005) suggests two reasons why the log-skew-t is appealing in economic modeling. First, it is easier—computationally—to implement the skew-t than some other distributions (like the stable Paretian model or the Lévy stable regression model) using standard maximum likelihood statistical techniques that are within reach of applied researchers. Second, the skew-t extends the normal distribution by permitting tails that are heavy and asymmetric. The log-normal is just a special case of the log-skew-normal when $\alpha = 0$.

5.1 Introduction

Normality is probably the most common assumption that econometricians make when conducting empirical studies using linear regression models. The error structure of unobserved variability is assumed to be normally distributed. The practice has been to use the student-t distribution with the appropriate degrees of freedom and rely on the central limit theorem for non-normal distributions. This practice can cause spurious results when the data sampled do not fit a normal distribution, but the results are used as such. When modeling performance arts data it is important that a normality test be conducted. Normality tests are used to test the following hypothesis:

$$\begin{cases} H_0: & \text{The data sampled are from a normal distribution} \\ H_1: & \text{The data are not sampled from a normal distribution} \end{cases} \tag{5.1}$$

I.L. Pitt, *Economic Analysis of Music Copyright*,
DOI 10.1007/978-1-4419-6318-5_5, © Springer Science+Business Media, LLC 2010

The Jarque–Bera or the Shapiro–Wilk normality tests are two powerful tests that can be used to test data for the departure from normality, depending on sample size.[1] The power of the Jarque–Bera test is poor for distributions with short tails and the test may also be biased. In such a case the Shapiro–Wilk test is recommended.[2]

Flexible forms of both the univariate and multivariate skew distributions whose empirical outcome might look *normal-like*, but with a lack of symmetry (such as the skew-normal and skew-*t* distribution and their logarithmic versions), have recently been developed.[3] Arellano-Valle and Azzalini (2006) introduced a further type of skew-normal distribution in a unified *formulation* that encompassed previous variants. Azzalini and Genton (2008) explore the skew-*t* distribution in more detail, and several reasons are given for the adoption of the skew-*t* distribution as a sensible general-purpose compromise between robustness and simplicity, both in treatment and interpretation of the outcome.

Walls (2005), among others, applied the skew-normal and the skew-*t* in his study of box-office revenue in the film industry. As will be discussed in the following sections, these skew distributions augment the normal and student-*t* distributions by adding a shape or skewness parameter (α) in the skew-normal case, and both a skewness parameter (α) and (ν) a degrees of freedom parameter are added to the skew-*t*. The skew family of distributions includes the standard $N(0, 1)$ as a special case.[4]

5.2 Skew Distributions and Their Probability Density Functions

5.2.1 The Skew-Normal Distribution

Azzalini (2008) provides a simplified exposition of the univariate skew-normal, and we adapt his limited treatment in the following subsections. Using Azzalini's definition, a continuous random univariate variable X is said to have a skew-normal *(SN)* distribution if it has the following density function:

$$f(x) = 2\phi(x)\Phi(\alpha x) \qquad (5.2)$$

where α is a fixed arbitrary number and,

$$\phi(x) = exp(-x^2/2)/\sqrt{2\pi}, \qquad \Phi(\alpha x) = \int_{-\infty}^{\alpha x} \phi(t)\, dt. \qquad (5.3)$$

Equation (5.3) denotes the standard normal (Gaussian) density function and its distribution (the latter evaluated at point αx). In other words, the random variable X is

$$X \sim SN(0, 1, \alpha) \qquad (5.4)$$

The component α is called the *shape* or *skewness parameter* because it regulates the shape of the density function, allowing for a continuous variation from normality to non-normality.[5] Dalla-Valle (2007) suggests that it is sometimes better to specify a parameter, δ, that varies in the range $(-1, 1)$, which is related to α in the following way:

$$\delta = \frac{\alpha}{\sqrt{1 + \alpha^2}} \quad \alpha = \frac{\delta}{\sqrt{1 - \delta^2}} \tag{5.5}$$

The density function $f(x)$ has the following formal properties:

1. When $\alpha = 0$, the skew-normal simplifies to the standard normal distribution.
2. As $|\alpha|$ increases the skewness of the distribution increases.
3. When $\alpha \to \infty$, the density converges to the so-called half-normal (or folded normal) density function.
4. If the sign of α changes, the density is reflected on the opposite side of the vertical axis.

Note that the square of a random variable X is distributed as a χ_1^2 random variable, irrespective of the value of α.

$$X^2 \sim \chi_1^2. \tag{5.6}$$

A result of this fact is that even moments of the skew-normal random variable are equal to the even moments of the normal random variable.[6] For ease of computation, location and scale parameters are added to the above random variable X and to its density function in Equation (5.2). The above random variable X and its density function Equation (5.2) can now be used to construct the linear transformation of random variables Y and X.

$$Y = \xi + \omega X \tag{5.7}$$

which is then said to have a location-scale skew-normal distribution with parameters (ξ, ω, α), and

$$Y \sim SN(\xi, \omega^2, \alpha) \tag{5.8}$$

(ξ, ω^2, α) are the location (which can be linear combinations of other variables), the scale, and the skewness parameters, respectively.

When $\alpha = 0$, we obtain, the $SN(\xi, \omega^2)$.

Selected characteristics of the random variable Y would include the mean value of the random variable Y:

$$E\{Y\} = \xi + \omega\sqrt{\frac{2}{\pi}}\,\delta \tag{5.9}$$

the variance is given by

$$var\{Y\} = \omega^2 \left(\frac{1 - 2\delta^2}{\pi} \right) \tag{5.10}$$

the skewness is specified as

$$\gamma_1 = \frac{4 - \pi}{2} \quad \frac{E\{X\}^3}{var\{X\}^{\frac{3}{2}}} \tag{5.11}$$

where

$$\delta = \alpha/\sqrt{1 + \alpha^2}, \quad E\{X\} = \sqrt{2/\pi}\delta \quad var\{X\} = 1 - 2\delta^2/\pi.$$

5.2.2 The Skew-t Distribution

The skew-t distribution has the following probability density function:[7]

$$f(x, \nu, \alpha) = 2TCDF\left(\alpha x \sqrt{\frac{1 + \nu}{x^2 + \nu}}, \nu + 1\right) TPDF\ (x, \nu) \quad -\infty < x, \alpha < \infty. \tag{5.12}$$

where ν, α, TCDF, and TPDF denote the degrees of freedom parameter, the skewness parameter, the cumulative distribution function of the t distribution, and the probability density function of the t-distribution, respectively.

For $\alpha = 0$, the skew-t reduces to a t-distribution. As α goes to infinity, the skew-t tends to the folded-t-distribution. The standard skew-t distribution can be generalized in a linear transformation with location (estimated regression coefficients or just the constant term), scale, skew, and degrees of freedom parameters as

$$Y \sim St(0, \omega^2, \alpha, \nu) \tag{5.13}$$

5.2.3 The Log-Skew-Normal Distribution

The log-skew-normal distribution can be defined in terms of the skew-normal distribution,[8] as follows:

$$f(x; \alpha, sd) = \frac{1}{x * sd}\phi(log(x)/sd; \alpha) \quad 0 < x, sd, < \infty; \quad -\infty < \alpha < \infty \tag{5.14}$$

with α denoting the skewness parameter, sd denoting the standard deviation of the corresponding normal distribution, and $\phi(x; \alpha)$ denoting the probability density of the skew-normal distribution. This is analogous to how the log-normal distribution is defined in terms of the normal distribution.

If $\alpha = 0$, the log-skew-normal distribution reduces to the log-normal distribution. The standard log-skew-normal distribution can be generalized with location and scale parameters in the usual way.

5.2.4 The Log-Skew-t Distribution

The log-skew-t distribution has the following probability density function:

$$f(x; v, \alpha, sd) = \frac{1}{x * sd}\text{STPDF}(log(x)/sd; v, \alpha, sd) \tag{5.15}$$

where $\alpha, sd > 0$; and v is a positive integer.

With STPDF denoting the skew-t distribution, and α, v, and sd denoting the shape parameters. For $\alpha = 0$, the log-skew-t reduces to a log-t distribution. The standard log-skew-t distribution can be generalized with location and scale parameters in the usual way as previously discussed.[9]

5.2.5 The Multivariate Skew-Normal Distribution

The preceding sections discussed the univariate attributes of the skew-normal distribution. A multivariate version of the skew-normal also exists,[10] a random variable X and its density function Equation (5.2) can now be used to achieve multivariate normality.

$$Y = \xi + \omega X \tag{5.16}$$

where $\xi = (\xi_1, ..., \xi_k)$ and $\omega = diag(\omega_1, ..., \omega_k)$ are location and scale parameters in the multivariate skew-normal covariance matrix respectively; the components of ω are assumed to be positive. The multivariate variables Y and X are such that all of its marginal components have a skew-normal

$$Y_k \sim SN_k\left(\xi_k, \omega_k^2, \alpha_k, \right) \tag{5.17}$$

or a skew-t distribution

$$Y_k \sim St_k\left(\xi_k, \omega_k^2, \alpha_k, v_k\right). \tag{5.18}$$

Their shapes are regulated by a vector parameter α; when $\alpha = 0$, we get the familiar multivariate normal distribution; linear transformations of any matrix are still multivariate skew-normal and the χ^2 distribution of certain quadratic forms is preserved.[11] Among the broad class of skew elliptical family, the multivariate skew-t

distribution offers ample flexibility for adapting itself to a wide range of practical situations, and still maintains mathematical tractability and a set of appealing formal properties.[12]

5.3 Model Specifications

Walls (2005) suggests that the difficulty of modeling film returns is similar to the problems of modeling asset returns in general: events that are different from the sample mean occur with a frequency that are improbably too large to have been drawn from a normal distribution. 'It is feasible to estimate a regression model with skew-normal or skew-t random disturbances using standard maximum likelihood techniques. The skew-t is appealing in that it extends the normal distribution by permitting tails that are heavy and asymmetric. The skew-normal and skew-t can be fitted using their log-transformed versions. These are referred to as the log-skew-normal and log-skew-t distributions.'[13] Individual skew-normal or skew-t copyright models can be estimated with different dependent and independent variables as shown in one example, Equation (5.19) and Table 5.1.

For example, the dependent variables consisting of various forms of license fees, credits, or royalty payments can then be fitted on a conditional vector of selected independent variables such as member type, age, tenure, license type, medium, title, and performance type. Diagnostic and visual inspection of the standard deviations can be used as one method to segment observations. In addition, if the data is available, titles can be broken down by music genre and gender of songwriter.

Table 5.1 Selected Variables in Estimating Copyright Regression Models

Dependent variables	Explanation
Royalty payments	Payments to song writers and publishers
License fee collected	License fee collected by PROs from music users
Performance credits	Credits earned for each song use
Independent variables	Explanation
Member type	Songwriter, composer or publisher
License type	Blanket or per program
Medium	Broadcast TV, local TV, radio, cable, Internet, etc.
Performance type	Features, themes, background, jingles and promos
Tenure	Membership in years for writers
Age	Age of member
Titles in catalog	Number of copyrighted songs in PRO catalog
Gender	Gender of songwriter
Segmentation	Segmentation based on selected criteria
Region	Midwest, west, south and northeast
Market size	Population rankings 1–126
Frequency band	AM vs FM
Genre	Type of music, pop, rock, jazz, classical, etc.

A basic equation for testing various models can be written as Equation 5.19:

$$
\begin{aligned}
Log(Y) = {} & \beta_0 + \beta_1(Member\ Type) + \beta_2(License\ Type) \\
& + \beta_3(Broadcast\ TV) + \beta_4(Local\ TV) + \beta_5(Radio) \\
& + \beta_6(Cable) + \beta_7(Internet) + \beta_8(Other) \\
& + \beta_9(Features) + \beta_{10}(Themes) + \beta_{11}(Back/ForeGround) \\
& + \beta_{12}(Jingles) + \beta_{13}(Promos) + \beta_{14}(Tenure\ 1\text{-}4) \\
& + \beta_{15}(Tenure\ 4\text{-}6) + \beta_{16}(Tenure\ 6\text{-}8) + +\beta_{17}(Tenure\ 8\text{-}10) \\
& + \beta_{18}(Segment1) + \beta_{19}(Segment2) + \beta_{20}(Age1) \\
& + \beta_{21}(Age2) + \beta_{22}(Age3) + \beta_{23}(Genre1) \\
& + \beta_{24}(Genre2) + \beta_{25}(Genre3) + \varepsilon_i
\end{aligned}
$$

$$(5.19)$$

In each model, ε_i is a random disturbance term that follows a log-normal, log-Skew-normal, or log-skew-t distribution depending on the model being estimated (Table 5.2).

Table 5.2 Estimated Models Error Structure

Model	Estimator	Error structure
Log-normal	OLS	$SN(0, 1)$
Log-skew-normal	Maximum Likelihood	$SN(\xi, \omega^2, \alpha)$
Log-skew-t	Maximum Likelihood	$t(\xi, \omega^2, \alpha, \nu)$

5.4 Interpretation of Dummy Variables in Semi-logarithmic Equations

The impact of dummy variables on any of the dependent variables when the specified model is semi logarithmic can be difficult to quantify. The impact of the dummy variables on the dependent variable $g*$ is computed as:

$$
g^* = \exp\left(\hat{\beta} - \frac{\hat{\sigma}^2 \hat{\beta}}{2}\right) - 1 \qquad (5.20)
$$

where $\hat{\beta}$ is the estimated coefficient on the dummy variable and $\hat{\sigma}^2$ is the estimated variance of $\hat{\beta}$. A discussion on the interpretation of dummy variables when the dependent variable is log-transformed is given in Halvorsen and Palmquist (1980) and Kennedy (1981). From their discussion we can develop estimates of the percentage impact of the dummy variables on the dependent variable. These estimates may not be appropriate for some explanatory variables since it may lack meaningful interpretation.

Notes

1. See Jarque and Bera (1980, 1987), Shapiro and Wilk (1965).
2. Thadewald and Büning (2007).
3. See these articles for a more extensive review Azzalini (1985, 1986), Azzalini and Capitanio (1999, 2003), Azzalini et al. (2003), Azzalini (2005), Dalla-Valle (2007), Azzalini and Genton (2008); Dalla-Valle (2007).
4. See additional applications in this volume, Genton (2004).
5. To view and plot the shape of the skew-normal density function, graphical demonstration programs can be found at NIST (2008).
6. Dalla-Valle (2007).
7. See Azzalini and Capitanio (1999, 2003).
8. Azzalini et al. (2003).
9. Azzalini et al. (2003), NIST (2008), Walls (2005).
10. See Azzalini and Capitanio (2003), Azzalini et al. (2003).
11. See Azzalini's website: http://azzalini.stat.unipd.it/SN/Intro/intro.html.
12. Azzalini and Capitanio (2003).
13. Walls (2005).

References

Arellano-Valle, R. and Azzalini, A. (2006). On the unification of families of skew-normal distributions. *Scandinavian Journal of Statistics*, 33:561–574.

Azzalini, A. (1985). A class of distribution which includes the normal ones. *Scandinavian Journal of Statistics*, 12:171–178.

Azzalini, A. (1986). Further results on a class of distribution which includes the normal ones. *Statistica*, 46:199–208.

Azzalini, A. (2005). The skew-normal distribution and related multivariate families. *Scandinavian Journal of Statistics*, 32:159–188.

Azzalini, A. (2008).   A very brief introduction to the skew-normal distribution. http://azzalini.stat.unipd.it/SN/intro.html.

Azzalini, A. and Capitanio, A. (1999). Statistical applications of the multivariate skew-normal distribution. *Journal of the Royal Statistical Society*, B61:579–602.

Azzalini, A. and Capitanio, A. (2003).   Distributions generated by perturbation of symmetry with emphasis on a multivariate skew-t distribution. *Journal of the Royal Statistical Society*, B65:367–389.

Azzalini, A., DalCappello, T., and Kotz, S. (2003). Log-skew-normal and log-skew-t distributions as models for family income data. *Journal of Income Distribution*, 11(3–4):12–20.

Azzalini, A. and Genton, M. (2008). Robust likelihood methods based on the skew-t and related distributions. *International Statistical Review*, 76:106–129.

Dalla-Valle, A. (2007). A test for the hypothesis of skew-normality in a population. *Journal of Statistical Computation and Simulation*, 77(1):63–77.

Genton, M., editor (2004). *Skew-Elliptical Distributions and Their Applications: A Journey Beyond Normality*. Chapman & Hall/CRC.

Halvorsen, R. and Palmquist, R. (1980). The interpretation of dummy variables in semi-logarithmic equations. *The American Economic Review*, 70(4):474–475.

Jarque, C. and Bera, A. (1980). Efficient tests for normality, homoscedasticity and serial independence of regression residuals. *Econometric Letters*, 6:255–259.

Jarque, C. and Bera, A. (1987). A test for normality of observations and regression residuals. *International Statistical Review*, 55:163–172.

Kennedy, P. (1981). Estimation with correctly interpreted dummy variables in semilogarithmic equations. *The American Economic Review*, 71(4):801.

NIST (2008). Dataplot Reference Manual, Chapter 8. http://www.itl.nist.gov/.

Shapiro, S. and Wilk, M. (1965). An analysis of variance test for normality. *Biometrika*, 52: 591–611.

Thadewald, T. and Büning, H. (2007). Jarque–Bera test and its competitors for testing normality – a power comparision. *Journal of Applied Statistics*, 34(1):87–105.

Walls, W. (2005). Modeling heavy tails and skewness in film returns. *Applied Financial Economics*, 15:1181–1188.

Chapter 6
Estimation of Skewness, Heavy Tails, and Music Success in a Performance Rights Organization

Abstract This chapter examines the economic accomplishments of individual members in a performing rights organization (PRO), sometimes referred to as a performing rights society. Skewness and heavy tail of returns in the form of member royalty payments are estimated using the skew-normal and skew-t distributions in a parametric approach. We found strong evidence of the so-called 'superstar effect' in which the average royalty payment made by a PRO is still dominated by extreme outcomes in which a few members earned a substantial share of royalty payments from blockbuster hits that have endured over time. There is little evidence of smaller niche members dominating or replacing the 'superstars'. Economists and others will benefit from this empirical study which emphasizes a new understanding of the music industry from a PRO, member royalty payment and *performance copyright* perspective.

6.1 Introduction

Connolly and Krueger (2005) in a lengthy survey found that in terms of concert revenue, 'superstars' received the lion's share of income.*

Walls (2005) found that the motion-picture market has a winner-take-all property where a small proportion of successful films earn the majority of box-office revenue. Furthermore, the average return across films is dominated by extreme events, namely those few films that populate the longer upper tail of distribution returns. Giles (2007) found that some popular tunes are dramatically more successful than others. Moreover, even among those recordings that reach the top of the charts, there is a great variation in their success, measured in terms of sales, or in terms of the length that they stay at 'number one.' Length of stay at the top of Billboard Charts has been one measure of success in the music industry. In Anderson (2008), *The Long Tail* is used to describe music consumption patterns in certain niche markets that are highly skewed. In Anderson's theory, obscure works and dormant musical works in publishers' catalogs were supposed to reinvigorate the music industry

---

*This chapter is adapted from Pitt (2010a).

struggling with declining CD sales and the onslaught of digital media.[1] All of these studies suggest that income in the music industry can be highly skewed, asymmetrical and depart from assumptions surrounding the normal distribution.

Licensed music is used in a variety of ways, or *performance types*, such as features, theme music, jingles, underscores, ring tones, or network station promos as shown in Table 6.1. The purchaser (music user) of the blanket license is allowed the non-exclusive and unlimited use of the PROs library of songs, once the fee for its use has been negotiated, for *non-dramatic public performances*. We can see in Table 6.2 that in 2007, when interest and other income and membership fees are excluded, ASCAP collected close to $594 million from domestic users and $266 million from foreign societies for a total of $860 million, an almost 10 percent increase from the year 2006. One indicator here is that a lot of American music is used abroad.

There are, however, other rights (and additional sources of income) to musical compositions that are licensed separately from ASCAP, BMI, and SESAC. SoundExchange handles the rights for the audio/sound recording of a song. The right to distribute songs on CDs, audio tapes, records, and downloads requires what is called a *mechanical license*. Mechanical rights are statutory and handled through the Harry Fox Agency, or by individual publishing companies. The right to use

Table 6.1 Selected Medium and Performance Type

Medium or music user	Performance type
Local radio	Features of variable lengths
Local TV	Opening/closing theme music
Network TV	Background or underscore music
Basic & premium cable TV	Jingles
Internet	Network promos
Background music	Ring-back tones
Others, concerts etc.	

Table 6.2 Consolidated Statements of Selected ASCAP's Receipts and Expenses

Domestic receipts	YE 2007 ($)	YE 2006 ($)	Change ($)	% Change
License Fees				
Television	109, 669	108, 122	1, 547	1.43
Cable	133, 859	113, 652	20, 207	17.78
Radio	238, 502	223, 854	14, 648	6.54
General	97, 380	90, 657	6, 723	7.42
New Media	8, 606	13, 643	−5, 037	−36.92
Symphonic & Concert	5, 889	5, 222	667	12.77
Interest & Other Income	3, 918	3, 766	152	4.04
Membership & Fees	395	–		
Total Domestic Receipts	598, 218	558, 916	39, 302	7.03
Royalties From Foreign Societies	265, 625	226, 559	39, 066	17.24
Total Receipts	863, 843	785, 475	78, 368	9.98
Expenses	103, 348	96, 078	7, 270	7.57
Excess Receipts over Expenses	760, 495	689, 397	71, 098	10.31

Source: http://www.ascap.com/about/annualReport/annual_2007.pdf.

songs in television programs, commercials, home video, motion pictures, and other audio visual projects is often referred to as a *synchronization license*, as music is synchronized with moving images. The synchronization license is normally negotiated between the producers of the audio visual programs and the music publisher.[2] Other derived sources of income for the composer, publishers, and performing songwriter could include corporate sponsorships, share of ticket sales from live concerts, online fan clubs, and the sale of T-shirts and other merchandise at websites or other places.

6.2 Royalty Payments for Songwriters, Composers and, Publishers

Chapter 2 (Sect. 2.12) provided an overview on the computation of royalty income based on performances. The royalty payments made to writers and publishers are typically referred to as 'distributions.' This is not to be confused with statistical distributions such as the normal or Chi-Square. PROs pay their songwriters, composers, and publishers for US performances approximately 6 months after the end of each-month performance period. In ASCAP's weighting rules, as described in its *Distribution Resource Documents*, performance credits are used as units of measure based on the results from its survey of music performances. For example, a feature performance may be awarded one use credit. Fractional use credits may be awarded for compositions performed as a theme, jingle or as a background, cue or bridge music.[3]

Table 6.3 shows that after administrative expenses were deducted, ASCAP distributed approximately $742 million in royalty payments close to 9 percent over the previous year to its various songwriters, composers, and music publisher members.

Table 6.3 ASCAP's Distribution of Royalty Payments ($000)

Member distribution	YE 2007	YE 2006	Change	% Change
Domestic & Foreign	$691, 390	$631, 765	$59, 625	9.44
Foreign Societies	$50, 209	$48, 502	$1, 707	3.52
Total Distributions	$741, 599	$680, 267	$61, 332	9.02

Source: http://www.ascap.com/about/annualReport/annual_2007.pdf.

6.3 Model Specification and Data Description

Walls (2005) suggests that the difficulty of modeling film returns is similar to the problems of modeling asset returns in general: events that are different from the sample mean occur with a frequency that are improbably too large to have been drawn from a normal distribution. Using maximum likelihood techniques, regression models with skew-normal or skew-*t* random disturbances can be estimated. Walls (2005), among others, applied the skew-normal and the skew-*t* in his study of box-office revenue in the film industry. A continuous random univariate variable X is said to have a skew-normal *(SN)* distribution[4] if it has the following density function:

$$f(x) = 2\phi(x)\Phi(\alpha x) \qquad (6.1)$$

In other words, the random variable X is

$$X \sim SN(0, 1, \alpha). \qquad (6.2)$$

Skew distributions augment the normal and student-t distributions by adding a shape or skewness parameter (α) in the skew-normal case. The component α in regulating the shape of the density function allows for a continuous variation from normality to non-normality. When $\alpha = 0$, the skew-normal simplifies to the standard normal distribution. For ease of computation, location (estimated regression coefficients or just the constant term) and scale (ω^2) parameters are also added to the above random variable X and its density function in Equation (8.1). The standard skew-t distribution can be generalized with location, scale, and a degree of freedom parameter (ν). The skew-t is appealing in that it extends the normal distribution by permitting tails that are heavy and asymmetric. The skew-normal and skew-t can be fitted using their log-transformed versions. 'These are referred to as the log-skew-normal and log-skew-t distributions.'[5] Individual composers and publishers are not identified in this analysis, given the proprietary nature of the study. Under these circumstances certain results that are typically reported in academic studies will be excluded.

The data were drawn from a random sample of ASCAP's domestic members that included 374 publishers and 626 writers in the first quarter of 2007 whose total credits accumulated were greater than zero (Table 6.4). The sample resulted in 989 observations being selected after it was scrubbed for missing data elements such as dates.

Table 6.4 ASCAP's Member Composition (1Q 2007)

Member type	Frequency	Percent
Writers/composers	626	62.6
Publishers	374	37.4
Total	1, 000	

6.4 Estimation Results

In each model, the dependent variable—Dollar Value (royalty payments) to ASCAP members—is fitted on a conditional vector of music performance attributes. The distribution of royalty payments is quantified conditional on member type (writer or publisher), license type (blanket or per-program), each type of medium (broadcast

TV, local TV, radio, etc.), performance type (features, themes, etc.), tenure (length of membership in years), and the sample broken down by tail segment variables derived from a normal density function superimposed on a frequency histogram of the dependent variable. A diagnostic and visual inspection of the standard deviations of Dollar Value (dependent variable) suggested one way of segmenting the observations.

$$
\begin{aligned}
Log(DollarValue) = & \beta_0 + \beta_1(Member\ Type) + \beta_2(License\ Type) \\
& + \beta_3(Broadcast\ TV) + \beta_4(Local\ TV) + \beta_5(Radio) \\
& + \beta_6(Cable) + \beta_7(Internet) + \beta_8(Other) \\
& + \beta_9(Features) + \beta_{10}(Themes) + \beta_{11}(Back/ForeGround) \\
& + \beta_{12}(Jingles) + \beta_{13}(Promos) + \beta_{14}(\text{Tenure } 1\text{--}4) \\
& + \beta_{15}(\text{Tenure } 4\text{--}6) + \beta_{16}(\text{Tenure } 6\text{--}8) + \beta_{17}(\text{Tenure } 8\text{--}10) \\
& + \beta_{18}(Lower\ Tail\ Segment1) + \beta_{19}(\text{Center Segment 2}) + \varepsilon_i
\end{aligned}
$$
$$(6.3)$$

- Dollar Value = Credits (the number of performance credits generated by medium and performance type) times a Credit Value (a quarterly fixed amount set by ASCAP),
- Member Type = 1, if member = Writer/Composer; Otherwise 0 if Publisher,
- License Type = 1 if License = Blanket; Otherwise 0 if Per Program,
- Medium indicator variables are Radio=1 if member received radio payments; Otherwise 0, and so on for Local Television, Broadcast TV, Cable, Internet, and Other payments, which include general licensing of bars, restaurants, etc.
- Performance Type indicator variables are Features =1 if member received features payments; Otherwise 0, and so on for Themes, Background/Foreground Music, Jingles, and Network Promos payments,
- Tenure is indicator variables for length of membership. Tenure 1–4 = 1 if members have been with ASCAP between 1 and 4 years and so on for Tenure 4–6, Tenure 6–8, Tenure 8–10 and Tenure Greater than 10 years is the omitted and relative category;
- Lower Tail (Segment 1) = 1 if the member is in the lower tail, Otherwise 0;
- Center (Segment 2) = 1 if the member is in the center, Otherwise 0;
- Upper Tail (Segment 3) = 1 if the member is in the right tail, Otherwise 0 and the omitted and relative category;
- ε_i = random disturbance term that follows a log-normal, log-skew-normal or log-skew-t distribution depending on the model being estimated.

Table 6.5 summarizes the logarithmic linear models used to test our assumptions.

Normality is probably the most common assumption that econometricians make when conducting empirical studies using linear regression models. The practice has been to use the student-t distribution with the appropriate degrees of freedom and rely on the central limit theorem for non-normal distributions. Incorrect probability judgments can be made in the analysis of economic data when normality is

Table 6.5 Estimated Models

Model	Estimator	Error structure	Decision
Log-normal (I)	OLS	$SN(0, 1)$	Reject
Log-skew-normal (II)	Maximum Likelihood	$SN(\xi, \omega^2, \alpha)$	Reject
Log-skew-t (III)	Maximum Likelihood	$t(\xi, \omega^2, \alpha, \nu)$	Accept

assumed, but asymmetry is present. In log-normal model I, we conducted Jarque–Bera and Shapiro–Wilk normality tests[6] on the residuals. Both tests performed well with each having a $p - value = [0.000]$. The null hypothesis was rejected at any reasonable significance level and indicated a departure from normality in our model specification.

The question now becomes how we estimate a general linear model in which the error term is not normally distributed, and performance royalty income distribution is not symmetrical due to the probability mass in the lower and upper tails. A histogram of the log-transformed dependent variable (Dollar Value) shown in Fig. 6.1 captured the asymmetry of royalty payments in the extreme in both the lower and upper tails with a relatively few members earning the most royalty payments. The graph suggests that when normalized by taking its log, the distribution departs from normality in the tail ends. This is not surprising since 'superstars' (with more titles) earn more royalty payments than newer members, and some members with popular hits at the beginning of their careers also earn more.

The log-normal Model I regression results are shown in Table 6.6 for comparative purposes. We proceed by estimating two additional models using Equation (6.3), the

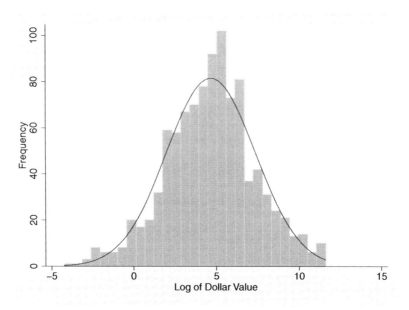

Fig. 6.1 Histogram of dependent variable

Table 6.6 Log-Normal Model I Estimates

Variable	Coefficient	Std. Error	t-stat
Constant	6.9658	0.3605	19.3233
Member Type			
Publisher/Writer/Composer	0.0262	0.0868	0.3014
License Type			
Blanket/Per Program	0.0841	0.1377	0.6105
Medium			
Broadcast TV	0.4905	0.1135	4.3234
Local TV	0.4324	0.1116	3.8756
Radio	0.5548	0.1041	5.3268
Cable	0.4155	0.1054	3.9428
Internet	0.4339	0.1524	2.8472
Other	0.4206	0.1075	3.9139
Performance Type			
Features	0.1573	0.1408	1.1172
Themes	1.1976	0.1546	7.7479
Back/Fore Ground	0.2449	0.1139	2.1506
Jingles	0.6018	0.2853	2.1096
Promo	0.9593	0.1813	5.2925
Tenure (Years)			
Between 1 and 4	0.1599	0.1467	1.0899
Between 4 and 6	0.2331	0.1337	1.7435
Between 6 and 8	0.1701	0.1409	1.2073
Between 8 and 10	−0.1585	0.1398	−1.1339
Tail Segment			
Lower Tail	−6.3769	0.2970	−21.4677
Center	−2.9235	0.2786	−10.4944
Log Likelihood	−1654.6		
Observations	989		

log-skew-normal Model II in which our interest is the coefficient on skewness α, and the log-skew-t Model III in which we look at both skewness (α) and tail thickness (df). Table 6.7 shows the regression results from Models II and III.

In the log-skew-normal Model II the coefficient on skewness($\alpha = -1.3468$) is significantly different from zero at the 0.05 level, and we depart from normality. If $\alpha = 0$, the log-skew-normal Model II would have been reduced to log-normal Model I. We can now safely reject the log-normal Model I as the preferred specification with this finding.

In the log-skew-t Model III the coefficient on skewness ($\alpha = -0.9718$) and the tail-weight coefficient (DF $= 14.4596$) are also significantly different from zero. The tail-weight coefficient indicates the lower and upper tails of the royalty payments distribution in our study are heavier than normal. If the tail-weight coefficient had been zero in the log-skew-t Model II, there would have been no difference between the log-skew-normal and the log-skew-t models, assuming α did not equal zero in both models. Following the log-skew-t results, we can safely reject both

Table 6.7 Log-Skew-Normal Model II and Log-Skew-t Model III Estimates

Variable	Log-skew-normal Model II			Log-skew-t Model III		
	Coefficient	Std. Error	t-stat	Coefficient	Std. Error	t-stat
Constant	8.0886	0.4027	20.0878	7.8593	0.4072	19.3018
Member type						
Publisher/writer/ composer	0.0218	0.0843	0.2585	0.0166	0.0837	0.1987
License type						
Blanket/per program	0.1007	0.1349	0.7468	0.0832	0.1364	0.6101
Medium						
Broadcast TV	0.4932	0.1173	4.2038	0.5036	0.1109	4.5411
Local TV	0.4263	0.1135	3.7558	0.4193	0.1086	3.8623
Radio	0.5040	0.0973	5.1800	0.5227	0.1010	5.1775
Cable	0.3957	0.1068	3.7043	0.4148	0.1029	4.0296
Internet	0.4207	0.1338	3.1451	0.4385	0.1453	3.0180
Other	0.4679	0.1033	4.5276	0.4814	0.1045	4.6090
Performance type						
Features	0.1037	0.1481	0.7003	0.0854	0.1384	0.6176
Themes	1.2573	0.1733	7.2563	1.2485	0.1535	8.1342
Back/fore ground	0.2478	0.1062	2.3338	0.2207	0.1101	2.0045
Jingles	0.6441	0.3028	2.1271	0.6967	0.2828	2.4634
Promo	0.9808	0.1747	5.6147	0.9870	0.1749	5.6438
Tenure (years)						
Between 1 and 4	0.1110	0.1319	0.8416	0.1214	0.1409	0.8611
Between 4 and 6	0.1823	0.1222	1.4912	0.1749	0.1293	1.3528
Between 6 and 8	0.1711	0.1396	1.2256	0.1803	0.1367	1.3192
Between 8 and 10	−0.1257	0.1530	−0.8213	−0.1508	0.1380	−1.0929
Tail segment						
Lower tail	−6.3413	0.2942	−21.5569	−6.2426	0.2881	−21.6663
Center	−2.9309	0.2795	−10.4850	−2.9528	0.2687	−10.9879
α (Skewness)	−1.3468	0.2516	−5.3521	−0.9718	0.2978	−3.2636
ω^2 (Scale)	1.6784	0.0970	17.3104	1.4295	0.1377	10.3842
ν DF (Tail weight)				14.4596	6.6779	2.1653
Log likelihood	− 6277.73			−6275.07		
Observations	989			989		

the log-normal and the log-skew-normal in favor of the log-skew-*t* as the preferred specification as shown in Fig. 6.2.

Figure 6.2 plots the estimated parameters of the skew-*t* density function when $(\omega^2(scale) = 1.4295, \alpha(skewness) = -0.9718$ and $\nu(DF) = 14.4596)$ in the shaded area and the corresponding normal density function as the solid line. The skew-*t* approximates the normal distribution quite well. The log-skew-*t* captures the extreme outcomes in music copyright income in which a few songwriters in the upper tail claim the greater share of royalty income. The log-skew-*t* model

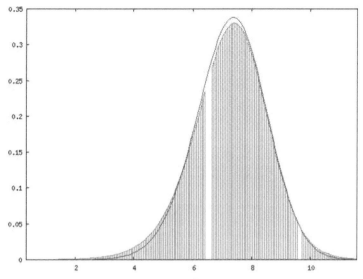

Fig. 6.2 Log-skew-T Model III density function ($\omega^2 = 1.4295$, $\alpha = -0.9718$, $v = 14.4596$)

demonstrates that when data is characterized as extreme outcomes, heavy tails and asymmetry, the normal (Gaussian) assumptions could lead to inaccurate probability statements.

We now turn to the interpretation of the dummy variables in the model with a cautionary note.[7] Table 6.8 shows the dummy variables elasticities. The distinction between publisher and writer, and the blanket and per-program license are not statistically significant in this particular model specification.

In the case of intellectual property, the asset is not itself consumed. Millions of others can enjoy the same music in the future. Each new generation of technology affords a new opportunity to sell them another time to consumers who may already own them.[8] The medium (television, radio, Internet, etc.) and performance types variables (themes, jingles, promos, etc.) and categorical variables are two of the key determinants in explaining the skewness in the distribution when both songwriters and publishers are included in the model. In the medium category of dummy variables elasticities, all of the variables are statistically different from zero, and all are positively related to royalty payments with radio performances having the greatest impact.

Music intensive radio stations use a lot of music due in part to the increase in the number of radio formats, genre, or radio audience segments that were introduced over many years. Radio genres have evolved into niches and sub-niches that define radio segmentation.[9] For example, 'rock music' has been sub-divided into 'classic rock,' 'modern rock,' 'alternative rock,' and many other categories such as 'hard rock Christian-themed,' 'soft rock,' and 'light rock.' Jazz has been sub-divided into 'traditional,' 'smooth jazz,' or 'new age.' Christian music has many sub-niches

Table 6.8 Model III Dummy Variables Elasticities

Variable	Coefficient	t-stat	g^*
Member type			
Publisher/writer/composer	0.0166	0.1987	0.0132
License type			
Blanket/per program	0.0832	0.6101	0.0767
Medium			
Broadcast TV	0.5036	4.5411	0.6445
Local TV	0.4193	3.8623	0.5120
Radio	0.5227	5.1775	0.6780
Cable	0.4148	4.0296	0.5061
Internet	0.4385	3.0180	0.5341
Other	0.4814	4.6090	0.6096
Performance type			
Features	0.0854	0.6176	0.0788
Themes	1.2485	8.1342	2.4442
Back/fore ground	0.2207	2.0045	0.2395
Jingles	0.6967	2.4634	0.9284
Promo	0.9870	5.6438	1.6426
Tenure (years)			
Between 1 and 4	0.1214	0.8611	0.1179
Between 4 and 6	0.1749	1.3528	0.1812
Between 6 and 8	0.1803	1.3192	0.1865
Between 8 and 10	−0.1508	−1.0929	−0.1482
Tail segment			
Lower tail	−6.2426	−21.6663	−0.9981
Center	−2.9528	−10.9879	−0.9497

such as 'Black Gospel' with an emphasis on music heard in predominantly Black churches, 'Contemporary Christian' music can be rock-driven or the type of Gospel music heard in evangelical southern states. Music intended for Spanish-speaking listeners can be broken down into 'Tejano,' 'regional Mexican,' and 'Spanish adult contemporary.' Still other radio stations base their musical content on nostalgia and musical time-periods such as 'hits' from the 1960s, 1970s, 1980s, and 1990s, or offer a 'mix' of these time periods in a 'Top 40' context. All these genres and formats increase the demand for musical works, and when performed composers, songwriters, and publishers are paid for their copyrighted songs.

Radio airplay also tends to stimulate music consumption in the form of CD sales, downloads from websites, sale of merchandise such as T-shirts, and concert tickets in which case the singer/songwriter might also benefit. Each individual audience member must first 'experience' the work by listening to it before the work is consumed. All of the performance type variables are significant except for features. The most significant performance type variable is theme-related musical compositions, followed by promotional spots. Theme music is the music used to open or close a program and may be heard day in and day out on radio or television. Sometimes a well-known song will be used as the opening and closing theme rather than a new song written for the program. It is the music that viewers might recognize as the theme of their favorite show or series. Promo or promotional spots that contain musical compositions are used to promote upcoming shows to increase viewers or listeners. For example, a popular television program in syndication can appear in multiple markets, on multiple stations and broadcast several times a week, thus increasing the number of performances of the musical composition. Length of membership variables is also not statistically significant in this specification when compared to the omitted category of members with more than 10 years of membership. It is worth noting, however, that the overall length of membership averages out to be 16.80 years, with newer member averaging 1.75 years, as shown in Table 6.9. Length of membership also reflects cases in which the copyright ownership was transferred to living heirs of deceased members. This may be the case that it is virtually impossible to predict ahead of time which member is likely to end up in the upper tail segment, given that length of membership is not significant.

Table 6.9 Length of Membership by Tail Segment (Includes Heirs of Deceased Members)

Segment	Mean	Min.	Max.
Lower tail	16.22	2.08	85.58
Center	16.87	1.75	94.50
Upper tail	21.39	3.83	64.08
Overall	16.80	1.75	94.5

Spurgeon (2008) suggests that it is often difficult to predict the demand of a copyright over time before the costs or investment is incurred in its creation and production. Each copyright is unique and consumers demand for each title can be independent of the demand for other titles. The transition interval from lower tail to upper tail segment is not necessarily the same for all songwriters and publishers, when you review the average length of membership by segment. The tail segment dummies are all highly significant and these variables represent the difference between the 'superstars' and the niche members with a steady stream of payments over time. Members who fall into the upper tail segment were omitted from this model as is required to prevent singularity. The signs on each tail segment coefficient are negative as expected when compared to the upper tail segment. The lower tail and center segments are all earning lower royalty payments than the upper tail segment. The lower tail segment contained a mix of relatively new and long-term members with an average length of membership of 16.2 years with a minimum of 2.1 years and a maximum of 86 years. Keep in mind that a single musical composition may have more than one credited song writer, legal heirs, or co-publishers. In that case, each credited writer then receives a proportional share of royalty payments. Members in the center segment—where there is a steady and consistent demand for their music in certain niche markets over a long period—averaged around 17 years with a minimum of 1.8 years and a maximum of 95 years. The upper tail segment contained recently [re]discovered artists, well-promoted unknowns, and well-known artists with a mean of 21.4 years, a minimum tenure of 4 years and a maximum of 64.1 years. Members such as those in the upper tail, with a catalog of multiple hits over many decades that have endured the test of time or the 'One Hit Wonders' and their experimental works, will receive the bulk of the royalty payments because there is a demand for their creative work in various media, and their songs are performed more frequently.

The goal for all members regardless of segment appears to be to maximize income over the shortest time span period in which their music is popular and in demand whether the music is a famous hit or an entire body of work. The time line of demand is irrelevant as the value of the copyright is continuously realized through collective licensing.[10]

Many others factors may play a role other than tenure in determining royalty payments. We discuss below the exogenous factors that could explain our heterogeneity findings on royalty payments across each segment made to creators for performances of their copyrighted compositions for their copyrighted performances may play a role that results in a relatively few creators earning a large share of royalty payments.

First, Galenson (2003) suggests that 'some great innovators make their most important discoveries suddenly, very early in their careers. In contrast, others arrive at their major contributions late in their lives, after decades of work. Which of these two life cycles a particular innovator follows is related systematically to his conception of his discipline, how he works, and to the nature of his contribution.' In other words, there is no known formula for music success and its financial rewards. Each musical composition is a unique combination of creativity, experimentation, innovation, talent, and luck.

Second, Grant and Wood (2004, pp. 99–121) observe that the ascendant trend [by major record producers] is to focus promotion and resources on only a diminishing few top-selling performing artists—implying an increasing impoverished range of 'diversity' in global music catalogs. Producers would rather 'bet' on popular stars (with a proven revenue generating stream) making a bad record rather than on some new or unknown artist and risking enormous amounts of capital in the process. Income distribution is, therefore, skewed toward artists with previous success, making it difficult for unknowns to break through.

Third, in the digital age, it has become increasingly difficult to measure the 'value' of music that is 'streamed' and consumed at various websites. As the sales of compact discs have declined in recent years, paid digital downloads have not been able to offset the decline in CD sales. This is in part due to the fact that these Internet companies may have trouble 'monetizing' their services when consumers have come to see Internet content as 'free.' Some of these Internet services are new and constantly evolving. For example, 'streaming' services may use both licensed and unlicensed copyrighted content on the same or different sites, and may offer free, paid subscriptions, or a combination of both. How to make sure that all of the 'upstream and downstream' revenues are captured and reported in a timely manner to music creators and performing artists can be time-consuming and expensive.

Fourth, the economic relationship between companies and their complicated myriad of 'network partners,' vendors, content suppliers, and [un]affiliated entities, and their ability to not disclose these relationships (some of which are proprietary) can mean that their revenue from performance copyrighted material can be hidden or buried in mounds of proprietary contracts. The task of requesting business contracts or documentation of relationships, with sometimes hundreds of network partners, that define such relationships can be long and arduous at best.

The fifth point we make, as in the case of ASCAP and BMI, is the presence of companies not wishing to pay, delaying payments or paying a reduced rate can petition the court under AFJ2 (2001) for relief in what is called a 'rate court' proceeding, using the industry parlance for a lawsuit. As you can expect, these proceedings often result in lengthy and costly delays that may take years before a final settlement is made, and the writers and publishers properly credited with past-due royalty payments. The legal costs (a necessity) only add to the administrative costs thus further reducing royalty payments.

6.5 Conclusion

This study is limited in scope to a sample of 989 members from a single quarter. The tails in our empirical distribution are skewed, heavier, and more asymmetrical than the tails of both the log-normal and the log-skew-normal distributions. Our results also showed that many of the composers and publishers are grouped into heavy tails of the empirical distribution in a departure from Anderson (2008) and his *Long Tail* analysis.

The large sum of royalty fees collected by the PROs are going to a relatively small number of publishers, 'superstars' performers, and songwriters in the upper tail segment of the distribution than on other members because their successful compositions are performed more frequently by radio and television stations, and other users of music. Success is still concentrated on a relatively few members. With our parametric results, we rejected both the log-normal and the log-skew-normal in favor of the log-skew-t to account for skewness, heavy tails, and asymmetry.

Walls (2005) suggests two reasons why the log-skew-t is appealing in economic modeling. First, it is easier—computationally—to implement the skew-t than some other distributions (like the stable Paretian model or the Lévy stable regression model) using standard maximum likelihood statistical techniques that are within reach of applied researchers. Second, the skew-t extends the normal distribution by permitting tails that are heavy and asymmetric. The log-normal is just a special case of the log-skew-normal when $\alpha = 0$. There is evidence of some correlated properties from one segment to the next, residual variances and some unobserved properties that the models failed to capture. The non-normal distribution in our study suggests that a refined longitudinal study (a pooled-time series cross section model) in which the same members are tracked and analyzed over various time intervals that coincide with certain key events such as important legislation and technological advances like the CD player, the iPod, and the Internet that have had a dramatic effect on songwriters' income might be worthwhile.

Notes

1. Anderson's 2008 is adapted from an earlier article that first appeared in *Wired* magazine in October 2004.
2. Brabec and Brabec (2008, pp. 171–214).
3. See *ASCAP's Distribution Resource Documents*, pp.1–30 available here http://www.ascap.com/reference.
4. See Chapter 5 and the following references: Azzalini (1985, 1986), Azzalini and Capitanio (2003), Azzalini et al. (2003), Dalla-Valle (2007), Azzalini and Genton (2008) for the theory development.
5. Walls (2005).
6. Jarque and Bera (1980, 1987), Shapiro and Wilk (1965).
7. A discussion on the interpretation of dummy variables when the dependent variable is log-transformed is given in Halvorsen and Palmquist (1980), Kennedy (1981). From their discussion we develop estimates of the percentage impact of the dummy variables on the dependent variable. These estimates may not be appropriate for some explanatory variables since they may lack meaningful interpretation. The impact of the dummy variables on the dependent variable g^* is computed as:

$$ g^* = \exp\left(\hat{\beta} - \frac{\hat{\sigma}^2 \hat{\beta}}{2}\right) - 1 \tag{6.4} $$

   where $\hat{\beta}$ is the estimated coefficient on the dummy variable and $\hat{\sigma}^2$ is the estimated variance of $\hat{\beta}$.
8. Grant and Wood (2004).
9. See http://ftp.media.radcity.net or The Radio Book 2008–2009 Edition for a listing.
10. Spurgeon (2008).

References

AFJ2 (2001). Second Amended Final Judgment, USA vs ASCAP, Civil Action No. 41 – 1395. United States District Court, S.D.N.Y. (White Plains), pp. 1–19.

Anderson, C. (2008). *The Long Tail*. Hyperion, New York, NY.

Azzalini, A. (1985). A class of distribution which includes the normal ones. *Scandinavian Journal of Statistics*, 12:171–178.

Azzalini, A. (1986). Further results on a class of distribution which includes the normal ones. *Statistica*, 46:199–208.

Azzalini, A. and Capitanio, A. (2003). Distributions generated by perturbation of symmetry with emphasis on a multivariate skew-t distribution. *Journal of the Royal Statistical Society*, B65:367–389.

Azzalini, A., DalCappello, T., and Kotz, S. (2003). Log-skew-normal and log-skew-*t* distributions as models for family income data. *Journal of Income Distribution*, 11(3–4):12–20.

Azzalini, A. and Genton, M. (2008). Robust likelihood methods based on the skew-*t* and related distributions. *International Statistical Review*, 76:106–129.

Brabec, J. and Brabec, T. (2008). *Music Money and Success: The Insiders Guide to Making Money in the Music Industry*. Schirmer Trade Books-Music Sales, New York, NY, 6th edition.

Connolly, M. and Krueger, A. (2005). Rockonomics: The economics of popular music. *NBER Working Paper*, (11282).

Dalla-Valle, A. (2007). A test for the hypothesis of skew-normality in a population. *Journal of Statistical Computation and Simulation*, 77(1):63–77.

Galenson, D. (2003). The two life cycles of human creativity. *NBER Reporter*, Fall:12–15.

Giles, D. (2007). Increasing returns to information in the US popular music industry. *Applied Economics Letters*, 14:327–331.

Grant, P. and Wood, C. (2004). *Blockbusters and Trade Wars: Popular Culture in a Globalized World*. Douglas and McIntyre, Vancouver, BC.

Halvorsen, R. and Palmquist, R. (1980). The interpretation of dummy variables in semi-logarithmic equations. *The American Economic Review*, 70(4):474–475.

Jarque, C. and Bera, A. (1980). Efficient tests for normality, homoscedasticity and serial independence of regression residuals. *Econometric Letters*, 6:255–259.

Jarque, C. and Bera, A. (1987). A test for normality of observations and regression residuals. *International Statistical Review*, 55:163–172.

Kennedy, P. (1981). Estimation with correctly interpreted dummy variables in semilogarithmic equations. *The American Economic Review*, 71(4):801.

Pitt, I. (2010a). Superstar effects on royalty income in a performance rights organization. *Journal of Cultural Economics* (forthcoming).

Shapiro, S. and Wilk, M. (1965). An analysis of variance test for normality. *Biometrika*, 52: 591–611.

Spurgeon, C. (2008). Economic principles and expert economic evidence. *CISAC*, (CJL08-3353):1–28.

Walls, W. (2005). Modeling heavy tails and skewness in film returns. *Applied Financial Economics*, 15:1181–1188.

Chapter 7
Economics of Songwriters' Performance Royalty Income: Tenure, Age, and Titles

Abstract This chapter examines the dynamic of 'superstar' effects of age, length in membership in a PRO, and number of song titles registered on songwriter's income when publishers are excluded. We found that royalty income distribution is still highly skewed and a key determinant of performance royalty income is due to the number of registered titles. This skewness of a relatively small number of songwriters earning more royalty payments than other members can be explained, in part, by successful members having a larger catalog of songs that are performed more frequently by radio and television stations, and other users of music. The standard skew-t distribution model generalized with location, scale, and a degree of freedom parameter (v) is used to analyze royalty income.

7.1 Introduction

Songwriting, in terms of creativity, can be just as challenging as many other art forms such as poetry, painting, sculpture, dance, or writing books due to the many intangibles involved in creating a successful song. The creative challenge to many aspiring songwriters is how to break through in a highly competitive environment and be successful, given the millions of songs that have already been written and recorded, the ever-changing radio formats, a fickle listening public, and the over-supply of many songwriters, some of whom may only approach songwriting on a part-time basis. In the music industry, it can be challenging to produce songs that are sufficiently distinctive and artistically appealing to a wide audience and so many genres and radio station formats. Yet without songwriters and their songs, there would be no sound recordings for the many music users and retailers whose revenue streams rely on music. It may take years for a song to become a hit, if ever, or it could just happen overnight if there is stock of creative material ready to take advantage of the latest genre.

Songwriters fall into one of two broad categories, the non-performing songwriter and the performing songwriter. The professional non-performing songwriter writes songs for recording artists who are not skilled songwriters. The non-performing while having the ability to write melodies, lyrics, and harmony of songs may lack singing ability, suffer from stage fright or they may have no desire to sing at all.

I.L. Pitt, *Economic Analysis of Music Copyright*,
DOI 10.1007/978-1-4419-6318-5_7, © Springer Science+Business Media, LLC 2010

The performing songwriter on the other hand is skilled musician who can also write their own material. Success for the songwriter comes from the commercial release of their creative output. The goal of most songwriters is to create a hit song that in the process sell millions of records and the record listed in one of the many Billboard Magazine charts posted each week. A few *lucky* performing songwriters will sign a recording contract with a major label, get to hear their music used on television, the radio, the cable networks, or on the Internet, and be rewarded for the creativity they each put into their work.

Table 7.1 provides a selected look at the successful Top 10 songwriters (who may also be performers as well) as of August 15, 2009 as ranked by *Billboard* magazine based on radio airplay from 1,617 US radio stations monitored by Nielsen BDS during the period April 1–June 30, 2009.[1] The songwriter/composer membership in a PRO, the number of titles registered, and their CAE/IPI numbers (which are not proprietary, listed at ASCAP's and BMI's websites and provided here to distinguish members with similar names.) are also displayed in the table to provide a contrast of PRO membership.

Table 7.1 *Billboard* Magazine's Top Ten Songwriters by PRO, April–June 2009

Rank	Songwriter	Titles	PRO
1	Nadir 'Redone' Khayat	229	BMI
2	Taylor Swift	70	BMI
3	Steffani 'Lady Gaga' Germanotta	62	BMI
4	Karl 'Max' Sandberg Martin[1]	170	STIM (ASCAP)
5	Lukasz Gottwald	182	ASCAP
6	Jason Mraz	107	ASCAP
7	Scott R. S. Mescudi	8	ASCAP
8	Ryan 'Alias' Tedder	155	ASCAP
9	Clifford J. 'T.I.' Harris Jr.	170	BMI
10	O. Omishore	20	ASCAP

[1] Member of STIM (Swedish Society), music in US licensed by ASCAP.
Sources: Ranking Data, *Billboard* magazine, August 15, 2009 Issue, p. 18. Used with permission of e5 Global Media. PRO membership data: http://www.ascap.com/ace and http://repertoire.bmi.com/ as of August 10, 2009.

7.2 Profile of a Non-performing Songwriter

For non-performing songwriters, their success will come from collaborating with other recording artists, record labels, and record producers. One such successful non-performing songwriter is Diane Warren. Walker (2008, p. 214) quotes a music industry executive describing Diane Warren as perhaps the'greatest writer of this generation and one of the greatest of all time.'

Diane Warren is described as a self-publishing songwriter, but not a performer, who has been written about in many music magazines and may not so well-known to the general public even though she is the writer of many hit songs.[2] Self-publishing is the practice of issuing your own mechanical and synchronization licenses without a major publisher (e.g., EMI, Sony, Universal) where there is a large enough body of work to make it profitable.[3] Some of the income benefits of self-publishing are apparent; the share of royalty income that would normally flow to the major publishers is retained by self-publishers, even though foreign administration rights might still be handled by in-country publishers in exchange for a share of royalty income. In addition, the self-publisher retains copyright ownership of their own material and can exploit it as they choose. The costs to the self-publisher would include publishing overhead expenses associated with copyright registration, demos, marketing, promotion, accounting, and so on to exploit old songs in their catalogs or shopping new songs to recording artists and record labels. Certain self-publishing administration activities can be sub-contracted out in what is referred to 'sub-publishing' where, for example, print music would be handled by a major print publisher such as Alfred Publishing Company, and the mechanical licensing handled by the Harry Fox Agency.[4]

The self-publisher would also establish a relationship with ASCAP, BMI, and SESAC to license and collect performance royalty fees on their behalf. For example, from a PRO royalty payment and songwriter/composer income perspective, as both the publisher and songwriter and copyright holder for any of her songs that have no other co-writers, Warren will received both the publisher and the songwriter share of royalty income. According to an article in the Fall 2006 issue of *Playback* magazine, among Warren's musical accomplishments was what the magazine called an 'astounding' feat of having seven of her songs recorded by seven different artists appear in the Billboard Hot 100 in the same week.[5]

Furthermore,

Diane Warren celebrated her 25th anniversary since joining ASCAP as a member in 1981. Warren has produced many number one hits across many music genres such as R&B, Country, Latin, Christian, Adult Contemporary and Dance charts, as well as Pop for an array of performers that include Elton John, Rebe McEntire, Johnny Mathis and Mary M. Blige among others. Her songs have been featured in close to 100 feature films. Warren has also received multiple nominations for Grammys Academy Awards and Golden Globes. Warren was also honored by ASCAP as Songwriter of the Year six times and has been inducted into the Songwriters Hall of Fame. Diane Warren is also the owner of her own independent publishing company, called Realsongs, and represents only one writer herself.[6]

Using the music industry executive's compliment and the *Playback* magazine except, we will illustrate the concept of the successful non-performing/songwriter/self-publisher using publicly available data on Diane Warren. In addition to the contemporary recordings artists mentioned in Table 7.2, Warren has been writing for some of the world's most notable other artists, including Elton John, Tina Turner, Barbara Streisand, and Aretha Franklin among others.[7]

Studies of the so-called 'superstar effect' have, in general, focused on the more well-known performers who in some cases also happen to be songwriters. It is these recording artists who are included as the 'superstars,' meaning that there is a marked skew in the income distribution of these performers, as they may earn the lion's share of performance royalty income when their compositions are used on the radio, on television, and on the Internet. The non-performing successful songwriter is the

Table 7.2 Diane Warren's Top 30 Hot 100 Songs, 1983–2000

Rank	Title	Label	Artist	Peak	Peak date
1	*Un-Break My Heart*	LaFace	Toni Braxton	1	12/7/96
2	*Because You Loved Me*	550 Music	Celine Dion	1	3/23/96
3	*I Don't Want To Miss A Thing*	Columbia	Aerosmith	1	9/5/98
4	*Have You Ever?*	Atlantic	Brandy	1	1/16/99
5	*Look Away*	Reprise	Chicago	1	12/10/88
6	*Blame It On The Rain*	Arista	Milli Vanilli	1	11/25/89
7	*Nothing's Gonna Stop Us Now*[1]	Grunt	Starship	1	4/4/87
8	*When I See You Smile*	Epic	Bad English	1	11/11/89
9	*Love Will Lead You Back*	Arista	Taylor Dayne	1	4/7/90
10	*How Do I live*	Curb	LeAnn Rimes	2	12/13/97
11	*Music of My Heart*	Mirimax	'N Sync & G. Estefan	2	10/16/99
12	*I Get Weak*	MCA	Belinda Carlisle	2	3/19/98
13	*If I Could Turn Back Time*	Geffen	Cher	3	9/23/89
14	*Rhythm of the Night*	Gordy	Debarge	3	4/27/85
15	*I Turn To You*	RCA	Christina Aguilera	3	7/1/00
16	*I Don't Want To Live Without Your Love*[2]	Reprise	Chicago	3	8/27/88
17	*How Can We Be Lovers*[3]	Columbia	Michael Bolton	3	5/5/90
18	*For You I Will*	Rowdy	Monica	4	4/19/97
19	*Don't Turn Around*[4]	Arista	Ace of Base	4	6/18/94
20	*Saving Forever For You*	Giant	Shanice	4	1/30/93
21	*If You Asked Me To*	Epic	Celine Dion	4	7/11/92
22	*I'll Be Your Shelter*	Arista	Taylor Dayne	4	7/14/90
23	*Set The Night To Music*	Atlantic	Robert Flack/M. Priest	6	11/16/91
24	*Who Will You Run To*	Capitol	Heart	7	10/3/87
25	*Time, Love and Tenderness*	Columbia	Michael Bolton	7	9/14/91
26	*The Arms Of The One Who Love You*	So So Def	Xscape	7	5/30/98
27	*Solitare*[5]	Atlantic	Laura Branigan	7	5/21/83
28	*When I Am Back On My Feet Again*	Columbia	Michael Bolton	7	8/4/90
29	*Just Live Jesse James*[6]	Geffen	Cher	8	12/26/89
30	*I'll Never Get Over You (Getting Over Me)*	Arista	Expose	8	7/17/93

Note: All songs written by Diane Warren, except for 1, 2, 4 written by Warren and Albert Hammond; 3. By Warren, Michael Bolton, and Desmond Child; 5. By Marine Clemenceau. 6. By Desmond Child and Warren.
Source: *Billboard* magazine, November 15, 2008, pp. 29–35.
Used with permission of e5 Global Media.

kind of 'superstar' that might be overlooked and rarely if ever studied in economic literature because it is often difficult to obtain income data due to confidentiality agreements. For example, the income data for painters might become available when their works are sold at auction houses, and that has been studied. In the world of sports, the individual pay packages and incentives of sports superstars are sometimes made public.

According to Walker (2008, p. 216), Warren wrote the hit song *Unbreak My Heart* for the singer Toni Braxton which sold 10 million copies and earned Warren millions as a self-publisher. In 2006, *Kiplinger* magazine in story on high income earners that included Diane Warren, among others, estimated that Warren collects royalty checks, presumably from all sources, in millions each year for the roughly 1,600 songs she has composed. The article goes on to quote Warren saying that the difference between being employed as a songwriter at a publishing company and owner of her own company and copyrights can be the 'the difference between earning $350 a week and making millions of dollars a year.'[8]

In the music industry world of arcane accounting, the songwriters' and publishers' share are sometimes referred to as each having 100 percent for a total of 200 percent. Warren would receive 100 percent of the publisher's and 100 percent of the writer's share of her song that is written by her and published through Realsongs, her publishing company. Table 7.2 shows the range of musical genres from ballads to pop hits, and the diverse cast of recording artists that Warren has collaborated with to produce hit songs. In a selected look at 30 of Warren's songs that reached the Billboard Top 100 chart between the years 1983 and 2000 in Table 7.3, of those 30 songs listed in the table, 53.33 percent were for just for five record labels. Furthermore, 40 percent of those same 30 songs were with six recording artists with whom Warren collaborated as shown in Table 7.4. Even as a self-publisher, collaboration with a major record label and their top-selling recording artists must still be done.

Table 7.3 Diane Warren's Top 30 Hot 100 by Record Label, 1983–2000

Label	Freq.	Percent	Cum.%
Arista	5	16.67	16.67
Columbia	4	13.33	30.00
Atlantic	3	10.00	40.00
Epic	2	6.67	46.67
Geffen	2	6.67	53.33
Reprise	2	6.67	60.00
550 Music	1	3.33	63.33
Capitol	1	3.33	66.67
Curb	1	3.33	70.00
Giant	1	3.33	73.33
Gordy	1	3.33	76.67
Grunt	1	3.33	80.00
LaFace	1	3.33	83.33
MCA	1	3.33	86.67
Mirimax	1	3.33	90.00
RCA	1	3.33	93.33
Rowdy	1	3.33	96.67
So So Def	1	3.33	100.00
Total	30	100	

Table 7.4 Diane Warren's Top 30 Hot 100 by Recording Artist, 1983–2000

Label	Freq.	Percent	Cum. %
Michael Bolton	3	10	10.00
Celine Dion	2	6.67	16.67
Cher	2	6.67	23.33
Chicago	2	6.67	30.00
Taylor Dayne	2	6.67	36.67
Ace of Base	1	3.33	40.00
Aerosmith	1	3.33	43.33
Bad English	1	3.33	46.67
Belinda Carlisle	1	3.33	50.00
Brandy	1	3.33	53.33
Christina Aguilera	1	3.33	56.67
Debarge	1	3.33	60.00
Expose	1	3.33	63.33
Heart	1	3.33	66.67
Laura Branigan	1	3.33	70.00
LeAnn Rimes	1	3.33	73.33
Milli Vanilli	1	3.33	76.67
Monica	1	3.33	80.00
Robert Flack/M. Priest	1	3.33	83.33
Shanice	1	3.33	86.67
Starship	1	3.33	90.00
Toni Braxton	1	3.33	93.33
Xscape	1	3.33	96.67
'N Sync & G. Estefan	1	3.33	100.00
Total	30	100	

The major publishers and labels can be a barrier to entry for independent songwriters by acting in ways to allow or prevent access to their signed recordings artists.

Music performance royalties in the form of income may act as one incentive for many songwriters, lyricists, and composers to continue to write new songs, intended for use in various mediums and performance types such as features, theme music, and jingles. Successive new works over a long period of time add to the artist's output or repertoire. This output can then be exploited by the copyright holders, including publishers for their mutual benefit. Perhaps, because of the unknown risks involved, music publishers may focus their capital investment on their current and best-selling performers with recording contracts, while relative unknown and untested songwriters may not receive the same level of investment as superstars.

In other words, royalty incentives work, aided in part by music publishers and record labels, by generally getting successful songwriters to write other successful songs, the more titles the more income depending on airplay. Table 7.5 illustrates how success, as measured by song titles at the publishing level, plays an important role in the music industry in the skewed distribution of income. Every quarter a publisher's airplay chart of their share of the top 100 songs on US radio stations is

Table 7.5 Top 10 Publishers Airplay Chart, April 1–June 30, 2009

Rank	Publisher	Share (%)	Shared titles
1	EMI Music	17.30	39
2	SONY/ATV Music	14.20	25
3	Warner/Chappell	14.10	35
4	Universal Music Group	11.90	24
5	Kobalt Music	7.40	15
6	Bug Music/Windswept	4.20	12
7	Stage Three Music	3.10	7
8	Cherry Lane Music	2.70	2
9	Big Loud Shirt	1.80	4
10	Croomstacular Music	1.70	3
	Industry Share (%)	78.40	

Ranking based on top 100 detecting songs from 1,617 US radio stations.
Source: Based on *Billboard* magazine, August 15, 2009, p. 18.
Used with permission of e5 Global Media.

computed and published in *Billboard* magazine using data from Nielsen BDS and the Harry Fox Agency.

Table 7.5 also illustrates the market share relationship between the major music publishers and independent music publishers, and their ability to attract recordings artists. EMI Music, SONY/ATV Music, Warner/Chappell, and Universal Music Group accounted for 57.50 percent of the top 100 songs in second quarter of 2009, while the top 10 publishers including some independents controlled 78.40 percent of the top 100 songs in terms of airplay.

7.3 Model Specification and Data Description

For the purposes of this monograph, the songwriter and composer source of income include only performance royalties, which are generated by public performances from radio airplay, broadcast and cable television airplay, the Internet, restaurants, bars, gyms, night clubs, or any public place where recorded music is played. The singer/songwriter may have other source of income such as mechanical, synchronization, and merchandising which are not considered here. Pitt (2010a) in modeling royalty income data among songwriters and publishers in a PRO, that members were grouped into heavy tails. The small number of 'superstars' in the upper tail segment of the income distribution earned significantly more royalty payments than other members because their successful compositions are performed more frequently by radio and television stations, and other music users.

Using maximum likelihood techniques, regression models with skew-normal or skew-*t* random disturbances can be estimated. A continuous random univariate variable X is said to have a skew-normal *(SN)* distribution[9] if it has the following density function:

$$f(x) = 2\phi(x)\Phi(\alpha x) \tag{7.1}$$

In other words, the random variable X is

$$X \sim SN(0, 1, \alpha). \tag{7.2}$$

Skew distributions augment the normal and student-t distributions by adding a shape or skewness parameter (α) in the skew-normal case. The component α in regulating the shape of the density function allows for a continuous variation from normality to non-normality. When $\alpha = 0$, the skew-normal simplifies to the standard normal distribution. For ease of computation, location (estimated regression coefficients or just the constant term) and scale (ω^2) parameters are also added to the above random variable X and its density function in Equation (8.1). The standard skew-t distribution can be generalized with location, scale, and a degree of freedom parameter (ν). The skew-t is appealing in that it extends the normal distribution by permitting tails that are heavy and asymmetric. The skew-normal and skew-t can be fitted using their log-transformed versions. 'These are referred to as the log-skew-normal and log-skew-t distributions' (Walls 2005).

The data were drawn from a random sample of ASCAP's domestic members that included 1,000 songwriters/composers in the first quarter of 2007 whose total credits accumulated were greater than zero. Individual songwriters are not identified in this analysis, given the proprietary nature of the study. Under these circumstances certain results that are typically reported in academic studies will be excluded. In each model, the dependent variable—Dollar Value (royalty payments) to ASCAP songwriter, members—is fitted on a conditional vector of member attributes. The distribution of royalty payments is quantified conditional on length of membership in a PRO, age, number of titles, member status, and the sample broken down into various earnings categories.

$$
\begin{aligned}
Log(DV) = \ &\beta_0 + \beta_1(Tenure\ 1\ and\ 6) + \beta_2(Tenure\ 6\ and\ 8) \\
&+ \beta_3(Tenure\ 8\ and\ 10) + \beta_4(Age\ Less\ than\ 35) \\
&+ \beta_5(Age\ Between\ 35\ and\ 50) + \beta_6(Titles\ 1\ and\ 25) \\
&+ \beta_7(Titles\ 25\ and\ 65) + \beta_8(Titles\ 65\ and\ 100) \\
&+ \beta_9(Low\ Earnings) + \beta_{10}(Medium\ Earnings) \\
&+ \beta_{11}(Survive) + \varepsilon_i
\end{aligned} \tag{7.3}
$$

Dollar Value = Credits (The number of performance credits generated by medium and performance type) times a Credit Value (a quarterly fixed amount set by ASCAP). *Tenure Category* is an indicator variable for length of membership. Tenure 1–6 = 1 if members have been with ASCAP between 1 and 6 years and so on for Tenure 6–8, Tenure 8–10, and Tenure greater than 10 years is the omitted and relative category. *Age Category* is an indicator variable for various age categories such as for members age less than 35 and ages between 35 and 50. The omitted category is those older than 50 years of age. *Titles Category* is an indicator variable for the number of song titles in ASCAP's catalog. Titles 1 and 25 are members with less than 25 titles, and so on. The omitted category is members with more than 100 titles. *Earnings Category* is an indicator variable for various income categories such as low, medium and the omitted category being high earners. *Survive* is an indicator variable for the surviving or non-surviving member at the time the sample was drawn. Survive = 1 if original songwriter/member is still alive; Otherwise 0 for an heir or estate. ϵ_i = random disturbance term that follows a log-normal, log-skew-normal, or log-skew-*t* distribution depending on the model being estimated.

Table 7.6 Estimated Models Error Structure

Model	Estimator	Error structure
Log-normal	OLS	$SN(0, 1)$
Log-skew-normal	Maximum likelihood	$SN(\xi, \omega^2, \alpha)$
Log-skew-*t*	Maximum likelihood	$t(\xi, \omega^2, \alpha, \nu)$

7.4 Estimation Results

The member profile shown in Table 7.7 indicated that the average length of membership in the PRO was 18.98 years, while the average age was 47.32 years. The Age variable includes the age when deceased members died and surviving heirs may be collecting royalties. The maximum age and membership include members whose copyrights were transferred to an estate or heir at the time of death. The average number of titles per member in the sample was around 64.10 songs, some of which are shared with other copyright holders who may or may not be members of the same performing rights society.

Our regression results are shown in Tables 7.8, 7.9, and 7.10. Table 7.8 is presented to illustrate the model under Ordinary Least Squares assumptions and Table 7.10 computes the dummy elasticities for the semi-logarithmic form.

The log-skew-t Model III is the preferred specification. All of the skew associated parameters are significant. Both α (*Skewness*) = -2.6080 ($t - stat = -4.9115$) and the ν (*Tail Weight*) = 4.4704 ($t - stat = 6.0106$) are both statistically significant at the 5 percent level. This indicates the presence of skewness and that the royalty income distribution is heavier than normal. Had the log-normal Model I

Table 7.7 Profile of Songwriters by Membership, Age and Titles (ASCAP First Quarter of 2007)

Variable	Mean	Std. Dev.	Min	Max
Membership (years)	18.98	17.58	2	95
Age	47.32	15.03	16	99
Titles in catalog	64.10	111.72	1	1, 110
Sample size = 1,000				

Table 7.8 Log-Normal Model I Estimates

Variable	Coefficient	Std. Error	t-stat
Constant	8.6378	0.1788	48.3125
Tenure			
Between 1 and 6	0.1290	0.1658	0.7777
Between 6 and 8	0.2011	0.1610	1.2494
Between 8 and 10	0.1024	0.1585	0.6460
Age			
Less than 35	0.1838	0.1681	1.0934
Between 35 and 50	−0.1087	0.1137	−0.9563
Titles			
Between 1 and 25	−0.4739	0.1524	−3.1087
Between 25 and 65	−0.2717	0.1556	−1.7462
Between 65 and 100	−0.2947	0.1956	−1.5070
Dollar Value			
Low Earnings	−5.8560	0.1440	−40.6660
Medium Earnings	−2.6910	0.1450	−18.5644
Status			
Survive	−0.0593	0.1643	−0.3612
R^2	0.73		
Log likelihood	−1772.56		

or the log-skew-normal Model II models been used, either one would have produced specification errors due to the presence of skew and heavy tails.

We now turn to the interpretation of the dummy variables in the model and its shortcomings. Halvorsen and Palmquist (1980) and Kennedy (1981) discuss the interpretation of dummy variables when the dependent variable is log-transformed. From their discussion we develop estimates of the percentage impact of the dummy variables on the dependent variable. We caution that these estimates may not be appropriate for some explanatory variables since they may lack meaningful interpretation or they may under- or over-estimate the relative explanatory power in the model.

The impact of the dummy variables on the dependent variable g^* is computed as:

$$g^* = \exp\left(\hat{\beta} - \frac{\hat{\sigma}^2\hat{\beta}}{2}\right) - 1 \tag{7.4}$$

where $\hat{\beta}$ is the estimated coefficient on the dummy variable and $\hat{\sigma}^2$ is the estimated variance of $\hat{\beta}$. In examining the dummy variables and their computed elasticities in Table 7.10, we observe that the length of membership(tenure), age, and surviving vs non-surviving member effects are not statistically significant in the Log-skew-t Model III. Although these variables are statistically insignificant in this model, this does not mean, however, that they may not be managerially relevant when it comes to administering their copyrighted songs through a PRO. The number of titles and income earnings categories are significant in the model. In examining the

Table 7.9 Log-Skew-Normal Model II and Log-Skew-t Model III Estimates

	Log-skew-normal Model II			Log-skew-t Model III		
Variable	Coeff. Est.	Std. Error	t-stat	Coeff. Est.	Std. Error	t-stat
Constant	10.7156	0.3282	32.6452	9.7850	0.2160	45.2996
Tenure						
Between 1 and 6	−0.0057	0.1104	−0.0518	0.0023	0.1149	0.0197
Between 6 and 8	−0.0131	0.1120	−0.1172	0.1192	0.1129	1.0554
Between 8 and 10	−0.1133	0.1023	−1.1073	0.0153	0.1068	0.1429
Age						
Less than 35	0.2679	0.1399	1.9142	0.1482	0.1157	1.2807
Between 35 and 50	−0.0101	0.0838	−0.1207	−0.0177	0.0804	−0.2196
Titles						
Between 1 and 25	−0.5061	0.1336	−3.7897	−0.4750	0.1171	−4.0565
Between 25 and 65	−0.3909	0.1261	−3.1009	−0.3328	0.1182	−2.8158
Between 65 and 100	−0.3910	0.1646	−2.3755	−0.2930	0.1465	−2.0004
Dollar Value						
Low Earnings	−5.9089	0.2512	−23.5269	−5.2456	0.1498	−35.0103
Medium Earnings	−3.5149	0.3027	−11.6101	−2.8932	0.1579	−18.3260
Status						
Survive	0.0093	0.1113	0.0837	−0.0198	0.1136	−0.1742
α (Skewness)	−5.5021	1.6704	−3.2939	−2.6080	0.5310	−4.9115
ω^2 (Scale)	2.3159	0.1188	19.4878	1.5507	0.1194	12.9927
ν DF (Tail Weight)				4.4704	0.7438	6.0106
Log Likelihood	−6186.52			−6162.93		
Observations	1, 000			1, 000		

Table 7.10 Model III Dummy Variables Elasticities

Parameter	Estimate	Std. Error	t-stat	g^*
Tenure				
Between 1 and 6	0.0023	0.1149	0.0197	−0.0043
Between 6 and 8	0.1192	0.1129	1.0554	0.1194
Between 8 and 10	0.0153	0.1068	0.1429	0.0096
Age				
Less than 35	0.1482	0.1157	1.2807	0.1520
Between 35 and 50	−0.0177	0.0804	−0.2196	−0.0207
Titles				
Between 1 and 25	−0.4750	0.1171	−4.0565	−0.3823
Between 25 and 65	−0.3328	0.1182	−2.8158	−0.2881
Between 65 and 100	−0.2930	0.1465	−2.0004	−0.2619
Dollar Value				
Low Earnings	−5.2456	0.1498	−35.0103	−0.9948
Medium Earnings	−2.8932	0.1579	−18.3260	−0.9453
Status				
Alive	−0.0198	0.1136	−0.1742	−0.0259

coefficients associated with the *Between 1 and 25*, *Between 25 and 65*, and *Between 65 and 100* variables in Table 7.10, we observe that all the signs are negative as expected when compared to the relative base (omitted) category of members with over 100 registered song titles, some of which may be shared with other copyright holders. The general conclusion here is that the more titles registered the more likely they will generate higher levels of income.

A songwriter, composer, or music publisher with a large catalog of songs including current and past hits, songs can have a significant advantage over rivals when it comes to exploiting royalty income through economies of scale. As the songwriter output of titles and their body of work increase over time the songwriter's royalty income should increase as well if there is a demand for the writer's music by consumers and that demand led to success in terms of airplay. Galenson (2000, 2003) studied the contemporary art market, careers and life cycles of artists such as painters using fine art auction transactions data to estimate the relationship between the artist's age and value of a painting at the date of a sale execution. Galenson (2005) further examined age and creativity by looking at the careers of 11 leading twentieth century American poets using the frequency with which poems were reprinted in anthologies as a measure of their importance. His study revealed that among those poets there were two distinctly different life cycles, one group produced their most important work early in their careers, in their 20s and 30s, whereas the other group produced their most important work considerably later, in their 40s, 50s, and even their 60s. Other studies have shown that age may not be such an important determinant in the measure of creativity or exceptional achievements among artists. Ginsburgh and Weyers (2006) and Simonton (1988) argue that it is the artist's cumulative output over time that is more relevant to achievement. The number of important, creative, or 'best quality' works is proportional to the total number of works produced, so that the ratio of quality to quantity is, on average, constant over the life cycle, leading to the so-called 'constant-probability-of-success model,' and creative achievements are generated at any moment in the life cycle. The songwriter's reputation is also enhanced over time as the relative number of song titles in their body of works increases over time. For some songwriters it may be their earlier works that produce the most in royalty income, while for others it is their work in later stages in life as they take advantage of a change in genre. Any or all of the copyright owner's exclusive rights may be transferred, conveyed by a will or pass as personal property as a gift under state property laws.[10]

7.5 Conclusion

The log-skew-*t* provides a parametric approach in which to estimate the skewness and heavy tails present in the data. The log skew-*t* extends the normal distribution by permitting tails that are heavy and asymmetric. The log-normal is just a special case of the log-skew-normal when $\alpha = 0$. Our analysis of the effects of royalty income using a sample of songwriters/composers showed that royalty income in a PRO is not normally distributed, but highly skewed. This is not so surprising since there is evidence of the so-called 'superstar effect' among the singer/songwriters present in the data in which a few songwriters earn a greater share of royalty payments.

Of the possible determinants in explaining the skewness in our data, the number of titles registered is a factor in explaining the skewness. We found that the greater the number of titles, the higher the level of royalty income generated by a sample of songwriters in a PRO because their successful compositions are performed more frequently by radio and television stations, and other users of music. Length of membership (tenure), age, and status effects are not statistically significant in the model presented, although they may be important to PRO administrators in terms of marketing and providing member services. The music catalogs themselves are often treated as 'financial' assets and a rich source of cash flow in terms of the income they generate from performance rights when the music is played on radio, television, and the Internet. The record labels may focus their investment dollars on a few already successful recording artists and on the successful non-performing songwriters who made such success possible. Novice but highly talented songwriters may not be a given an opportunity to break through simply because risk averse music executives may simply choose already successful writers with proven hit-making ability. The successful recording artist when paired with the successful songwriter may reinforce forcing each other's reputation and, thus, value to record labels and music publishers. A songwriter, composer, or music publisher with a large catalog of songs, including current and past hits, can have a significant advantage over rivals and new entrants when it comes to exploiting royalty income through economies of scale.

Notes

1. The ranking does not take into account publishing splits among songwriters for a given song, but divides credits equally among each listed songwriter.
2. See *Billboard* Magazine, November 15, 2008, pp. 29–32; Walker (2008, pp. 214–223) and Steinblatt (2006).
3. Walker (2008, pp. 214–223).
4. Walker (2008, p. 218).
5. See Steinblatt (2006). *Playback* magazine is a magazine for ASCAP members.
   Reaching the Billboard Charts is a measure of success in the music industry.
6. See Steinblatt (2006).
7. Walker (2008, p. 215).
8. *Source*: Article by Kimberly Lankford and Sean O'Neill entitled *Success With Your Money: 5 Millionaires Tell How They Did It* in the December 29, 2006 *Kiplinger* magazine's special issue and available online at http://www.kiplinger.com/features/archives/2006/12/millions.html.
9. See Chap. 5 and the following references: Azzalini (1985, 1986), Azzalini and Capitanio (2003), Azzalini et al. (2003), Dalla-Valle (2007), Azzalini and Genton (2008) for the theory development.
10. Walker (2008).

References

Azzalini, A. (1985). A class of distribution which includes the normal ones. *Scandinavian Journal of Statistics*, 12:171–178.

Azzalini, A. (1986). Further results on a class of distribution which includes the normal ones. *Statistica*, 46:199–208.

Azzalini, A. and Capitanio, A. (2003). Distributions generated by perturbation of symmetry with emphasis on a multivariate skew-*t* distribution. *Journal of the Royal Statistical Society*, B65:367–389.

Azzalini, A., DalCappello, T., and Kotz, S. (2003). Log-skew-normal and log-skew-*t* distributions as models for family income data. *Journal of Income Distribution*, 11(3–4):12–20.

Azzalini, A. and Genton, M. (2008). Robust likelihood methods based on the skew-*t* and related distributions. *International Statistical Review*, 76:106–129.

Dalla-Valle, A. (2007),). A test for the hypothesis of skew-normality in a population. *Journal of Statistical Computation and Simulation*, 77(1):63–77.

Galenson, D. (May 2000). The careers of modern artists. *Journal of Cultural Economics*, 24(2):87–112.

Galenson, D. (2003). The two life cycles of human creativity. *NBER Reporter*, Fall:12–15.

Galenson, D. (2005). Literary life cycles: Measuring the careers of modern american poets. *Historical Methods*, 38(2):45–60.

Ginsburgh, V. and Weyers, S. (2006). Creativity and life cycles of artists. *Journal of Cultural Economics*, 30:91–107.

Halvorsen, R. and Palmquist, R. (1980). The interpretation of dummy variables in semi-logarithmic equations. *The American Economic Review*, 70(4):474–475.

Kennedy, P. (1981). Estimation with correctly interpreted dummy variables in semilogarithmic equations. *The American Economic Review*, 71(4):801.

Pitt, I. (2010a). Superstar effects on royalty income in a performance rights organization. *Journal of Cultural Economics* (forthcoming).

Simonton, D. (1988). Age and outstanding achievement: What do we know after a century of research? *Psychological Bulletin*, 104:251–267.

Steinblatt, J. (2006). 'Wonder Woman:The Amazing, True Life Adventures of One Of America's Greatest Hitmakers'. *Playback* magazine. Fall, pp. 40–52.

Walker, J. (2008). *This Business of Urban Music: A Practical Guide to Achieving Success in the Industry, From Gospel to Funk to R&B to Hip-Hop.* Billboard Books.

Walls, W. (2005). Modeling heavy tails and skewness in film returns. *Applied Financial Economics*, 15:1181–1188.

Chapter 8
Economics of Radio Blanket License: Format, Region, and Market Size

Abstract In this chapter, we take a look at one of the sources of income for a PRO, the licensing fees paid by one set of music users, commercial radio stations. PROs deduct a percentage off the licensing fees collected to cover the administrative costs of music copyright licensing. The remaining amount is then distributed to songwriters, composers, and publishers as income from music performances. The income for PROs, songwriters, composers, and publishers are dependent on many factors affecting the radio blanket license fees paid by music users. It is, therefore, important to understand the determinants that drive the licensing fee income. An econometric model has been developed that looks at the fee structure involved in the radio blanket license, and explains the variation of the blanket fees in terms of radio format, station owners, region, market size, and recorded plays.

8.1 Introduction

The relationship between the radio industry and the music industry is one that has been described as turbulent for many years, particularly with the record labels demanding a new performance right for sound recordings on terrestrial radio. Dertouzos (2008) found that a significant portion of industry sales of albums and digital tracks can be attributed to radio airplay. Commercial radio station operators earn revenue by delivering millions of listening consumers, whether at home or on the road, to meet the marketing needs of advertisers. Stations, whose primary programming consist of music, use music to attract those listeners segmented by ratings companies like Arbitron and Neilsen BDS into various demographic factors such age, gender, ethnicity, education, income, market size, and region. On the other hand, the music industry is in the business of selling music to the general public in various formats such as the CD and digital downloads. In the past, radio exposure was a key success factor in selling music until the advent of music television such as MTV and the Internet. Table 8.1 provides the size of the radio station market in terms of advertising revenue for the period 2006–2010 with local radio being the largest contributor.

I.L. Pitt, *Economic Analysis of Music Copyright*,
DOI 10.1007/978-1-4419-6318-5_8, © Springer Science+Business Media, LLC 2010

Table 8.1 Selected Radio Revenues, 2006–2010E ($ mil.), January 2010 Forecast

Radio	2006	2007	2008	2009E	2010E
Network & Satellite Radio	1,178	1,226	1,220	1,098	1,119
Local Radio—National[a]	3,553	3,343	2,929	2,349	2,319
Local Radio—Local[a]	15,478	15,133	13,607	10,737	10,439
Total Radio	20,209	19,702	17,756	14,184	13,878
Y/Y Change	30	−507	−1,946	−3,572	−306
Y/Y % Change	0.15%	−2.51%	−9.88%	−20.12%	−2.16%

E = Estimated
[a]Excludes online advertising revenues
Source: B. Wieser, www.magnaglobal.com.

8.2 Radio Blanket License

The blanket and per-program licensing fees for terrestrial commercial are multi-year licenses that cover an extended licensing period. The RMLC, the radio industry lobby group, and the PROs negotiate either a flat fee blanket licensing agreement to cover all the commercial radio stations in the RMLC group or as in past years a fee based on the percentage of radio station revenue.

Once the licensing fee has been agreed to, there is a complex process of allocating the fee to individual stations within the industry. Radio stations can choose either a blanket license to cover music intensive use or a per-program license to cover stations that air talk, sports, and less music intensive programming. The per-program is still a blanket license meaning that once the per-program fee has been paid, stations can still use all of the licensed music in a PRO's repertoire in their selective programming schedules. Radio stations operating under a blanket or per-program license are divided into various groupings that take into consideration the top 100 metropolitan areas and ratings by Arbitron. In some cases, stations are allowed to change between a blanket and per-program licensing twice each year provided that appropriate notice is provided to the PRO.

Radio programming formats are always changing as stations switch from one programming format to another, depending on the station owner's pursuit of advertising revenue and other factors. License fee paid by the radio broadcasters to PROs in their licensing agreement would also cover stations wishing to simultaneously stream their terrestrial signal onto the Internet without a change in programming content. Licensing fees paid to ASCAP and BMI are made only for the underlying musical composition, the lyrics and musical notation, and not the sound recording. This is where the concept of intellectual property rights, in which a single song can have multiple copyrights attached to it, becomes rather confusing to the general public with so many licensing agencies collecting on different copyrights. This confusion has led to many disagreements and lawsuits between station owners and factions within the music industry.

Web-only radio stations, satellite radio stations such as Sirius-XM, and digital cable streaming certain content over the Internet must also obtain a digital audio performance license from SoundExchange, under the Digital Performance in Sound

Recordings Act and the Digital Millennium Copyright Act, which covers the digital audio portion of a sound recording. There is now pending legislation that if enacted would create a new performance right, the right for recording artists to collect royalty payments when their music is played on terrestrial broadcast stations.

Radio as a single entity account for the largest share of blanket licensing fees collected by ASCAP, almost as large as both broadcast television and cable combined. Table 8.2 shows the dollar amounts collected by ASCAP in performance licensing fees 2007 that are a fraction of the radio industry advertising revenue first shown in Table 8.1. Table 8.2 also shows that radio's share of ASCAP's blanket licensing fees amounted to 39.87 percent; cable's share reached 22.38 percent, television fees reached 18.33 percent and 'new media' (Internet fees) accounted for 1.44 percent of domestic receipts in 2007.

Table 8.2 ASCAP's Blanket and Per-Program Licensing Fees (Consolidated Income Statement)

Domestic receipts	YE 2007 ($)	%Share	%Cum.
License Fees			
Radio	238, 502	39.87	39.87
Cable	133, 859	22.38	62.25
Television	109, 669	18.33	80.58
General	97, 380	16.28	96.86
New Media	8, 606	1.44	98.29
Symphonic & Concert	5, 889	0.98	99.28
Interest & Other Income	3, 918	0.65	99.93
Membership Fees	395	0.07	100.00
Total Domestic Receipts	598, 218	69.25	
Royalties Foreign Societies	265, 625	30.75	
Total Receipts	863, 843		

Source: Based on data from   http://www.ascap.com/about/annualReport/annual_2007. pdf.

Table 8.2 also shows the domestic and foreign license fees collected by ASCAP in 2007. Domestic fees accounted for close to 69.25 percent of 2007 receipts, while foreign collections accounted for the remaining 30.75 percent. On the foreign collections side, ASCAP collected $265 million from foreign affiliates in Britain, Canada, Germany, Japan, and elsewhere for distribution to its members.

8.3 Survey of Radio Performances

As required by AFJ2 (2001), ASCAP conducts a *sample survey* of radio performances. The sample survey consists of hundreds of thousands of hours of non-dramatic radio performances or detected airplay data from a sample of commercial and college radio stations, National Public Radio, and satellite radio. Table 8.3 takes a selected look at some of the variables involved in a typical radio performance sample survey conducted by ASCAP and its partners that would also include the

Table 8.3 Selected ASCAP and Radio Performances Survey Variables

Variable	Measurement type
Station	Commercial, non-commercial, satellite
Radio band	AM vs. FM
License type	Blanket vs. per program
Region	West, midwest, south & northeast
Genre	Pop, Spanish language, sport/news/talk, urban contemporary, country, religious, jazz, classical and ethnic

times of the day, all days of the year, every region of the country, and all types and sizes of stations.

8.4 Model Specification and Data Description

The radio blanket fee paid by commercial radio station owners out of advertising revenue to performing rights organizations for the use of copyrighted songs in their repertory covers some of their administrative costs and is an important source of performance royalty income for many songwriters, composers, and music publishers. Licensing fees collected by ASCAP, BMI, and SESAC and later distributed as performance royalties are paid directly and separately to the songwriter, composer, and music publisher. Moreover, the performance right royalty income may be the only direct source of income for some performing songwriters long after their songs are no longer available at retail outlets. Music played on the radio can impact the demand for music sales at retail outlets.

A continuous random univariate variable X is said to have a skew-normal *(SN)* distribution[1] if it has the following density function:

$$f(x) = 2\phi(x)\Phi(\alpha x). \tag{8.1}$$

In other words, the random variable X is

$$X \sim SN(0, 1, \alpha). \tag{8.2}$$

Skew distributions augment the normal and student-t distributions by adding a shape or skewness parameter (α) in the skew-normal case. The component α in regulating the shape of the density function allows for a continuous variation from normality to non-normality. When $\alpha = 0$, the skew-normal simplifies to the standard normal distribution. For ease of computation, location (estimated regression coefficients or just the constant term) and scale (ω^2) parameters are also added to the above random variable X and its density function in Equation (8.1). The standard skew-t distribution can be generalized with location, scale, and a degree of freedom parameter (ν). The skew-t is appealing in that it extends the normal distribution by permitting tails that are heavy and asymmetric. The skew-normal and skew-t can be fitted using their log-transformed versions. These are referred to as the log-skew-normal and log-skew-t distributions.[2] This study relied on proprietary and licensed data from many sources including Mediaguide for commercial radio stations airplay data; and BIA Financial Network for market size and region data that appear in the Appendix. All non-commercial radio stations were excluded from this study. Individual radio stations and owners are not identified in this analysis, given the proprietary nature of the study. Under these circumstances certain results that are typically reported in academic studies will be excluded. The model is specified as follows:

$$
\begin{aligned}
Log\ (LFEE) = \ & \beta_0 + \beta_1(Frequency) + \beta_2(Genre) \\
& + \beta_3(License\ Type) + \beta_4(Station\ Owners) \\
& + \beta_5(Region_j) + \beta_6(Market\ Size_j) \\
& + \beta_7(Fee\ Category_j) + \beta_8(Plays\ Category_j) \\
& + \varepsilon_i
\end{aligned}
\tag{8.3}
$$

Frequency is an indicator variable for AM/FM Bands. Radio frequency = 1 if FM; otherwise 0 if AM. *Genre* is an indicator variable for radio format. Pop/Other = 1 if station genre = Pop music; otherwise 0 for all other formats. *License Type* is an indicator variable for type of license. Blanket/Per Program = 1 if license fee = Blanket; otherwise 0 if Per Program. *Station Owners Category* is an indicator variable for number of stations owned by a single entity. Owner50 = 1 if station owners held more than 50 stations; otherwise 0. *Regions Category* is an indicator variable for US regions. Midwest = 1 for midwest region, with the other regions being northeast, south, and west. *Market Size* is an indicator variable for Arbitron's Market Size Groupings: large market (rank 1–25) = 1, otherwise 0; medium market (rank 26–125) = 1, otherwise 0; and small market (rank 126+) = 1, otherwise 0. *Fee Category* is an indicator variable for low, medium, and high licensing fee categories. Fee Cat.1 = 1 if licensing fees paid were low; otherwise 0. Fee Cat. 2 = 1 if licensing fees were medium; otherwise 0, and so on. *Plays Category* is an indicator variable for the number of low, medium, and high performances. Plays1 = 1 if the number of airplays/performances recorded in a sample survey were low; otherwise 0, and so on. ε_i = random disturbance term that follows a log-normal, log-skew-normal, or log-skew-t distribution depending on the model being estimated.

In each model, the dependent variable (LFEE)—radio blanket licensing fees paid by commercial radio stations to a PRO—is fitted on a conditional vector of the radio survey attributes. The distribution of radio licensing fees is quantified conditional on frequency, radio format or genre, license type, number of stations owners, region, market size, and fee and airplay categories. In the radio format or genre category, we reduced various radio programming formats to Pop format and Other to reflect how music genres continue to mix and evolve into different sounds and perspectives. Pop here refers to a subset of popular music played on radio stations and can include stations that offer a mix of mostly Top 40 type music. 'Other' radio format would include stations that focused on country, jazz, urban contemporary, religious, Spanish language programming, or other types of programming.

For the purposes of this study, we grouped station ownership into a category of station owners with more than 50 stations in the data and those with fewer than 50 stations. Region data included commercial radio stations in the midwest, south, northeast, and western regions of the United States. Market size is based on Arbitron's ranking of 1–25 for large market size, rank 25–125 for medium market size, and rank 126–302 for small markets. The Appendix provides a breakdown of the regions and market size used in compiling the dataset.[3] Fee and Plays categories are selected licensing fee and airplay groupings.

8.5 Estimation Results

Our regression results are shown in Tables 8.4, 8.5, and 8.6. We present Table 8.4 to illustrate the model under Ordinary Least Squares assumptions.

Table 8.6 computes the dummy elasticities for the semi-logarithmic form of the chosen model. All of the skew associated parameters—α (*Skewness*)$= -1.3551$, $t-stat = -6.9041$, and the ν (*Tail Weight*)$= 5.1636 (t - stat = 8.1298)$—are statistically significant at the 5 percent level and the log-skew-t Model III is chosen as

Table 8.4 Log-Normal Model I Estimates

Variable	Coefficient	Std. Error	t-stat
Constant	10.0460	0.1004	100.0810
Frequency			
AM/FM Band	0.4503	0.0652	6.9051
Genre			
Pop/Other	0.0559	0.0314	1.7820
License Type			
Blanket/Per Program	0.4821	0.0662	7.2781
Stations Owners			
Owner50	0.2515	0.0320	7.8655
Region			
Midwest	−0.0662	0.0463	−1.4301
Northeast	−0.1063	0.0458	−2.3227
West	−0.0869	0.0473	−1.8379
Market Size			
Large	0.9203	0.0526	17.5113
Medium	0.2329	0.0434	5.3676
Fee Bands			
Fee Cat. 1	−2.7327	0.0447	−61.1942
Fee Cat. 2	−1.2222	0.0395	−30.9809
Airplays			
Plays1	−0.1227	0.0380	−3.2269
Plays2	−0.0162	0.0387	−0.4183
R^2	0.82		
Log likelihood	−1956		
Observations	1,968		

Table 8.5 Log-Skew-Normal Model II and Log-Skew-t Model III Estimates

Variable	Log-skew-normal Model II			Log-Skew-t Model III		
	Coeff. Est.	Std. Error	t-stat	Coeff. Est.	Std. Error	t-stat
Constant	10.8715	0.1105	98.3949	10.6602	0.1022	104.3300
Frequency						
AM/FM Band	0.4118	0.0726	5.6740	0.4384	0.0623	7.0324
Genre						
Pop/Other	0.0433	0.0288	1.5059	0.0507	0.0265	1.9103
License Type						
Blanket/Per Program	0.4553	0.0712	6.3920	0.4269	0.0618	6.9125
Stations Owners						
Owner50	0.2135	0.0287	7.4309	0.2017	0.0272	7.4152
Region						
Midwest	−0.1377	0.0452	−3.0446	−0.1317	0.0397	−3.3141
Northeast	−0.1662	0.0451	−3.6881	−0.1428	0.0395	−3.6167
West	−0.1143	0.0500	−2.2854	−0.1335	0.0411	−3.2454
Market Size						
Large	0.9708	0.0532	18.2414	0.9276	0.0478	19.4254
Medium	0.1792	0.0365	4.9100	0.1433	0.0358	4.0071
Fee Bands						
Fee Cat. 1	−2.5978	0.0409	−63.4701	−2.4687	0.0408	−60.4858
Fee Cat. 2	−1.3203	0.0342	−38.6544	−1.2763	0.0351	−36.3739
Airplays						
Plays1	−0.1063	0.0341	−3.1153	−0.0967	0.0315	−3.0662
Plays2	−0.0077	0.0345	−0.2230	−0.0072	0.0319	−0.2268
α (Skewness)	−2.3658	0.2271	−10.4173	−1.3551	0.1963	−6.9041
ω^2 (Scale)	0.9603	0.0326	29.4248	0.6529	0.0365	17.8849
ν DF (Tail Weight)DF				5.1636	0.6351	8.1298
Log Likelihood	−22247			−22198		
Observations	1,968			1,968		

the preferred specification. The coefficient on radio frequency (AM/FM = 0.4384, t-stat = 7.0324) is significant in the log-skew-t Model III. This is to be expected given the ratio of FM stations to AM stations in many metropolitan areas, more FM stations would incur higher licensing fees, particularly the music intensive stations with a blanket license.

In August of 2009, there were a total of 14,923 (10,750 commercial and 4,173 non-commercial) radio stations on the air in the United States with 31 different segments and sub-segment formats. Of the total number of radio stations on the air, 9,431 stations or 63.20 percent were FM band.[4] The genre coefficient (Pop/Other = 0.0507, t-stat = 1.9103) is also very close to being significant at 0.05 level. More music intensive radio stations catering to pop music and its various sub-segments in larger urban metro areas could have higher licensing fees than other stations with different programming formats in rural areas.

Table 8.6 Model III Dummy Variables Elasticities

Variable	Estimate	Error	t-stat	g^*
Frequency				
Band	0.4384	0.0623	7.0324	0.4082
Genre				
Pop/Other	0.0507	0.0265	1.9103	0.0506
License Type				
Blanket/Per Program	0.4269	0.0618	6.9125	0.3990
Stations Owners				
Owner50	0.2017	0.0272	7.4152	0.1989
Region				
Midwest	−0.1317	0.0397	−3.3141	−0.1310
Northeast	−0.1428	0.0395	−3.6167	−0.1419
West	−0.1335	0.0411	−3.2454	−0.1327
Market Size				
Large	0.9276	0.0478	19.4254	0.6444
Medium	0.1433	0.0358	4.0071	0.1423
Fee Bands				
Fee Cat. 1	−2.4687	0.0408	−60.4858	−0.9960
Fee Cat. 2	−1.2763	0.0351	−36.3739	−0.8764
Airplays				
Plays1	−0.0967	0.0315	−3.0662	−0.0964
Plays2	−0.0072	0.0319	−0.2268	−0.0072

In a recent Recording Industry Association of America (RIAA) survey on the popularity of various music genres shown in Table 8.7, Oldies, Religious, Other Country and Children are the genres to show year over increases in popularity. Although Rock, Country, Rap/Hip-hop, and R&B/Urban led the chart in terms of popularity, Country is the only genre to show a year-over-year increase by 3.48 percent in popularity, among the top five genre by consumer preference. Meanwhile, R&B/Urban (−13.56 percent), Classical (−17.39 percent) and Jazz (−57.69 percent) showed some of the biggest year-over-year declines. Genre can be viewed as being representative of listener choices and stations strive to increase their listenership in order to increase ratings and therefore advertising revenue.

In an interesting correlation of album sales and genre popularity, among the top selling genre, *Billboard* magazine reports that 'the biggest recent market shares losers have been R&B (which includes Rap), Country, and Latin. R&B peaked in 2000 with sales of 199.7 million units or 25 percent of the US album market, but has since tumbled to 77 millions units or 18 percent of sales. Since 2001, the genre [R&B] has underperformed in the overall market except for 2004. Annual sales of country music outperformed the overall US album market in 2004–2006, but have since exceeded the annual decline in total sales, falling 16.3 percent in 2007 and 24 percent in 2008. Latin sales amounted to 25.1 million units in 2008, a 21.1 percent decline over 2007.'[5] The choice of radio genre is important because a genre that performs exceptionally well as measured by one of the ratings services is the one that is likely to attract advertising dollars.

Table 8.7 RIAA Consumer Music Preferences (Year-Over-Year Change)

Genre	2007 (%)	2008 (%)	Change %	Change
Rock	32.4	31.8	−0.6	−1.85
Rap/Hip-hop[1]	10.8	10.7	−0.1	−0.93
R&B/Urban[2]	11.8	10.2	−1.6	−13.56
Country	11.5	11.9	0.4	3.48
Pop	10.7	9.1	−1.6	−14.95
Religious[3]	3.9	6.5	2.6	66.67
Classical	2.3	1.9	−0.4	−17.39
Jazz	2.6	1.1	−1.5	−57.69
Soundtracks	0.8	0.8	0	0.00
Oldies	0.4	0.7	0.3	75.00
New	0.3	0.3	0	0.00
Children's	2.9	3	0.1	3.45
Other[4]	7.1	9.1	2	28.17

[1] 'Rap': includes Rap and Hip-Hop.
[2] 'R&B': includes R&B, Blues, Dance, Disco, Funk, Fusion, Motown, Reggae, Soul.
[3] 'Religious': includes Christian, Gospel, Inspirational, Religious, and Spiritual.
[4] 'Other': includes Big Band, Broadway Shows, Comedy, Contemporary, Electronic,
EMO, Ethnic, Exercise, Folk, Gothic, Grunge, Holiday Music, House Music,
Humor, Instrumental, Language, Latin, Love Songs, Mix, Mellow, Modern,
Ska, Spoken word, Standards, Swing, Top-40, and Trip-Hop.
Source: www.riaa.com.

The license type coefficient (Blanket/Per Program = 0.4269, t-stat = 6.9125) is significant. Stations with blanket licenses are usually more music intensive than 'per-program' stations featuring talk, sports, and news programming with limited use of music. The station owners coefficient (Owner50 = 0.2017, t-stat = 7.4152) is significant. The distribution of the radio blanket license fee is highly skewed when the licensing fee paid is aggregated up by station owner. For example, at the time of this writing and according to licensed data from www.bia.com, Clear Channel owned approximately 1,196 stations (or 35.24 percent) with various programming formats some of which are music intensive, and was the largest station group owner at the time. Other large station owners included Cumulus Broadcasting, CBS radio, and Citadel Communications as shown in Table 8.8.

All of the region category variables (midwest, northeast, and west) are significant when compared to the (omitted and relative) southern region category. These regions are lower in terms of radio licensing fees relative to the south with its popularity of country music which is centered in Nashville, Tennessee. The market size categorical variables in terms of large and medium size metro areas are also significant. The large- and medium-size markets are paying more in licensing fees in comparison to smaller-sized markets as one would expect.

Stations in larger markets with a bigger reach attract more listeners and therefore more advertisers and advertising revenue when ratings are factored in. Many of the stations that operate under a blanket license in the midwest, northeast, south and west and broken down into small, medium and large marketing areas that are ranked by Arbitron using measures such as Cume, Time Spent Listening (TSL), and Average Quarter-Hour Persons (AQH) ratings.[6] Cume is short for cumulative

Table 8.8 Top 25 Radio Station Owners (Ranked by Stations Owned)

Station Owner	AM Stat.	HD/F2 Stat.	HD/F3 Stat.	FM Stat.	Total Stat.	% Share
Clear Channel	248	345	2	601	1, 196	35.24
Cumulus B'cast & Media	93	13	0	246	352	10.37
CBS Radio	34	75	11	102	222	6.54
Citadel Comm.	54	–	–	151	205	6.04
Entercom	33	61	–	79	173	5.10
Gap I & Gap II	32	0	0	84	116	3.42
Cox Radio Inc	15	19	1	70	105	3.09
Saga Comm.	30	4	1	61	96	2.83
Salem Comm.	66	–	–	27	93	2.74
Univision	15	15	1	57	88	2.59
Cherry Creek Radio	23	–	–	45	68	2.00
Regent Comm.	13	2	–	49	64	1.89
Beasley Broadcast Group	17	13	2	26	58	1.71
Three Eagles Comm.	18	–	–	36	54	1.59
Radio One Inc	11	1	–	41	53	1.56
Entravision Comm.	11	4	–	36	51	1.50
Aloha Station Trust LLC	8	11	–	30	49	1.44
Bicoastal Media LLC	19	–	–	30	49	1.44
ABC/Disney	44	1	–	3	48	1.41
Bonneville Intl. Corp	7	18	–	21	46	1.36
Nassau B'cast I LLC	15	–	–	29	44	1.30
Midwest Comm.	16	–	–	27	43	1.27
MultiCultural Radio	40	–	–	1	41	1.21
Mapleton Comm.	11	–	–	30	41	1.21
Emmis Comm.	2	16	–	21	39	1.15
Total	875	598	18	1, 903	3, 394	100

Source: Based on licensed data from www.bia.com, August 13, 2009.

audience or the number of different persons listening to a radio station for at least 5 minutes during any time period. TSL is an estimate of the number of quarter-hours the average person spends listening during a specified hour. AGH is defined as the average number of persons listening to a particular station for at least 5 minutes during a 15-minute period.

The Fee Band categorical variables are all significant (Fee Cat. 1 $= -2.4687$, t-stat $= -60.4858$, and Fee Cat. 2 $= -1.2763$, t-stat $= -36.3739$) and lower than the omitted category of larger licensing fees paid. In cases where music intensive stations are paying licensing fees based on a percentage of revenue, you would expect to find the larger reach in terms of radio listeners and ranking by Arbitron, the more in licensing fees paid. The number of radio performances (airplay) Plays1 category is significant when compared to the omitted category and we do not break out the number of radio performances by genre.

8.6 Airplay Analysis

Radio airplay is one of the ways new songs, new songwriters, and composers are exposed to listening audiences in various regions and markets. The pace at which a song crosses over from one genre (a crossover hit) to the next and in the process increase record sales can be influenced by many factors such as the number of plays on a radio station; the number of Top 40 stations in a particular market; the relationship between a record label and a radio station; the competition for newly released music by radio stations; and the number of listeners segmented by age, ethnicity, and other factors in each market. For example, Table 8.9 shows a selected sample of the detected radio airplay of just one title, *Day 'N' Nite*, by the songwriter and recording artist named 'Kid Cudi.' Mediaguide first detected the song using its software on April 3, 2008 and recorded 175,473 performances of the song at time the data was retrieved.

Table 8.9 Example of Selected Mediaguide Detected Airplay Report (Period 08/11/09 to 08/17/09 US Only)

	Song Title: *Day 'N' Nite* First Detected: 04/03/08				Recording Artist: 'Kid Cudi' Plays-to-Date: 175,473		
State	Stations	AM	MID	PM	EVE	OVN	TP Plays
AL	6	3	8	2	12	6	31
AR	3	0	0	2	0	0	2
AZ	8	24	32	27	41	52	176
CA	36	65	92	71	84	112	424
CO	7	21	31	24	24	39	139
DC	4	1	6	6	4	6	23
FL	17	21	48	40	42	67	218
GA	4	14	19	16	13	19	81
IA	2	0	0	0	1	0	1
IA/IL	1	0	0	1	0	0	1
ID	3	8	10	8	15	8	49
IL	10	9	12	13	15	12	61
IN	5	7	10	5	9	17	48
KS	1	0	0	0	0	0	0
KY	1	6	9	4	5	6	30
LA	5	18	22	18	27	28	113
MA	12	8	10	9	6	11	44
MD	3	0	0	1	0	0	1
MI	1	0	6	9	13	7	35
MN	8	4	5	2	6	6	23
MO	4	2	2	2	3	3	12
MO-KS	4	3	8	7	5	7	30
MS	2	0	0	0	1	0	1
NC	3	10	20	13	19	22	84
NC/SC	9	1	16	9	9	16	51
NE/IA	3	1	0	4	2	0	7
NJ	2	0	3	1	1	4	9
NM	3	8	14	10	12	16	60
NV	4	8	12	7	15	15	57
NY	14	6	11	11	17	17	62
OH	13	1	7	4	12	6	30
OK	9	0	12	9	9	15	45
OR	5	3	11	8	10	9	41
PA	4	12	16	19	29	26	102

Table 8.9 (continued)

State	Stations	AM	MID	PM	EVE	OVN	TP Plays
RI	10	3	9	5	4	10	31
SC	2	6	4	5	2	10	27
TN	5	9	14	15	20	17	75
TN/VA	9	0	0	0	1	0	1
TX	1	17	30	31	33	43	154
UT	29	18	23	18	19	24	102
VA	5	2	9	3	10	8	32
WA	11	7	20	8	28	22	85
WI	1	8	11	10	25	13	67
PR	1	0	0	2	0	6	8
Total	290	334	572	459	603	705	2,673
Share		12.50%	21.40%	17.17%	22.56%	26.37%	100.00%

AM=Morning, MID=Midday, PM=Afternoon, EVE=Evening,
OVN=Overnight and TP=Total Plays for the week.
Source: Based on licensed data from Mediaguide, Inc., © 2009.

Table 8.10 Example of Radio Formats in Detected Airplay Report (Period 08/11/09 to 08/17/09 US Only)

Dominant format	Freq.	Percent	Cum.%
CHR/Pop	100	34.48	34.48
R&B/Hip-Hop	64	22.07	56.55
CHR/Rhythmic	57	19.66	76.21
College Variety	9	3.10	79.31
Regional Mexican	9	3.10	82.41
Hot AC	7	2.41	84.83
Spanish CHR/Rhythmic	7	2.41	87.24
Spanish Pop	7	2.41	89.66
AC Misc	5	1.72	91.38
Pop (NC)	4	1.38	92.76
Urban AC	4	1.38	94.14
Dance	3	1.03	95.17
Latin Misc	2	0.69	95.86
Tropical	2	0.69	96.55
AC	1	0.34	96.90
Active Rock	1	0.34	97.24
Alternative	1	0.34	97.59
Classical	1	0.34	97.93
Jazz	1	0.34	98.28
Mainstream Rock	1	0.34	98.62
News/Talk	1	0.34	98.97
Sports	1	0.34	99.31
Triple A (C)	1	0.34	99.66
Triple A (NC)	1	0.34	100
Total	290	100	

Radio format for the data in Table 8.9
Source: Based on licensed data from Mediaguide, Inc. © 2009.

The song itself was number 5 on Billboard's chart of the Top 20 Publishing Songs; and Scott Ramon 'Kid Cudi' Seguro Mescudi, the full name cited by *Billboard* magazine for the artist, was also named the number 7 songwriter for the week of August 15, 2009.[7] For the week of 08/11/09 to 08/17/09, Mediaguide detected 2,673 radio performances of the hit title on 290 radio stations in various regions in the United States, each station, presumably, paying for a blanket or per-program licensing fee for the use of the copyrighted composition. Most of the detected performances occurred in the midday, evening, and overnight hours.

Table 8.10 is a frequency distribution for the Mediaguide airplay data in Table 8.9. The song was detected on 290 radio stations and a cumulative 56.55 percent of those stations were either a Pop or a Hip-Hop station, representing a skew toward a younger demographic in terms of age of radio listeners. It is worth noting that the song cuts across many genres and the singer/songwriter has what is called 'crossover appeal.' The crossover appeal and popularity of this particular songwriter increased as the many music outlets in which his music composition was played. The number of radio rations in various regions and markets, the crossover appeal across genres creating a hit song, and the number of airplays are all factors that help to explain the skewness in songwriter/composer income.

8.7 Conclusion

The radio format is important as it represents the programming choices of station managers whose analyses of marketing trends, target audiences, advertisers demand, and other demographic factors play a role in playlist composition. The songwriter will continue to receive performance rights royalty payments long after a song stopped selling in retail stores. Of course, not every song in the repertory of a PRO—and covered under a blanket license—gets the same amount of airplay each year and there are many factors why this is the case. Commercial radio relies on a strong selection of hit songs, including the many sub-segments of Top-40 music, in order to attract the listening audience, particularly those in the 18–34 age category that advertisers find appealing. Certain songs will have a long or short shelf-life on radio depending on the radio station format, consumer preferences, and advertisers needs, and this can affect the songwriter's income from performance royalty income.

Mediaguide airplay data showed the many genres or radio formats a single song could encompass making such a diverse mix of programming and station branding quite challenging for radio programmers. Whether an artist's crossover appeal is a planned marketing strategy or it is spontaneous, a song with a wide demographic appeal, a target audience and advertising interest is often played on radio. Market size, airplay, genre, region, and frequency are some of the key determinants of music performances for the songwriter and composer. These factors play a role in licensing fees collected by PROs and they can have an impact on the income of the songwriter, composer and music publisher, and the PRO administering the performance copyrights.

There is also another added difficulty for the novice songwriter on how to write songs, and the music publisher on how to market songs to different and unique core audiences across a broad demographic spectrum. This analysis was limited in scope to commercial radio stations and did not take into consideration playlists by individuals radio stations, whether the type of song in the playlist data was a new song or old hit, airtime of songs, and the number of radio performances by record label. All these factors would be useful in further explaining the skewness in songwriters' income.

A further study of music performances by record label would be beneficial to analyze the consolidation in radio station ownership following the 1996 Telecommunications Act, and to test whether the major labels have an advantage over independent labels in terms of getting their songs and recordings artists played on the commercial radio. College and non-commercial radio may be one of the outlets where new music from unknown songwriters can often be heard because there are fewer advertising related concerns and risk-averse programming practices.

Notes

1. See Chapter 5 and the following references: Azzalini (1985, 1986), Azzalini and Capitanio (2003), Azzalini et al. (2003), Dalla-Valle (2007), Azzalini and Genton (2008) for the theory development.
2. Walls (2005).
3. Many thanks to Mike Riley for compiling the data for us.
4. See http://ftp.media.radcity.net/ZMST/insideradio/TOTALFormats.html.
5. *Billboard* magazine, January 17, 2009, p. 24.
6. See http://www.arbitron.com/radio_stations/tradeterms.htm.
7. *Billboard* magazine, August 15, 2009, pp. 18–19.

References

AFJ2 (2001). Second Amended Final Judgment, USA vs ASCAP, Civil Action No. 41 – 1395. United States District Court, S.D.N.Y. (White Plains), pp. 1–19.

Azzalini, A. (1985). A class of distribution which includes the normal ones. *Scandinavian Journal of Statistics*, 12:171–178.

Azzalini, A. (1986). Further results on a class of distribution which includes the normal ones. *Statistica*, 46:199–208.

Azzalini, A. and Capitanio, A. (2003). Distributions generated by perturbation of symmetry with emphasis on a multivariate skew-*t* distribution. *Journal of the Royal Statistical Society*, B65:367–389.

Azzalini, A., DalCappello, T., and Kotz, S. (2003). Log-skew-normal and log-skew-t distributions as models for family income data. *Journal of Income Distribution*, 11(3–4):12–20.

Azzalini, A. and Genton, M. (2008). Robust likelihood methods based on the skew-*t* and related distributions. *International Statistical Review*, 76:106–129.

Dalla-Valle, A. (2007). A test for the hypothesis of skew-normality in a population. *Journal of Statistical Computation and Simulation*, 77(1):63–77.

Dertouzos, J. (2008). *Radio Airplay and the Record Industry: An Economic Analysis*. National Association of Broadcasters. Unpublished.

Walls, W. (2005). Modeling heavy tails and skewness in film returns. *Applied Financial Economics*, 15:1181–1188.

Chapter 9
Concluding Remarks

Abstract This monograph integrated applied economic and statistical theory into a framework for the study of income in a performing rights organization. We test the empirical assumptions of Anderson (2008) and his Long Tail theory in an application of music performance copyright. The hope behind this study is that it would continue to broaden the scope in the study of cultural economics along the lines of Ginsburg and Throsby (2006). Putting aside all of the legal, regulatory, and contestable markets' case studies that have been done on PROs in general, there has been few, if any, empirical studies of PRO members in economic literature. This study, among others, is the first step in bridging that empirical gap. This study is limited in scope, for obvious reasons and due in part to the proprietary nature of the data involved when it comes to royalty income and licensing fees in contractual agreements. We did not address all of the questions when it comes to the many issues involved in music copyright because of data limitations, time constraints, and other factors. We will, however, define some of the unanswered questions in the following sections that may worth further economic and policy analyses.

9.1 Music Users: Radio, Television, and Internet

Music is being consumed by more people in many new ways as the Internet and devices, such as the iPod that made music even more portable, have changed the listening habits of consumers. The widespread use of digital technology in the music industry has dramatically changed the landscape for radio and television broadcasters, Internet sites, publishers, record labels, songwriters, composers, authors, music producers, performing rights agencies, and performing/non-performing songwriters alike.

Passage of the Telecommunications Act of 1996 has had a dramatic effect on the radio industry as deregulation led to relaxed ownership rules. Several companies acquired a large number of radio stations through mergers and acquisitions. More importantly, the consolidation meant that the station group owners in order to increase economies of scale and scope use the same programming choices across different stations in different markets, promoting the same (and small number) of popular singer/recording artists. This type of consolidation could also produce a scarcity in music by limiting the number of new, unknown, or independent artists that appear on radio.

Initially, the radio stations' market-by-market differentiation created a huge opportunity for advertisers to connect with various listening segments in local markets favored by those advertisers. Just as competition for listeners from iPods, satellite radio, and the Internet intensified, advertising growth diminished aided in the part by the on-going recession in 2009. This led many radio stations to cut programming and labor costs by replacing local programming with syndicated and pre-recorded programming from other markets.

From a new or novice songwriter and radio listeners' perspective, in general, with more radio time slots allocated to syndicated programming, it is probably a safe bet to assume that some radio programmers would play it safe, avoid the use of some unknown artists, and use only familiar chart toppers and old hits with more of a mass market type of appeal in local markets.

As major advertisers such as auto, real estate, and finance firms abandoned or reduced their print, radio and television advertising, radio station revenue fell dramatically as was shown in Table 2.7. In addition, merger and acquisition costs left many radio station owners saddled with an enormous debt burden in which some of these stations were on the brink of bankruptcy in 2009, unable to service their massive debt. In the event of a large number of radio stations filing for bankruptcy, the industry could face a new round of mergers, restructuring, asset sales, and further consolidation in already fragmented market. These changes can have an impact on the income of songwriters, composers, and music publishers. One policy question worth investigating is given the high debt/leverage in the radio industry, what has been or will be is the economic impact of a large number of radio stations concentrated in the hands of just a few station-owners in terms of new and independent songwriters getting airplay, competition in the industry, and effects of refinancing their debt on operation costs.

9.2 Music Creators: Composers, Songwriters, and Music Publishers

One of the debates in the music industry has been whether performing artists should focus more on the economic aspects of creating a hit song or on the artistic qualities of music. Our analysis showed the importance of hit songs, particularly how they are used in radio programming decision making. Today's songwriter and composer must master not only basics of music composition, but also many other aspects of the business side of music such as the technical aspects of sound recording and the four P's of marketing—product, pricing, promotion, and placement. Songwriter and composers are the creative engines that drive the music industry. Songwriters, composers, and music publishers all depend on the sound recording for a fraction of their income. Songwriters and composers play a vital role to many recording artists who do not write or compose their own music, and who otherwise would not have a career without them. On the other hand, non-performing songwriters depend on the recording artists to bring their works to life and benefit when their music is broadcast and performance rights income is earned.

The world of songwriting is dynamic with changing consumers' tastes and preferences happening practically overnight; and new business models being introduced with increasing frequency. The fragmentation and segmentation of the music industry can make it impossible sometimes for some new artists to get airplay on some large radio stations. For most songwriters, their income from performance rights royalty income depends on the amount of their music played on radio, television, the Internet, and other places. Just as cassette tapes replaced vinyl records because they were more portable, CDs replaced tapes because they had a better sound quality and digital recordings diminished CD sales, the innovation in digital technology has fueled a new cycle in competing business models of many music publishers. The music publisher and the performing songwriter dependent on income generated by mechanical and performance rights royalties have been hard hit by music listeners' ability to download their favorite music from websites on the Internet.

The Internet with its audio-visual capabilities makes it easier for music listeners to find the right image, sound, personal taste they are looking for, and identify with a band's message long before they appear on radio, television, in a live local concert or a physical CD is made available at a local retailer. In July of 2009 according to *Billboard* magazine, the top four music publishers, Universal (31.46 percent), Sony (25.51 percent), Warner (20.91 percent), and EMI (8.6 percent) had the largest market share in terms of total album sales, while independent labels made up the remaining 13.5 percent.[1]

Many other changes in the music industry include performing artists and songwriters having more licensing/copyright control, retail distribution of their own songs by bypassing the traditional record labels. Consumers now having the ability to download their favorite songs from the Internet have also impacted income from royalties. Some people consider the downloading of unlicensed music from the Internet as piracy or theft of intellectual property.

One of the biggest changes in the music industry has been rise of the independent artist, and the independent record label that competes with the major record labels and music publishers in terms of funding the creation, distribution, and marketing of sound recordings. Some successful artists are now able to make more money (on their own or with an independent record label) by touring, merchandising T-shirts, and direct sales of CDs to specific fans in growing niche markets. Artists can also sell downloads of their songs directly to their fans from their own websites. MySpace, youTube, Facebook, Hulu, and other Internet sites are some of the new platforms for the easy, legal, and reliable access to music content.

Table 9.1 from NARM using Nielsen's SoundScan data shows that in 2008, roughly 105,575 (an increase of 25,880) new albums were released in both physical and digital formats by the major and independent labels. Table 9.2 shows the major record labels released 81.88 percent of all new albums in 2008. In addition, new releases distributed by independent labels had been consistent around the 37 million new release album sales until 2008, when that number dropped to 27 million.[2]

Table 9.1 New Album Releases, 2007–2008

Releases	2007	2008	Change	% Change
Physical	54,536	56,205	1, 669	3.06
Share%	68.43	53.24		
Digital	25,159	49,370	24, 211	96.23
Share%	31.57	46.76		
Total	79,695	105,575	25, 880	32.47

Source: Based on data from http://www.narm.com/2009Conv/Nielsen09Presentation.pdf, citing Nielsen's SoundScan State of the Industry Data 2008.

Table 9.2 New Release Album Sales by Label, 2008

Label	Sales	% Share
Major	122, 000, 000	81.88
Independent	27, 000, 000	18.12
Total New Release	149, 000, 000	

Source: Based on data from http://www.narm.com/2009Conv/ Nielsen09Presentation.pdf citing Nielsen's SoundScan State of the Industry Data 2008.

According to Nielsen SoundScan of those new releases that sold more than 25,000 copies or more, 950 albums accounted for 153 million sales or 82 percent of all new release sales.

Furthermore, of the new albums released in 2008, five albums totaling 10.6 million in sales accounted for 2.48 percent of all album sales. As shown in Table 9.3 the album by artist, 'Lil Wayne' led the group with 2,874,000 in album sales or a 27.09 percent share. Even with all the changes in the music industry we can see marked skewness in new releases of albums, recordings artists, and records labels, and the major hurdle that independent labels and songwriters need to overcome in getting their music played on commercial radio stations.

Table 9.3 Top New Album Releases by Artist, 2008

Album	Sales	% Share
Lil Wayne	2, 874, 000	27.09
Coldplay	2, 144, 400	20.21
Taylor Swift	2, 112, 000	19.90
AC/DC	1, 915, 000	18.05
Metallica	1, 565, 000	14.75
Total New Releases	10, 610, 400	100.00
Total Album Sales	428, 000, 000	

Source: Based on data from http://www.narm.com/2009Conv/ Nielsen09Presentation.pdf, citing Nielsen's SoundScan State of the Industry Data 2008.

In a study released in April 2009 and conducted by Thomson (2009) that calculated the 'airplay share' for five different categories of record labels to determine whether the ratio of major label to non-major label airplay has changed over the past 4 years, the author found 'no change or little measurable change in airplay share from 2005 to 2008, with major label songs consistently securing 78 to 82 percent of airplay. There was a slight increase in airplay for 'indies' on a few formats (Country and Non-Commercial, in particular) but otherwise the data from year to year stayed pretty much the same.'[3] Thomson findings are consistent with the new album release data from Nielsen SoundScan as shown in Table 9.2 in that album sales depend on the strength of new releases from major record companies.

However, according to *Billboard* magazine, it is not unusual to find some leading players in independent digital music joining forces and forming marketing and services partnerships with major labels such as Universal and Sony, the very companies they were created to oppose.[4] Even with the release of new albums, there has been cut backs at the labels, due to the heavy debt burden, from the recent mergers and acquisition which can impact the record label's investment and marketing decisions on unknown, new, or emerging songwriters, and therefore songwriters' and composers' income. Strobl and Tucker (2000) found that, at least in the UK, 'one of the most important factors in guaranteeing chart survival is initial popularity. Apart from the reputation and popularity of the artist, audience exposure and substantial promotional campaigns are likely to play key role in the result, and it is, of course, those albums signed under the label of the more powerful record companies that are likely to be relatively more promoted.'

9.3   Performance and Mechanical Royalty Income

As the sale of CDs, cassette tapes, and other physical formats have plummeted in recent years, artists and publishers looked to public performance and synchronization income to offset the income from sliding CD sales. Performing rights organizations such as ASCAP, BMI, SESAC, and SoundExchange soon took on an added dimension in the music industry as publishers and record labels turned to multiple performance and sound recording rights in musical works to counter the decline in CD revenue. It remains to be seen exactly how mechanical rights agencies will be impacted financially (at least initially) by the continued slide in the sales of CDs due in part to digital downloads and the closing of retail outlets further limiting shelf-space devoted to music sales.

The *Wall Street Journal* reports that the Borders bookstore chain is now converting the shelf space that previously sold music and DVDs, whose popularity has faded with bookstore shoppers, into stocking books aimed at the teenage book-buying segment, further decreasing the availability of music at retail outlets.[5] According to *Billboard* magazine, one the most striking trends during the last 5 years has been the rise of non-traditional music chains such as Amazon.com, QVC, and TV direct-phone sales at the expense of traditional mass marketers such as Wal-Mart and Target, music chains such as Best Buy and Borders and local independent retailers. The combined non-traditional category now accounts for 23.5 percent of album sales, up from just 5 percent in 2004.[6]

9.4 Bypassing the PRO: Impact of Direct or Source Licensing

With the fear of legal ramifications from attempting to influence market forces and
other anti-trust matters, some performing and mechanical rights organizations are
reluctant to discuss the issue of direct or source licensing. These organizations
could, however, be impacted by the case in which some music users and publishers
are seeking to negotiate what is called 'source licensing' or direct licensing, as an
alternative to the blanket licenses issued by copyright licensing agencies. As CD
sales continue to plunge and digital sales have failed to fully offset CD sales, music
publishers and music users are looking for ways to increase revenue through direct
or source licensing. Direct or source licensing means that some music users, for
example broadcasters on a per-program license, could go directly to the source, in
this case the music publisher, who is the copyright holder of a song, and negotiate a blanket performance licensing fee for the works in their catalogs, bypassing
intermediary performing rights organization such as ASCAP and BMI.[7]

In the case of mechanical rights organizations, music publishers are seeking
direct payment of digital mechanical royalties from music users and retailers in a
cost-saving effort. For example, music publishers are seeking the right to be paid
directly by iTunes, the biggest online music retailer. The idea behind source licensing is that the publishers will save money on the percentage licensing fee deducted
by PROs for administration costs and presumably pass those savings on to the music
user. Source licensing may also be applicable to independent performing artists
working outside of the major labels and publishers who are paid directly by online
music companies.

Recall that PROs have the *non-exclusive licensing rights* to the millions of copyrighted musical compositions in their catalogs, and their primary source of income
is a percentage of the blanket license fee collected. However, copyright holders are
still free to negotiate their own licensing arrangements with others. In the Internet
era, where it is possible to distribute, market, and quantify in real time the listening
habits and airplay or musical performances of a work online, some independent and
unsigned artists are bypassing the traditional labels and royalty collecting agencies
altogether, and negotiating directly with such online companies as Last.fm.

Last.fm has a program called 'Artist Royalty Program' where it pays independent
and unsigned artists who join the program a performance royalty from their revenue
streams.[8] Presumably, the advantage to the independent songwriter and composer in
the Last.fm royalty program is that he or she might be paid months sooner and avoid
some of the administration costs associated with a traditional PRO. One promising
area of further research is what are the likely economic impacts over the long run
as to whether direct or source licensing when combined with other new market
forces such as Last.fm. Is direct or source licensing a threat that might erode or
eliminate the need for certain functions performed by performing and mechanical
rights agencies or a better income opportunity for songwriters and composers who
choose not to affiliate with a PRO?

The PROs will also be impacted when their blanket-license agreements with
radio, the cable, and TV industries expire not so much from declining CD sales,

but from deals tied to a percent of advertising revenue especially as those music users face significant market pressures due to the recession.

The advertising market worsened in 2009 as our preliminary data showed in Chapter 2. It is not clear when economic growth returns how the advertising industry will look in terms of the amount spent on digital media or emerging markets. During the 2009 recession, many companies in the automotive, financial services, and travel-related industries dramatically lowered radio, television, and print advertising spending. Would these companies be willing to pay as much for advertising services like they did before the economic slump? Media companies rely on the growth in advertising revenue to sustain profitability. PRO's compulsory licensing fees in turn are revenue based and performance royalty income is based on licensing fees.

9.5 New Business Models

The industry has now turned to what it calls a '360' deal in which the artist and the record label will share profits in deals besides the usual mechanical, performance, and synchronization licensing. According to *Billboard* magazine, in a new competing-retailer distribution model with different versions of songs and recording artists, the group 'Journey' signed an exclusive distribution deal with big-box retailer Wal-Mart, bypassing the record label, for the release of an album of new material, a re-recorded greatest hits disk and a DVD of live performances. Not to be outdone, Journey's record label, Sony BMG, apparently hoping to cash in on the Wal-Mart package, assembled a pre-existing CD/DVD of 'Greatest Hits' from 2003 for exclusive sale at Best Buy.[9]

Touring and merchandising sales have become another source of revenue to offset the income from declining CD sales for many musicians. *Billboard* magazine reports that nearly 300 touring acts are expected to perform in the Summer of 2009 at various music venues such as stadiums, arenas, amphitheaters, clubs, theaters, casinos, fairs, and festivals in the both the United States and abroad.

The merchandise being sold include a 'Build Your Own Stonehenge Model' targeting 'heavy metal' fans by a band called 'Spinal Tap.' The singer and songwriter 'Beyoncé' is selling a 'boombox handbag' for $75 that may actually cost more than a functional radio at a local retailer. Other trinkets include mugs, sun-glasses, guitar picks, 'foam fingers,' and something called a 'beer koozie' designed to keep beverages cold.[10]

In a widely reported story, the artist 'Madonna' abandoned her record label and signed with 'Live Nation,' a concert promoter, in yet another new business model in the music industry. However, the economic impact of the merger between Live Nation and Tickemaster has yet to be determined in terms of ticket prices, all of which can affect the income of songwriters, composers, and record labels.

9.6 Legislation and Competing Agendas

Although we did not analyze pending legislation, it is worth noting some of the main issues affecting the music industry in terms of intellectual property of musical works. The legislation will no doubt have future economic impacts that will be studied later. *The Performance Rights Act*—the right for musicians and vocalists whose recordings are played on *terrestrial* radio stations to be compensated—and the *Local Radio Freedom Act*—introduced to prevent any new sound recording performance tax, fee, or royalty on terrestrial radio stations—are pending new legislation. When enacted this legislation will either create an entire new category of audio performance rights or dismiss the audio performance rights altogether. SoundExchange is already collecting royalties for the record labels, musicians, and vocalists for certain audio digital performances on digital radio and satellite television and want to broaden that limited audio digital performance royalty to terrestrial broadcast stations.

The *Performance Rights Act legislation* is backed by the RIAA and many of the large record labels on the grounds that the legislation will repeal an exemption that they have long viewed as an anomaly in the US copyright law that supposedly gave radio broadcasters a 'free ride.'[11]

Critics, such as Dertouzos (2008), claim that recording artists *already* receive promotional benefits such as free publicity, name recognition and a boost in record sales, concert tickets, and merchandise from traditional radio airplay offsetting the need for further audio performance royalty payments for vocalists and background musicians, while stations owners benefit from listeners and advertising dollars. The Performance Rights Act (H.R. 848) is opposed by the National Association of Broadcasters, the industry lobbying group, many small non-commercial, minority-owned, religious radio station owners, and others. Some local radio stations and others consider the legislation a threat to new artists and consider it a new 'performance tax' designed to fund and bailout the recorded music industry for failing to anticipate and adapt to the consumer preference of digital music over the CD format.[12] The critics are skeptical that the recording artists will receive their fair share of the licensing fees generated due to allegations of abuse by labels of artists, and the fact that the record companies would receive 50 percent of the revenue generated and that the labels might see royalties as high as 20 percent of revenues. The critics also claim that a new content fee would jeopardize the viability of small struggling radio stations in the current recessionary climate.[13] Many in the industry are left wondering how the infringement issues surrounding multiple rights existing in one work would be resolved when a music user obtains a sound recording license for the audio portion and not the performing rights license for the musical composition.

9.7 Econometric Models

Even with the limited data analysis that we presented here, it is not hard to see how the use of data such as compulsory licensing fees and radio, television, and Internet performances when combined with other data such as retail album sales, digital downloads, live concert ticket sales, and so on can provide marketing insights and other ways in which to increase income for songwriters, composers, and music publishers. In era of the declining CD album sales, data collection, mining, and analysis are becoming increasingly important in terms of understanding the listening, buying, and music use habits of consumers. Greater data availability would be very valuable to future students in promoting further studies of art and cultural economics. In our parametric study, we showed how the log-skew-t model is the preferred specification that can be used to account for skewness, heavy tails, and asymmetry when modeling income data in the arts industry. Walls (2005) suggests two reasons why the log-skew-t is appealing in economic modeling. First, it is easier—computationally—to implement the skew-t than some other distributions (like the stable Paretian model or the Lévy stable regression model) using standard maximum likelihood statistical techniques that are within the reach of applied researchers. This approach avoids the mistakes that can be made when ordinary least squares estimators are used.

Second, the skew-t extends the Normal distribution by permitting tails that are heavy and asymmetric. The log-normal is just a special case of the log-skew-normal when $\alpha = 0$. One of the limitations in data analysis and economic modeling, is what is the best time period to use capture the variation in any of the models. For example, *Billboard* magazine charts are computed on a weekly basis, PRO payment schedules are on a quarterly basis, radio station format changes can occur on a monthly or annual basis, and some stations also broadcast other types of programming such as news where very little music is used, and different stations in different markets may be sampled at different times.

We did not examine airplay by type of radio station—commercial vs non-commercial—or by record label—major vs independent. Given the stiff competition for advertising dollars in a slumping economy, many radio stations are probably risk-averse and may chose to follow the programming formats that best maximizes revenue. The non-Normal distribution in our study suggests that a refined longitudinal study (a pooled-time series cross-section model) in which the same members are tracked and analyzed over various time intervals that coincide with certain key events such as important legislation and technological advances such as the CD player, the iPod, and the Internet that have had a dramatic effect on songwriters' income might be worthwhile.

Perhaps with the insights, data mining and econometric techniques presented here, organizations such as the International Confederation of Societies of Authors and Composers (CISAC) could be persuaded to make some of their proprietary member data widely available on a quarterly basis so that the music industry could be widely studied like other industries such as the airline or banking industries.[14]

Notes

1. *Billboard* magazine, July 2009, p. 8.
2. See http://www.narm.com/2009Conv/Nielsen09Presentation.pdf.
3. Thomson (2009).
4. Bruno (2009).
5. Trachtenberg (2009).
6. *Billboard* magazine, January 17, 2009, p. 24.
7. See Passman (2000, pp. 237–238).
8. See www.last.fm.

9. See *Billboard* magazine, June 21, 2008, p. 56.
10. See *Billboard* magazine, May 23, 2009, pp. 18–22.
11. See www.CISAC.org. As of June 2008, CISAC membership includes 225 authors' societies from 118 countries and indirectly represents more than 2.5 million creators within all the artistic repertoires: music, drama, literature, audio-visual, graphic, and visual arts.
12. See www.CISAC.org.
13. See www.CISAC.org.
14. See www.cisac.org.

References

Anderson, C. (2008). *The Long Tail*. Hyperion, New York, NY.

Bruno, A. (2009). 'Evolutionary Road: As They Align With Major Labels, Indie Aggregators Come of Age'. *Billboard* magazine. August 1, p. 10.

Dertouzos, J. (2008). *Radio Airplay and the Record Industry: An Economic Analysis*. National Association of Broadcasters. Unpublished.

Ginsburg, A. and Throsby, D., editors (2006). *Handbook of the Economics of Art and Culture*, volume 1. North Holland.

Passman, D. (2000). *All You Need to Know About the Music Business*. Simon & Schuster.

Strobl, E. and Tucker, C. (2000). The Dynamics of Chart Success in the UK Pre-Recorded Popular Music Industry. *Journal of Cultural Economics*, 24:113–134.

Thomson, K. (2009). Same Old Song: An Analysis of Radio Playlists in a Post-FCC Consent Decree World. Technical report, Future of Music Coalition.

Trachtenberg, J. (2009). 'Borders Aims to Capitalize on Teens With New Shops'. *Wall Street Journal*. July 21, p. B6.

Walls, W. (2005). Modeling heavy tails and skewness in film returns. *Applied Financial Economics*, 15:1181–1188.

Appendix

Radio Rankings by Share of Population (June 2010)

Table 1 Radio Rankings by Share of Population (June 2010)

Rank	Market	State	Population	% Share	Cum.%	Market Size	Region
1	New York	NY	18, 246, 500	6.97%	6.97%	L	NE
2	Los Angeles	CA	12, 721, 700	4.86	11.84	L	WE
3	Chicago	IL	9, 383, 100	3.59	15.42	L	MW
4	San Francisco	CA	7, 025, 500	2.68	18.11	L	WE
5	Dallas-Ft. Worth	TX	6, 373, 200	2.44	20.54	L	MW
6	Houston-Galveston	TX	5, 834, 300	2.23	22.77	L	MW
7	Atlanta	GA	5, 377, 200	2.06	24.83	L	SO
8	Philadelphia	PA	5, 128, 600	1.96	26.79	L	NE
9	Washington	DC	5, 021, 700	1.92	28.71	L	SO
10	Boston	MA	4, 632, 800	1.77	30.48	L	NE
11	Detroit	MI	4, 601, 900	1.76	32.23	L	MW
12	Miami-Ft. Lauderdale-Hollywood	FL	4, 055, 800	1.55	33.78	L	SO
13	Seattle-Tacoma	WA	3, 954, 100	1.51	35.30	L	WE
14	Puerto Rico	PR	4, 104, 200	1.57	36.86	L	SO
15	Phoenix	AZ	4, 101, 700	1.57	38.43	L	WE
16	Minneapolis-St. Paul	MN	3, 243, 700	1.24	39.67	L	MW
17	San Diego	CA	3, 040, 400	1.16	40.83	L	WE
18	Nassau-Suffolk	NY	2, 686, 500	1.03	41.86	L	NE
19	Tampa-St. Petersburg-Clearwater	FL	2, 772, 200	1.06	42.92	L	SO
20	Denver-Boulder	CO	2, 822, 800	1.08	44.00	L	WE
21	St. Louis	MO	2, 716, 000	1.04	45.04	L	MW
22	Baltimore	MD	2, 687, 000	1.03	46.06	L	SO
23	Portland	OR	2, 498, 300	0.95	47.02	L	WE
24	Charlotte-Gastonia-Rock Hill	NC-SC	2, 426, 700	0.93	47.95	L	SO

I.L. Pitt, *Economic Analysis of Music Copyright*,
DOI 10.1007/978-1-4419-6318-5, © Springer Science+Business Media, LLC 2010

160

Appendix

Table 1 (continued)

Rank	Market	State	Population	% Share	Cum.%	Market Size	Region
25	Pittsburgh	PA	2, 256, 200	0.86	48.81	L	NE
26	Riverside-San Bernardino	CA	2, 256, 000	0.86	49.67	M	WE
27	Sacramento	CA	2, 164, 300	0.83	50.50	M	WE
28	Cincinnati	OH	2, 155, 400	0.82	51.32	M	NE
29	Cleveland	OH	2, 056, 600	0.79	52.11	M	NE
30	Salt Lake City-Ogden-Provo	UT	2, 197, 400	0.84	52.95	M	WE
31	San Antonio	TX	2, 087, 400	0.80	53.74	M	MW
32	Kansas City	MO-KS	1, 932, 600	0.74	54.48	M	MW
33	Las Vegas	NV	1, 949, 300	0.74	55.23	M	WE
34	Orlando	FL	1, 802, 500	0.69	55.92	M	SO
35	San Jose	CA	1, 783, 500	0.68	56.60	M	WE
36	Columbus	OH	1, 776, 700	0.68	57.28	M	NE
37	Milwaukee-Racine	WI	1, 798, 600	0.69	57.97	M	MW
38	Austin	TX	1, 762, 900	0.67	58.64	M	MW
39	Indianapolis	IN	1, 694, 300	0.65	59.29	M	MW
40	Middlesex-Somerset-Union	NJ	1, 626, 100	0.62	59.91	M	NE
41	Providence-Warwick-Pawtucket	RI	1, 577, 300	0.60	60.51	M	NE
42	Raleigh-Durham	NC	1, 621, 200	0.62	61.13	M	SO
43	Norfolk-Virginia Beach-Newport News	VA	1, 605, 900	0.61	61.74	M	SO
44	Nashville	TN	1, 562, 800	0.60	62.34	M	SO
45	Greensboro-Winston Salem-High Point	NC	1, 414, 600	0.54	62.88	M	SO
46	Jacksonville	FL	1, 344, 500	0.51	63.40	M	SO
47	West Palm Beach-Boca Raton	FL	1, 249, 400	0.48	63.87	M	SO
48	Oklahoma City	OK	1, 338, 300	0.51	64.38	M	MW
49	Memphis	TN	1, 294, 700	0.49	64.88	M	SO
50	Hartford-New Britain-Middletown	CT	1, 218, 100	0.47	65.34	M	NE
51	Monmouth-Ocean	NJ	1, 227, 400	0.47	65.81	M	NE
52	New Orleans	LA	1, 030, 700	0.39	66.21	M	SO
53	Buffalo-Niagara Falls	NY	1, 108, 500	0.42	66.63	M	NE
54	Louisville	KY	1, 136, 000	0.43	67.07	M	SO
55	Richmond	VA	1, 132, 900	0.43	67.50	M	SO
56	Rochester	NY	1, 080, 200	0.41	67.91	M	NE

Table 1 (continued)

Rank	Market	State	Population	% Share	Cum.%	Market Size	Region
57	Birmingham	AL	1,066,700	0.41	68.32	M	SO
58	Greenville-Spartanburg	SC	1,037,800	0.40	68.72	M	SO
59	McAllen-Brownsville-Harlingen	TX	1,112,600	0.43	69.14	M	MW
60	Tucson	AZ	1,007,800	0.39	69.53	M	WE
61	Dayton	OH	964,700	0.37	69.89	M	NE
62	Ft. Myers-Naples-Marco Island	FL	945,600	0.36	70.26	M	SO
63	Albany-Schenectady-Troy	NY	905,700	0.35	70.60	M	NE
64	Honolulu	HI	895,500	0.34	70.94	M	WE
65	Tulsa	OK	900,600	0.34	71.29	M	MW
66	Fresno	CA	914,100	0.35	71.64	M	WE
67	Grand Rapids	MI	874,100	0.33	71.97	M	MW
68	Albuquerque	NM	848,500	0.32	72.30	M	WE
69	Allentown-Bethlehem	PA	810,800	0.31	72.61	M	NE
70	Wilkes Barre-Scranton	PA	773,400	0.30	72.90	M	NE
71	Knoxville	TN	794,300	0.30	73.21	M	SO
72	Omaha-Council Bluffs	NE-IA	763,500	0.29	73.50	M	MW
73	Sarasota-Bradenton	FL	694,700	0.27	73.76	M	SO
74	El Paso	TX	729,100	0.28	74.04	M	MW
75	Bakersfield	CA	732,100	0.28	74.32	M	WE
76	Akron	OH	694,300	0.27	74.59	M	NE
77	Wilmington	DE	698,300	0.27	74.85	M	SO
78	Harrisburg-Lebanon-Carlisle	PA	665,700	0.25	75.11	M	NE
79	Baton Rouge	LA	673,600	0.26	75.37	M	SO
80	Monterey-Salinas-Santa Cruz	CA	658,100	0.25	75.62	M	WE
81	Gainesville-Ocala	FL	665,200	0.25	75.87	M	SO
82	Stockton	CA	666,400	0.25	76.13	M	WE
83	Charleston	SC	683,600	0.26	76.39	M	SO
84	Syracuse	NY	635,300	0.24	76.63	M	NE
85	Little Rock	AR	662,100	0.25	76.88	M	SO
86	Greenville-New Bern-Jacksonville	NC	659,900	0.25	77.13	M	SO
87	Daytona Beach	FL	606,200	0.23	77.37	M	SO
88	Springfield	MA	605,200	0.23	77.60	M	NE
89	Columbia	SC	626,600	0.24	77.84	M	SO
90	Des Moines	IA	631,800	0.24	78.08	M	MW

Table 1 (continued)

Rank	Market	State	Population	% Share	Cum.%	Market Size	Region
91	Spokane	WA	615, 500	0.24	78.31	M	WE
92	Toledo	OH	603, 800	0.23	78.54	M	NE
93	Colorado Springs	CO	609, 700	0.23	78.78	M	WE
94	Lakeland-Winter Haven	FL	600, 100	0.23	79.01	M	SO
95	Mobile	AL	576, 300	0.22	79.23	M	SO
96	Ft. Pierce-Stuart-Vero Beach	FL	550, 500	0.21	79.44	M	SO
97	Melbourne-Titusville-Cocoa	FL	538, 900	0.21	79.64	M	SO
98	Wichita	KS	581, 300	0.22	79.87	M	MW
99	Madison	WI	579, 500	0.22	80.09	M	MW
100	Boise	ID	596, 000	0.23	80.31	M	WE
101	Visalia-Tulare-Hanford	CA	579, 000	0.22	80.54	M	WE
102	Johnson City-Kingsport-Bristol	TN-VA	531, 700	0.20	80.74	M	SO
103	Lexington-Fayette	KY	550, 400	0.21	80.95	M	SO
104	York	PA	530, 000	0.20	81.15	M	NE
105	Lafayette	LA	538, 000	0.21	81.36	M	SO
106	Chattanooga	TN	550, 900	0.21	81.57	M	SO
107	Huntsville	AL	516, 200	0.20	81.77	M	SO
108	Ft. Wayne	IN	525, 500	0.20	81.97	M	MW
109	Augusta	GA	515, 100	0.20	82.16	M	SO
110	Victor Valley	CA	518, 100	0.20	82.36	M	WE
111	Modesto	CA	509, 300	0.19	82.56	M	WE
112	Lancaster	PA	506, 100	0.19	82.75	M	NE
113	Roanoke-Lynchburg	VA	486, 600	0.19	82.94	M	SO
114	Worcester	MA	510, 800	0.20	83.13	M	NE
115	Morristown	NJ	479, 200	0.18	83.31	M	NE
116	New Haven	CT	486, 000	0.19	83.50	M	NE
117	Portsmouth-Dover-Rochester	NH	479, 700	0.18	83.68	M	NE
118	Oxnard-Ventura	CA	478, 700	0.18	83.87	M	WE
119	Santa Rosa	CA	459, 300	0.18	84.04	M	WE
120	Ft. Collins-Greeley	CO	485, 000	0.19	84.23	M	WE
121	Reno	NV	477, 800	0.18	84.41	M	WE
122	Jackson	MS	480, 400	0.18	84.59	M	SO
123	Bridgeport	CT	459, 400	0.18	84.77	M	NE
124	Pensacola	FL	479, 800	0.18	84.95	M	SO
125	Lansing-East Lansing	MI	460, 500	0.18	85.13	M	MW
126	Youngstown-Warren	OH	425, 300	0.16	85.29	S	NE
127	Fayetteville	NC	446, 400	0.17	85.46	S	SO
128	Flint	MI	419, 300	0.16	85.62	S	MW

Table 1 (continued)

Rank	Market	State	Population	% Share	Cum.%	Market Size	Region
129	Palm Springs	CA	433, 200	0.17	85.79	S	WE
130	Canton	OH	401, 900	0.15	85.94	S	NE
131	Reading	PA	403, 200	0.15	86.09	S	NE
132	Fayetteville	AR	423, 400	0.16	86.26	S	SO
133	Shreveport	LA	401, 000	0.15	86.41	S	SO
134	Saginaw-Bay City-Midland	MI	380, 200	0.15	86.55	S	MW
135	Appleton-Oshkosh	WI	383, 700	0.15	86.70	S	MW
136	Springfield	MO	396, 700	0.15	86.85	S	MW
137	Corpus Christi	TX	386, 000	0.15	87.00	S	MW
138	Beaumont-Port Arthur	TX	370, 100	0.14	87.14	S	MW
139	Newburgh-Middletown	NY	378, 300	0.14	87.29	S	NE
140	Burlington-Plattsburgh	VT-NY	364, 400	0.14	87.43	S	NE
141	Atlantic City-Cape May	NJ	362, 400	0.14	87.56	S	NE
142	Salisbury-Ocean City	MD	365, 700	0.14	87.70	S	SO
143	Trenton	NJ	361, 100	0.14	87.84	S	NE
144	Flagstaff-Prescott	AZ	354, 100	0.14	87.98	S	WE
145	Tyler-Longview	TX	371, 700	0.14	88.12	S	MW
146	Eugene-Springfield	OR	354, 300	0.14	88.25	S	WE
147	Quad Cities	IA-IL	357, 100	0.14	88.39	S	MW
148	Stamford-Norwalk	CT	354, 400	0.14	88.53	S	NE
149	Rockford	IL	360, 900	0.14	88.66	S	MW
150	Peoria	IL	354, 700	0.14	88.80	S	MW
151	Killeen-Temple	TX	385, 700	0.15	88.95	S	MW
152	Ann Arbor	MI	361, 400	0.14	89.09	S	MW
153	Fredericksburg	VA	350, 400	0.13	89.22	S	SO
154	Montgomery	AL	360, 200	0.14	89.36	S	SO
155	Biloxi-Gulfport-Pascagoula	MS	350, 900	0.13	89.49	S	SO
156	Macon	GA	346, 400	0.13	89.62	S	SO
157	Savannah	GA	348, 500	0.13	89.76	S	SO
158	Myrtle Beach	SC	333, 800	0.13	89.88	S	SO
159	Asheville	NC	312, 500	0.12	90.00	S	SO
160	Huntington-Ashland	WV-KY	309, 200	0.12	90.12	S	SO
161	Tallahassee	FL	323, 300	0.12	90.25	S	SO
162	Wilmington	NC	312, 700	0.12	90.37	S	SO
163	Evansville	IN	305, 400	0.12	90.48	S	MW
164	Utica-Rome	NY	291, 000	0.11	90.59	S	NE
165	Poughkeepsie	NY	287, 800	0.11	90.70	S	NE
166	Hagerstown-Chambersburg-Waynesboro	MD-PA	292, 700	0.11	90.82	S	NE

Table 1 (continued)

Rank	Market	State	Population	% Share	Cum.%	Market Size	Region
167	Portland	ME	275, 300	0.11	90.92	S	NE
168	Wausau-Stevens Point	WI	270, 400	0.10	91.02	S	MW
169	Erie	PA	277, 600	0.11	91.13	S	NE
170	San Luis Obispo	CA	273, 200	0.10	91.23	S	WE
171	Lincoln	NE	290, 100	0.11	91.35	S	MW
172	Concord	NH	269, 200	0.10	91.45	S	NE
173	Anchorage	AK	280, 900	0.11	91.56	S	WE
174	Wenatchee	WA	271, 500	0.10	91.66	S	WE
175	Ft. Smith	AR	274, 600	0.10	91.76	S	SO
176	Morgantown-Clarksburg-Fairmont	WV	261, 800	0.10	91.86	S	SO
177	New London	CT	275, 900	0.11	91.97	S	NE
178	New Bedford-Fall River	MA	256, 800	0.10	92.07	S	NE
179	South Bend	IN	264, 300	0.10	92.17	S	MW
180	Lubbock	TX	272, 400	0.10	92.27	S	MW
181	Merced	CA	263, 200	0.10	92.37	S	WE
182	Odessa-Midland	TX	263, 400	0.10	92.47	S	MW
183	Binghamton	NY	245, 300	0.09	92.57	S	NE
184	Lebanon-Rutland-White River Junction	NH-VT	239, 400	0.09	92.66	S	NE
185	Charleston	WV	242, 400	0.09	92.75	S	SO
186	Kalamazoo	MI	253, 900	0.10	92.85	S	MW
187	Green Bay	WI	247, 900	0.09	92.94	S	MW
188	Columbus	GA	247, 800	0.09	93.04	S	SO
189	Tupelo	MS	239, 500	0.09	93.13	S	SO
190	Dothan	AL	237, 700	0.09	93.22	S	SO
191	Amarillo	TX	235, 200	0.09	93.31	S	MW
192	Richland-Kennewick-Pasco	WA	234, 700	0.09	93.40	S	WE
193	Manchester	NH	229, 100	0.09	93.49	S	NE
194	Salina-Manhattan	KS	227, 000	0.09	93.57	S	MW
195	Cape Cod	MA	216, 900	0.08	93.66	S	NE
196	Traverse City-Petoskey	MI	225, 500	0.09	93.74	S	MW
197	Topeka	KS	228, 900	0.09	93.83	S	MW
198	Chico	CA	224, 500	0.09	93.92	S	WE
199	Waco	TX	231, 500	0.09	94.01	S	MW
200	Danbury	CT	223, 600	0.09	94.09	S	NE
201	Clarksville-Hopkinsville	TN-KY	276, 000	0.11	94.20	S	SO
202	Frederick	MD	228, 100	0.09	94.28	S	SO
203	Rocky Mount-Wilson	NC	222, 200	0.08	94.37	S	SO
204	Yakima	WA	232, 800	0.09	94.46	S	WE
205	Bend	OR	208, 700	0.08	94.54	S	WE
206	Laredo	TX	235, 700	0.09	94.63	S	MW

Table 1 (continued)

Rank	Market	State	Population	% Share	Cum.%	Market Size	Region
207	Bowling Green	KY	210, 500	0.08	94.71	S	SO
208	Medford-Ashland	OR	203, 300	0.08	94.79	S	WE
209	Santa Maria-Lompoc	CA	208, 400	0.08	94.87	S	WE
210	Cedar Rapids	IA	211, 100	0.08	94.95	S	MW
211	Terre Haute	IN	208, 200	0.08	95.03	S	MW
212	Duluth-Superior	MN-WI	201, 800	0.08	95.10	S	MW
213	Hilton Head	SC	212, 300	0.08	95.18	S	SO
214	Santa Barbara	CA	203, 400	0.08	95.26	S	WE
215	Fargo-Moorhead	ND-MN	202, 000	0.08	95.34	S	MW
216	Muncie-Marion	IN	196, 300	0.08	95.41	S	MW
217	Champaign	IL	199, 100	0.08	95.49	S	MW
218	Florence	SC	198, 400	0.08	95.57	S	SO
219	St. Cloud	MN	200, 500	0.08	95.64	S	MW
220	Las Cruces	NM	208, 100	0.08	95.72	S	WE
221	Sunbury-Selinsgrove-Lewisburg	PA	189, 400	0.07	95.79	S	NE
222	Winchester	VA	194, 600	0.07	95.87	S	SO
223	Laurel-Hattiesburg	MS	204, 200	0.08	95.95	S	SO
224	Bangor	ME	189, 400	0.07	96.02	S	NE
225	Alexandria	LA	190, 400	0.07	96.09	S	SO
226	Olean	NY	186, 000	0.07	96.16	S	NE
227	Ft. Walton Beach	FL	183, 600	0.07	96.23	S	SO
228	La Crosse	WI	187, 800	0.07	96.30	S	MW
229	Elmira-Corning	NY	180, 800	0.07	96.37	S	NE
230	Redding	CA	178, 300	0.07	96.44	S	WE
231	Charlottesville	VA	182, 200	0.07	96.51	S	SO
232	Tuscaloosa	AL	189, 900	0.07	96.58	S	SO
233	Lake Charles	LA	183, 000	0.07	96.65	S	SO
234	Rochester	MN	184, 400	0.07	96.72	S	MW
235	Bryan-College Station	TX	194, 700	0.07	96.80	S	MW
236	Twin Falls (Sun Valley)	ID	171, 500	0.07	96.86	S	WE
237	Muskegon	MI	172, 400	0.07	96.93	S	MW
238	Joplin	MO	177, 200	0.07	97.00	S	MW
239	Lafayette	IN	178, 000	0.07	97.07	S	MW
240	Panama City	FL	164, 700	0.06	97.13	S	SO
241	Bloomington	IL	169, 900	0.06	97.19	S	MW
242	Dubuque	IA	162, 800	0.06	97.26	S	MW
243	Marion-Carbondale	IL	161, 300	0.06	97.32	S	MW
244	Eau Claire	WI	163, 200	0.06	97.38	S	MW
245	Abilene	TX	162, 400	0.06	97.44	S	MW
246	Pueblo	CO	158, 100	0.06	97.50	S	WE
247	Pittsburg	KS	157, 900	0.06	97.56	S	MW
248	Columbia	MO	164, 600	0.06	97.63	S	MW

Table 1 (continued)

Rank	Market	State	Population	% Share	Cum.%	Market Size	Region
249	LaSalle-Peru	IL	152, 500	0.06	97.68	S	MW
250	State College	PA	152, 500	0.06	97.74	S	NE
251	Waterloo-Cedar Falls	IA	152, 600	0.06	97.80	S	MW
252	Sussex	NJ	147, 700	0.06	97.86	S	NE
253	Lufkin-Nacogdoches	TX	155, 000	0.06	97.92	S	MW
254	Parkersburg-Marietta	WV-OH	145, 600	0.06	97.97	S	NE
255	Lima	OH	150, 000	0.06	98.03	S	NE
256	Grand Junction	CO	149, 200	0.06	98.09	S	WE
257	Wheeling	WV	141, 500	0.05	98.14	S	SO
258	Florence-Muscle Shoals	AL	143, 100	0.05	98.20	S	SO
259	Monroe	LA	148, 900	0.06	98.25	S	SO
260	Hamptons-Riverhead	NY	136, 200	0.05	98.30	S	NE
261	Billings	MT	141, 100	0.05	98.36	S	WE
262	Kalispell-Flathead Valley	MT	135, 200	0.05	98.41	S	WE
263	Texarkana	TX-AR	134, 100	0.05	98.46	S	SO
264	Wichita Falls	TX	142, 600	0.05	98.52	S	MW
265	Battle Creek	MI	133, 500	0.05	98.57	S	MW
266	Grand Island-Kearney	NE	133, 900	0.05	98.62	S	MW
267	Valdosta	GA	138, 000	0.05	98.67	S	SO
268	Albany	GA	131, 400	0.05	98.72	S	SO
269	Altoona	PA	123, 500	0.05	98.77	S	NE
270	Montpelier-Barre-St Johnsbury	VT	121, 700	0.05	98.81	S	NE
271	Augusta-Waterville	ME	119, 600	0.05	98.86	S	NE
272	Harrisonburg	VA	120, 600	0.05	98.91	S	SO
273	Columbus-Starkville-West Point	MS	124, 100	0.05	98.95	S	SO
274	Rapid City	SD	122, 500	0.05	99.00	S	MW
275	Mankato-New Ulm-St Peter	MN	119, 200	0.05	99.05	S	MW
276	Williamsport	PA	115, 100	0.04	99.09	S	NE
277	Elkins-Buckhannon-Weston	WV	114, 100	0.04	99.13	S	SO
278	Sioux City	IA	120, 500	0.05	99.18	S	MW
279	Sheboygan	WI	113, 500	0.04	99.22	S	MW
280	Watertown	NY	122, 900	0.05	99.27	S	NE
281	Ithaca	NY	102, 300	0.04	99.31	S	NE
282	Bismarck	ND	106, 800	0.04	99.35	S	MW
283	Decatur	IL	107, 400	0.04	99.39	S	MW
284	Bluefield	WV	104, 600	0.04	99.43	S	SO
285	Lewiston-Auburn	ME	104, 800	0.04	99.47	S	NE

Table 1 (continued)

Rank	Market	State	Population	% Share	Cum.%	Market Size	Region
286	Lawton	OK	123, 400	0.05	99.52	S	MW
287	Cookeville	TN	104, 700	0.04	99.56	S	SO
288	Sebring	FL	101, 900	0.04	99.60	S	SO
289	San Angelo	TX	110, 900	0.04	99.64	S	MW
290	Hot Springs	AR	97, 800	0.04	99.68	S	SO
291	Grand Forks	ND-MN	100, 300	0.04	99.72	S	MW
292	Jackson	TN	97, 200	0.04	99.75	S	SO
293	Jonesboro	AR	97, 400	0.04	99.79	S	SO
294	Cheyenne	WY	87, 200	0.03	99.82	S	WE
295	Beckley	WV	78, 300	0.03	99.85	S	SO
296	Mason City	IA	77, 300	0.03	99.88	S	MW
297	Meridian	MS	76, 900	0.03	99.91	S	SO
298	Brunswick	GA	77, 200	0.03	99.94	S	SO
299	Clovis	NM	80, 600	0.03	99.97	S	WE
300	Casper	WY	73, 500	0.03	100.00	S	WE
Total			261, 662, 000	100%			

Source: Based on licensed data from www.bia.com, NE=Northeast, SO=South, MW=Midwest and WE=West, L=Large, M=Medium and S=Small

Author Index

Subject Index

360 deal, 82, 155
80-20 split, 13, 20

A

A&R executives, 82
ABC, 46
Advance payment, 11
Advertisers, 150
Album sales, 6
Amphitheaters, 155
AOL, 48
AQH measure, 143
Arbitron, 36
Arenas, 155
Artist management and development, 67
ASCAP, 41, 153
Audience segmentation, 28

B

Background/foreground music, 55
Bankruptcy, 150
Barrier to entry, 12
Billboard Magazine, 5, 13, 155
Blanket license, 3, 42
BMI, 41, 153
Business models, 5
Bypassing record label, 71

C

Cable, 4, 46
Cable fees, 137
Cash flow crisis, 36
Casinos, 155
Cassette tapes, 5
Catalog, 13
Catalog licensing, 66
CBS Radio, 33
CBS television, 46
CD format, 5

Census survey, 51
Central limit theorem, 95, 109
Christian Copyright Licensing Incorporated
    (CCLI), 18
CISAC, 62
Citadel Communications, 33
Clear Channel Communications, 33
Click-throughs, 49
Clubs, 155
Commercial stations, 28
Commercial success, 13
Compulsory license, 15
ComScore, 49, 83
Concert promoters, 71
Consolidation, 150
Copyright Act, 15
Copyright Arbitration Royalty Panel, 42
Copyright control, 151
Copyright infringement, 42
Copyright laws, 4
Copyright owner, 42
Copyright Royalty Board (CRB), 42
Cost savings, 83
Creative life cycles, 116
Creative marketing, 66
Creative process, 81
Credit value, 62
Cross-ownership rules, 32
Cultural good, 10, 44
Cultural products, 10, 13, 14
Cum measure, 143
Cumulus Media, 33
Curious economics, 13

D

Debt, 150
Deep catalog, 13
Demand for music, 13
Demand for tickets, 75

Printed in Poland
by Amazon Fulfillment
Poland Sp. z o.o., Wrocław

13900977R00112